AN INTRODUCTION TO
GAELIC POETRY

AN INTRODUCTION TO GAELIC POETRY

Derick Thomson

LONDON
VICTOR GOLLANCZ LTD
1974

Printed in Great Britain by
The Camelot Press Ltd, London and Southampton

Dedicated to Carol

Contents

Preface and Acknowledgments

THE WRITING OF a book of this nature was an undertaking I had long promised myself and other people, before the Publisher's invitation introduced a note of urgency to the project. In the event it has been slowly matured and quickly blended, and it can only be hoped now that its flavour will pass.

Many friends and teachers and students could be thanked for their interest over the years in Gaelic poetry, and I have felt enriched and encouraged by this interest. The last quarter-century has deepened our understanding of the Gaelic poetic tradition in important ways, as scholars have probed it more thoroughly and more sympathetically. And in the same period the tradition has enjoyed a new lease of life in contemporary writing and in public interest. It is not a bad time to take stock.

I wish to express my own and the Publisher's thanks to all living authors whose work has been translated in this book, and to their Publishers who have given permission to quote or translate. I should like to mention in particular Michael Carmichael who gave permission, as Trustee, to quote from *Carmina Gadelica*; The Scottish Gaelic Texts Society; William Maclellan; Messrs Oliver and Boyd; An Comunn Gaidhealach; Gairm Publications; and Victor Gollancz Ltd. In addition I should like to thank Donald Macaulay, George Campbell Hay and Iain Crichton Smith for permission to use their translations of a number of poems.

GLASGOW,   D. S. THOMSON
FEBRUARY 1973

An Introductory Note

SCOTTISH GAELIC LITERATURE throughout its history has been dominated by verse to an unusual extent. Prose has indeed enjoyed great popularity in an oral context, in heroic and romantic tales, in historical and other anecdotage, although verse was widely cultivated and enjoyed in the oral context also. But the written and printed literature of the Scottish Gaels over the last four centuries has included a high proportion of verse, and although the balance in recent times has begun to change significantly in favour of prose, as far as printed work goes, verse continues to hold a central and dominant place. It is still probably the most important touchstone of literary taste, and it still stands at the frontiers of innovation.

That this is so can hardly be explained solely in terms of the ancient prestige that poetry enjoyed, in Gaelic as in Irish and Welsh society, for such a prestige is not uncommon in early times. Yet part of the explanation may lie in that, and it is certainly true that the practice of poetry rested on a highly organized and prestigious basis. The system of organized learning and recording into which the poets fitted in early times is best known in an Irish context, but it is clear that many parts of that system functioned in Gaelic Scotland.[1]* At one time the office of bard had occupied a modest place in the poetic hierarchy, but the later bards took over some of the functions of their superiors, the *filid*, as well perhaps as some of the magical functions of the pagan druids. Consequently when we examine the surviving bardic verse (the verse, that is, of professional poets in the main) in Gaelic Scotland, and the office and traditions associated with the bards, we find a wide range of work and function represented. The most generously represented type of poetry is indeed the praise-poetry. This had been the responsibility of the bards in ancient times, and was taken over by the *filid*, it is claimed, about the twelfth century, so that our late medieval bards may be said to exercise this function of praise as *filid*. We have examples of battle incitement, traditionally a bardic product. Where the bard produces versified history and genealogy he is presumably filling the role of the *seanchaidh* or

* For Notes, see p. 307.

chronicler. We have examples of mythological and heroic tales woven into verse by late medieval poets, such as the telling of the Cú Chulainn-Conlaoch story (the Gaelic Sohrab and Rustum), in the Book of the Dean of Lismore, a notable sixteenth-century manuscript anthology. Niall MacMhuirich, about the year 1690, enters into a learned poetic dispute with two Irish poets, deploying a formidable knowledge of traditional ancient history and story. Again, a poet may set down his version of the seven deadly sins, or naturalize in a Rannoch setting the idea of Brant's *Ship of Fools*. Meantime there were poets who chronicled contemporary events, or even, very occasionally, private emotions: an account of pre-Flodden emotions, a mid-sixteenth century love-song in praise of an Islay lady, an account of a six-day spree in Dunvegan Castle (probably in the year 1613), a satirical description of the bagpipes and a spluttering executant. By the nineteenth century, however, the predominant impression, in current tradition, of the Mac-Mhuirich bards was that they were clever magicians, powerful, unscrupulous, able to control the winds and the fate of enemies.[2] A parallel belief, in the power of poetic satire, is well attested in Gaelic Scotland and Ireland.

The power of the bards was partly at least a temporal power, growing out of possessions, and often boosted by closeness to the chief. They formed hereditary lines (as did the brehons or judges, the harpers, leeches and others), and held lands in virtue of their office. We have evidence from Irish sources of certain bardic families becoming very wealthy and powerful,[3] and the Scottish evidence itself points to conditions of comfort in a material sense and strong influence in a social and political sense. The Mac-Mhuirich farms in South Kintyre were on excellent land and were extensive, and the MacMhuirich bards' closeness to their Chief (originally the Lord of the Isles and later Clanranald) is well attested. The MacMhuirich bardic line is the most remarkable by far in Scotland, stretching from the early thirteenth century when the Irish poet known as Muireadhach Albanach or Scottish Murray came in flight to Scotland to the late eighteenth.[4] It was an off-shoot, or an extension, of the Irish bardic family of the Ó Dálaighs, which has a remarkable record in Ireland. There were other hereditary bardic lines, such as that of the Ó Muirgheasáins, bards latterly to the MacLeods of Harris and Dunvegan: their Irish ties were so strong that they did not shed the Ó in their names as long as they continued to compose bardic verse. A third bardic line, that of the MacEwens, is known to us in a little detail, and a number of others in less, while there are probably lines which are represented in the extant records only by their last practitioner: this may be the case with Fionnlagh Ruadh, bard to the Chief of the MacGregors in the early sixteenth century. We know hardly anything of the poets who must have adorned the rich and powerful court of the Chief of Macintosh, or indeed many other courts, both small and large. We catch a hint of the poet's ceremonial functions, as where Hugh MacDonald of Sleat says that the white inauguration dress worn by the Lord of the Isles was afterwards given to the poet,[5] a practice reminiscent of that by which Ó Dálaigh poets gained possession of the bridal dresses of girls married in Desmond and Duhallow.[6] Martin Martin, in the late seventeenth century, recorded some details he had heard of how the bardic schools were run, and how poets composed their set pieces in the dark, and with a boulder on their bellies.[7]

The organization and practice of poetry had clearly reached such a pitch that they deeply affected society. We may suspect strongly that this influence was at one time restricted largely to the richer and more powerful sector of society, but whether by the breakdown of the native order, and the resulting democratization of Gaelic society, or by other means also, the influence of the poetic tradition spread much more widely, producing in earlier times, and to some extent down to the present, an unusually high level of literary awareness and appreciation in the populace at large. Quite apart from the more learned verse which in this way began to influence taste, there were other verse traditions whose origins and early history are obscure to us, but which we find in full flower in the sixteenth and seventeenth centuries.

The present account seeks to distinguish and characterize these various traditions, and to follow movements in poetry down to our own day. Although it notes in passing some of the connections and influences that link the work of one generation or one poet to another, it attempts to concentrate mainly on the poetry itself, leaving a fuller exposition of matters of literary history for another work. There are many gaps in the present account which could not readily be excused in a literary history: a passing reference only to the songs of MacDonald of Dalness, a cursory mention only of Eachann MacLeòid, an eighteenth-century poet of some individuality, no account of the eighteenth–nineteenth-century poet Allan MacDougall, selective treatment of nineteenth-century verse, and so on. I am conscious at many points of the compression of the treatment of poets and periods. Each of the chapters might well have been the subject of a book, and no doubt will be some day. It is to be hoped, at any rate, that parts of this account will stimulate further interest in the topics raised, for there is much detailed work to be done.

Within the ordained compass of the work there has been a sustained attempt to preserve a balance, or a series of balances, both between chapters and between the treatment of individual topics, and I would hope to be able to defend the decisions taken in this respect, at least within reason. It may, however, be admitted that some of the allocations to chapters are somewhat arbitrary. The chapter on Songs is perhaps the one most open to cavil. Some items there could as properly have been included in the chapter on eighteenth-century poetry, but usually there is some consideration that tips the balance one way or the other. The inclusion, for example, of *"Eala nan Cuantan"* in the chapter on Songs implies a judgement that its deepest affinities are with "song to be heard" rather than with "literature to be read". Such a judgement is a subjective one, and is open to challenge. Indeed, many of the judgements made are subjective to some degree, or to a large degree, and I am not convinced that literary judgements can be otherwise.

The Publishers wished to have a book liberally illustrated by quotation, in translation. As a practising publisher (though a spare-time one) I was conscious of their standing and authority in the matter, and was ready in any case to perform this service. The most difficult problems have been in this part of the work. The problems of translation are notorious, and common, and there are writers who have particularly strong gifts in this field. I can hardly claim to be of that band. The translations are not made according to a dogmatic theory, but there are elements of rigidity in them that ought to be explained. In general the translations are my own, though where a debt is owed to someone else it is generally declared, and in particular there are six or seven poems translated by Iain Crichton Smith, while in a few instances I have used translations, made by poets, of their own poetry: these are acknowledged. Among my own principles as a translator there may be reckoned (1) the transfer of sense with the greatest fidelity consistent with the norms of the language used for translation; (2) the retention of the physical "shape" of the poem: this implies translating line-for-line in the main, and observing some correspondence between line-length in the original and the translation; (3) as a partial consequence of the second principle, a close adherence to the rhythmical movement of the original (in many cases there is a close or one-for-one correspondence between both syllable-counts and rhythmic sequence); (4) a disclaimer of the ultimate perfection of getting sense, sound, structure, rhyme and rhythm right, all at once. It seems to me that this last ideal is entirely impossible. We live, blessedly, in a polyglot world, and translation implies difference. Thus where there is rhyme in the translation it is almost inevitable that the other elements of the equation are not in balance. Yet some instances of rhyming translation have been included, and perhaps there should have been more. In the rhythmical translations some slight changes in sense have been allowed to preserve rhythm, e.g. as in a line "with your dark sable cloak", where the original has "black cloak", but uses a word of three syllables for "cloak".[8] There are also instances of line-fillers like "now" and "then" being used. But where there is a serious departure from fidelity it is confessed. It should be added that a few translations are frankly presented as prose.

There remains a residue of cases, of passages that seem untranslatable. I do not think that anything of crucial importance has been omitted on this pretext. Any translation made on the principles described above will tend to be in a somewhat lower key than the original, since I do not claim to be deploying the whole battery of skills that a poet working in his chosen language employs. There is no complete substitute for appreciation of poetry in a particular language short of learning that language and learning it well. In particular, there are many examples of verbal wit that can hardly be fully translated, for they may often depend on the whole range of a word's connotations, and there is only one kind of computer, to date, that can be programmed in the right way to appreciate this. In similar fashion, humour of situation and humour of character often depend for their effect on a knowledge of the culture's stereos, and an intimate knowledge at that.

The purpose of these explanations is to reassure readers that the poetry they are about to investigate is even better than the translations suggest.

All but the most urgent footnotes are placed near the end of the book, with a reference at the beginning of the chapter to the pages on which they are to be found. A full Bibliography of works referred to is added, together with an Index of Poets, with cross-references to Gaelic and English name-forms, and a General Index which excludes the names of poets. This apparatus should make it relatively easy both to locate discussions of particular works and to suggest further reading.

AN INTRODUCTION TO
GAELIC POETRY

I

The Bardic Poets

THE PLACE WHICH the professional poets held in the Gaelic society of Scotland, and the sector they occupied in the world of poetry, has already been discussed in broad terms. It is unfortunate that by the time we have contemporary sources reporting on these poets and their work, the world they belonged to was already disintegrating. Using the fragments we have of the whole corpus of such verse, together with historical evidence, and adding the inferences we can make from the later tradition of Gaelic poetry, we have enough ectoplasm to fashion a shadowy figure of the medieval professional bard in Gaelic Scotland. Our knowledge of the system as it existed in Ireland gives body and definition to the figure. It is more than usually helpful to know the background to the poetry in this case, since that background colours the poetry so positively, but ultimately it is the poetry that is our concern: what the surviving poetry says, and its way of saying it.

The system of which the bardic poet formed part, closed shop though it attempted to be, could not succeed in cutting itself off from a slightly larger world, and could not have survived economically (which was indeed one of its main purposes) had it been cut off from some sort of public. The understanding and appreciation which allowed a patron to decide whether a poem was worth a horse or two, or a number of milch-cows, allowed him also to try his hand at making poems, if he was so inclined. Poetry is perennially saved from esotericism by the need for a public. We can argue over the size of this necessary public, then and now, but not over the need for it. There is indeed room for argument still, over the size of the public for bardic verse. It may be suspected that it was rather larger than is usually assumed. At any rate, there is a good deal of evidence that people who had never been professional poets could compose bardic verse. Most often, however, such people were members of the ruling class, and their verse was both more occasional and less stringent technically than that of the professional poets. Despite these qualifying remarks, work of this kind is to be included in this chapter. There is also some verse that makes a bridge between the bardic world and the vernacular world of sixteenth- and seventeenth-century Gaelic Scotland, and this will be considered in Chapter 2. The title of the chapter is to be interpreted fairly loosely, though the types of poetry discussed can be classified closely enough.

Excluding that bridging poetry of the sixteenth and seventeenth centuries and excluding also heroic ballads, the surviving corpus of bardic poetry in Scotland consists of approximately 160 items, ranging in size from fragmentary quatrains to poems of over two hundred lines in length. Some of this is not as yet dated accurately, but clearly the bulk of it belongs to the period 1450 to 1650, and more than half of it—a rough total of eighty-six items—belongs to the century between 1450 and 1550. Approximately forty poems can be assigned to the period 1600 to 1700, and a mere handful, hardly exceeding ten poems, to the post-1700 period. This curious bunching of surviving poems is to be explained by the nature of the surviving sources. Of these the sixteenth-century Book of the Dean of Lismore is by far the richest source, with some eighty-eight items of Scottish interest, excluding heroic ballads. This explains the relatively high total of poems from the period 1450–1550, and the still higher relative total of early sixteenth-century poems. The figure for the seventeenth century is boosted by the survival of a handful of manuscripts connected with the MacMhuirich bardic family, especially the Red Book of Clanranald, and in particular by the survival of a good number of poems by two leading members of the MacMhuirich family, the seventeenth-century poets Cathal and Niall MacMhuirich.

Of this surviving total of bardic items, some forty are anonymous. A few poets are well represented, as for example Cathal MacMhuirich by thirteen poems, Niall MacMhuirich by nine, the sixteenth-century Sir Duncan Campbell of Glenorchy by nine also, Fionnlagh Ruadh, bard to the Chief of Clan Gregor in the early sixteenth century, by seven, John MacMhuirich, Donnchadh Mac Dhubhghaill Mhaoil and Giolla Críost Táilliúr by four each, and the remainder by one, two or three items.

The restricted range of surviving sources introduces a territorial bias. The Book of the Dean of Lismore is heavily biased towards work of Perthshire and Argyllshire origin. The Dean's collection only just impinges on Inverness-shire and the Hebrides, while the later MacMhuirich collections are biased towards the Macdonald

lands in the islands. When we allow for such bias, and for the
chance and selective nature of our sources, it seems a fair inference
that bardic poetry was once practised fairly freely, and on a wide
scale, and we can conjecture that wherever a Gaelic Chief held
established court, from the thirteenth century to the sixteenth, and
as we have seen in certain localities until the late seventeenth, there
was likely to be some bardic activity. The scale of this activity
might vary widely, from the court of the Lords of the Isles, where
there were probably a number of professional bards, to humbler
and more peripheral courts, favoured by a visit from a bard on
circuit. We should not forget that in some of these establishments,
as for instance the court of the Isles and the court of the Campbell
Chiefs, the Chief himself might turn his hand to verse as a cultural
pastime. The main centres of such activity, at least in the later
centuries of this period, are marked by the existence of those bardic
dynasties already referred to, but an important part of the bardic
system was the bardic circuit, or even the prolonged foray, which
brought Irish poets such as Aonghus nan Aor (and perhaps
Muireadhach Albanach himself) to Scotland, and Scottish poets
such as Giolla Críost Brúilingeach and Maol-Domhnaigh Ó
Muirgheasáin to Ireland. And, more important in a domestic sense
than these larger gestures, the bardic circuit on the one hand, and
the bard's close involvement in his Chief's affairs, on the other,
allowed these poets to spread their influence at home, as when we
find Niall Mór MacMhuirich, a Clanranald poet, at Dunvegan, or
his younger kinsman Cathal lamenting the death of a daughter of
the Mackenzie family of Gairloch.

All this verse is, of course, connected with privileged families, in
one way or another. It may be that at rare moments a poet may
speak for his fellows, for his countrymen even, as the anonymous
poet who composed a battle incitement before Flodden, and it may
be that a poet's more personal and lyrical verses may survive
(though this happens even more rarely). The system could tolerate
such idiosyncrasies but was certainly not designed for them.

Were it not, however, for the chance discovery of the Dean of
Lismore's manuscript in the second half of the eighteenth century,
we would scarcely have known that any bardic verse existed in
Scotland before 1500, and would have no idea of its spread and
variety. Though the Dean's collection shows a bias towards work
of Argyllshire and Perthshire provenance, this is not to be interpreted in any narrow chauvinistic fashion. What he includes is

what comes his way, and among that was a sizeable collection of Irish verse including such items as a series of poems by the fourteenth-century poet Gearóid Iarla: poems which are not known from other sources. This Irish contribution, and in particular the number of poems by members of the Ó Dálaigh bardic family, related by then distantly to the MacMhuirichs, may suggest to us that the Dean drew heavily on MacMhuirich and related sources. In this sense the inclusion of the Irish poems may simply underline the Dean's dependence on a particular Argyllshire source. It argues more than that, however: an acceptance of poetry of this genre, whatever its provenance. It could not, I think, be argued that the Dean's appreciation of bardic verse was a fine one. Some of his versions suffer badly from mutilation—a mutilation that most probably took place in transmission. But it can scarcely be doubted that he had an understanding of bardic verse, and that his taste was catholic. The latter conclusion is well enough demonstrated by the wide range of poems and subjects which he includes: much religious verse, an important collection of heroic ballads, love poetry, genealogical verse of high density, standard panegyric, political verse, satire, humorous verse, and poems that can, at least loosely, be described as obscene. We can draw the further conclusion from a study of the Dean's collection that the standard literary language in Gaelic Scotland was regarded as suitable for this wide range of verse, though if we were to go by the evidence of the Dean's book alone, we might think that the amateurs were as much responsible as the professionals for the extension of this verse's range.

This catholicity and range are best seen in the Dean's collection, for our other sources are more strictly professional, so that once again we find ourselves indebted to James MacGregor for an enlargement of our understanding of the earlier history of Gaelic verse in Scotland. A short list may be given of more unusual subjects of poems: praise of a prize horse, a request for a bow, the destruction of wolves, anti-clerical views, satire of the "Ship of Fools" type, the antithesis of love v. lust, classical and biblical justifications for avoiding courtship, allegory in which a sexual encounter is described in terms of chess/backgammon, a description of Arthur's court seen in terms of the bardic poet's ideal, and an account of a six-night spree in Dunvegan. All but the last two occur in the Dean's collection.

We can return to some of these, but it would be as well to begin with what is, after all, the staple of the bardic poet's production:

verse which recounts genealogy and history (either factual or fictitious), and which praises both the quick and the dead. Sometimes the history is almost totally unrelieved, except by pseudo-history, as in the earliest surviving poem with a specifically Scottish subject, but probably by an Irish author, the *Duan Albanach*, dated by Professor K. H. Jackson about 1093. The poem begins with a courtly address to the Gaelic men of learning of Scotland:

> O all ye learned ones of Alba,
> O stately yellow-haired company[1]*

and going on to ask and answer a question about the first invasion of Alba (by Albanus), proceeds through legend and sketchy history to a list of kings of Alba, with lengths of reign. Some of this is accurate, some not, but even the earlier part has much authentic information in it, drawing on old, native sources. There is, however, no poetry, as distinct from verse, in all this. Nor is there much poetry in the verses that the Dean's brother addressed to John, the Chief of the Macgregors who died in 1519, a *cairtmhil* or 'chartered warrior'' in the poet's eyes: .. ....

> It is timely to recount to you, blue-eyed one,
> (listen, O John, to your history)
> The enumeration of your line—what's the harm in doing so?
> it was royal, gentle, of noble repute.

> Patrick your father is known to you;
> Malcolm was Patrick's father:
> he was the son of Black John whose heart was not black,
> it is right to place him in the foremost count.

> . . . . . .

> One knows about the father of that John,
> namely Malcolm who did not conceal generosity,
> son of Little Duncan, whose conduct was not paltry:
> war-hounds untouched by a side-stroke.[2]

Despite a long section of potted genealogy, there is some life and fire in the poem in praise of the Chief of the Campbells, composed

* For Notes, see pp. 307–8.

probably by one of the MacEwen bardic family befween 1638 and 1661. This is the poem which makes an elaborate parallel between the courts of Argyle and King Arthur. A handful of its thirty-seven stanzas may be quoted:

> His of right are the young warriors of the Isles,
> let him not allow the charter that is his to slip his grasp;
> the leadership of the Gael is his by right,
> he is the one whose hosts range most widely.

> From Ireland to the outmost bounds of Lewis
> the warriors of the rugged lands, stern of deed,
> are his, as of right, all ready to obey his command;
> each one of these is an auxiliary of his

> If he follows in the steps of his forefathers
> servants will stay with him,
> companies of poets will be in his stronghold—
> they will not move to their native territories.[3]

This carefully angled panegyric is followed by a flattering comparison with Arthur's court, seen very much through the eyes of a Gaelic professional bard:

> Tales of wonder were told
> to generous Arthur daily and nightly;
> he was not interested in tasting a bite
> until the bones of a tale were laid before him.

> Out from their pavilion and into the assembly
> went a full complement of men of art and learning of every kind;
> gold was distributed by the kings
> to the hearty exuberant throng as they sat over their drink.

When the genealogical section begins the reader is taken back in somewhat unorthodox steps of ten, eleven and twelve generations at a time, and this rapid progression is summed up near the end of the poem:

> Three score and four generations
> of your warrior stock from Archibald

to the generation of Adam who did not do violence to understanding,
in the line of that generous, valiant company that kept their
honour well.

There you have the culminating point of your story,
with warrant of chronicle behind it,
from the lips of wise men, omitting no one,
O young, modest man whose cheeks are fresh and joyous.

More often than not genealogy plays a more subdued part in the
praise-poem, whether it be a panegyric or an elegy, and often this
effacing of the chronicler allows the poet to come into his own.
There was doubtless a time when the functions of chronicling and
of panegyric had been more distinct, performed by different
officials. When these and other poetic functions merged, in a less
strictly stratified society, there were poets whose leanings took
them in one direction or another: towards genealogy or literary
history or lyricism for example, and although they may try their
hand at various kinds of verse-making their individual characteristics show. The mid-seventeenth-century MacEwen poets (if we
are right in ascribing various Campbell panegyrics to them) have a
leaning towards genealogy and chronicle, whereas the Mac-
Mhuirichs are clearly more attracted to lyricism. Neither Cathal
MacMhuirich's poem of welcome to Donald, son of John of
Moidart (late 1640s) nor Niall MacMhuirich's elegy for the same
man (*c.* 1686) carry genealogical detail, but they are shot through
with lyricism. Niall's elegy may be quoted in contrast to the
Campbell poem we have sampled:

(Joy in the Hebrides . . .)
Joy in the Hebrides has come to an end, the death of one man
has brought entire affliction; though it is (but) the beginning of
grief there is deep depression throughout the lands.

Since the death of the warrior of the blood of Conn, every heart
is sick and wounded, others pay no respect to the clan, hence-
forth it will be easy to take their pledges (from them).

The son of big-bodied spirited John of Moidart, the shortness
of his life has wounded me sharply; wretched is my state now

that this man is dead: that has consumed (as with fire) my flesh and my blood.

I never saw one like him for openness of disposition, for purity of character, for liberality, for excellence in (giving) goods and chattels—and the urbanity of our chief, alas, is in the clay.

He was the great nourisher and fosterer of our schools of poets; his death, O God, is a heavy loss for us; [the cutting short of] his life has stolen my strength from me; what are these but ill tidings (threatening) danger to the foundations (of our poetic institutions)?

He was a lion in the fierceness of his exploits, but would not indulge in anything shameful, a man who was foremost in showing the way to peace, my beloved was he who gave protection to the destitute and to the learned poets.

My heart is stricken with sorrow, mourning him—a man with no possessions is a destitute person—I am in a state of distraction, I scarcely know who I am (?), O God, thinking of my ruler and my king.

Lively was his courage on the field of battle, a leader who did not refuse battle, a hand that was not feeble in the hard fight, Donald who held victory in his fair palm.

In support of his king's great party, he bore arms from the time he came of age (?); he responded to the fury of the battle-fields, a steadfast, noble warrior, for such my beloved one was.

Stalk (=hero?) that was most powerful in every battle-field, whose tenderness to the unfortunate was most pleasantly given; the heart of this one contained true love, lying on the ground is the beloved of men of learning.

Salmon of Shiel, powerful salmon, and last in line of the kings from [the Earldom of] Ross, here in this western land of the grey geese, the pledge that I gave him has been heard of far and wide.

After the going of this body that has been laid in the grave,
wretched is my tarry in an empty world, since I do not see—
though it was my privilege to speak of it—the leader of the hosts
for whom I make a (=this) poem.

Many a man in fair Uist, and many a woman is in a paroxysm of
grief, because their chief has been hidden in the clay: the guardian
of warrior-bands who did not flee from a pursuing host.

Donald, while he was alive, never kept back from me anything
that I asserted was due to me as a reward; in the gap of danger
he was not weak, my white sun, he who did not hoard
cattle.[4]

The typical praise-poem lies in between the extremes of chronicle
and lyric, and is central to the whole tradition of bardic poetry.
Its structure and conventions will be discussed later in this chapter. The poets who made such praise-poems had to be ready to
turn their attention to other kinds of verse also. One such kind was
political verse, for the official poet was among other things a P.R.O.
and public apologist. His services could be used to incite his own
party, or to vaunt its exploits, or to excuse failure. It is unfortunate
from the point of view of the historian that so little has survived
of this type of verse, since even its bias might be useful as a corrective to the bias of other documents. A poem about the fleet of
John MacSween of Knapdale, probably composed in 1310, and
ascribed to Artúr Dall MacGurcaigh (?), throws a strange and
interesting light on a dark corner of history. MacSween, who was
the third lord of that ilk in Knapdale, supported King Edward I of
England, and later Edward II, and this alliance brought him into
conflict with the Campbells, and also with Robert the Bruce, who
eventually took from him his lands in Knapdale. These lands came
into the possession of John of Argyll and Sir John Menteith. In 1310
King Edward II granted Knapdale to John MacSween and his
brothers, provided they could recover it by force of arms from
John of Menteith, Edward's enemy. Our poem evidently relates
to MacSween's expedition, which failed.

The poem, however, was composed before the expedition set
out, certainly before action was joined, and its purpose was in
part to incite: it is a *brosnachadh catha*, an incitement to battle, a
type of composition that is well attested in Gaelic. Naturally there

is a note of boastfulness in it, an aggrandisement of the hero and his possessions. But the poet describes MacSween's fleet, and we must assume that it gives us some factual information here:

Tryst of a fleet against Castle Sween,
welcome the venture in the Land of the Gael;
horsemen traversing the waves,
brown barks are being cleaned out for them.

Tall men are arraying the fleet
which takes its course on the swift sea-surface;
every hand holds a trim warspear
in the battle of targes, polished and comely.

The prows of the ships are arrayed
with quilted hauberks as with jewels,
with warriors wearing brown belts;
Norsemen—nobles at that.

The prows of the brown-sailed ships
are decked with swords which have gold and ivory settings;
[the second?] rank is composed of bright pointed spears;
shields hang from the long sides of the ships.

Behind the shields on the dappled ships
is a gleaming pile of stones of gold;
[a festooning] of fair hats and collars
beside the yards which are so sharp and strong.

. . . . . .

Fair ladies sit on the floor of the ships;
there are high beds for stately damsels;
speckled cushions are arranged for them,
couches for the ladies where each may lie alone.[5]

The content of this passage is interesting. The poem was composed less than fifty years after the battle of Largs, and Norse traditions would be very strong in the West of Scotland at this time. We should expect to find Norse fashions in ship design, in warlike array, and in weapon design, and this seems to be precisely what we do find in this passage, coupled at that with a reference to the crews as "Lochlannaigh is ármuinn" (Norsemen . . . nobles). Lochlannach means a Scandinavian, particularly a Norseman, and *ármunn* is a loanword in Gaelic, coming from Norse *ármaðr* "steward". Whether the members of the crews were predominantly Norse or not, this would be regarded as a compliment, as the Norsemen formed a sort of warrior-caste.

The fourth stanza quoted above would seem to describe a typical Scandinavian manned warship of the Dark Ages. The first line describes the swords, and we may set beside it the descriptions of archaeologists, as Shetelig,[6] who says that the groove between the pommel and the upper crossbar, and the cross-pieces, were often adorned with silver wire (and it may be that for *déad* "ivory", in line 2 of the stanza, we should read *tét* "string or wire"). Brøndsted writes of Viking swords: "The blade was frequently worked in damascene, and the hilt inlaid with gold, copper, silver, or *niello*, so that the Viking sword was often a weapon of great splendour."[7] Brøndsted also refers to the rows of shields along the gunwales of the famous Norwegian Viking ship at Gokstad.[8] Thus, although these details of Norse design and fashion do not survive (to my knowledge) from Western Scotland in an archaeological sense, they are clearly attested here in a literary source.

The presence of the ladies, with their speckled cushions and beds, may remind us again of the Gokstad ship-burial, discovered on the shore of Oslo Fjord in 1880, and dated *c.* 900 A.D., where a chieftain had been buried, lying finely dressed and armed in his bed. In the prow of the ship there were five beds, and in the chamber there were scraps of wool and gold-embroidered silk.[9]

Although this exotic detail sets the poem apart in some ways, it fits well enough into the bardic pattern, with its use of conventions such as pathetic fallacy:

> The streams of Sliabh Monaidh
> welcome MacSween of Sliabh Mis;
> shoals of the fish of the estuaries come to meet him.

> . . . . . .

> Branches bow down their knees . . . ,

and the reference to the welcome given by the men of learning:

> Alba's men of learning come,
> they welcome the valiant hero of Mis.

There are other, more specific, examples of the *brosnachadh* or battle incitement, in particular a group of three productions that are probably linked: the Harlaw Brosnachadh, ascribed to Lachlann MacMhuirich, and dated 1411, a short poem in the Red Book of Clanranald, in praise of MacDonald (of the Isles), and a prose-poem on the army and arming of John of the Isles, which belongs to the 1480s (as may also the Red Book poem). The first of these has a peculiar interest, indeed several points of peculiar interest. It is composed using alliteration but not rhyme, in an archaic heptasyllabic metre with trisyllabic line-endings and is one of the last, if not the last poem to be composed in this metre, while it may also rank as the earliest surviving poem in vernacular Scottish Gaelic, as opposed to the Classical literary language. Its other peculiar interest is that it is an alphabetic poem, working its way through the alphabet with couplets each giving four epithets beginning with the same letter, all in praise of the Clan Donald, as though one were to say in English:

> Be angry, be ardorous,
> be ape-like, be athletic;
> be bloody, be blustering,
> be bear-like, be barbarous.

This gives some notion of the movement and tone of the Incitement, but in more sober translation it opens as follows:

> O children of Conn, remember
> Hardihood in time of battle:
> be watchful, be daring,
> be dexterous, winning renown;
> be vigorous, pre-eminent;
> be strong, nursing your wrath;
> be stout, be brave,
> be valiant, triumphant . . .

and it ends:

> O Children of Conn of the Hundred Battles,

now is the time for you to win recognition,
O raging whelps
O sturdy bears,
O most sprightly lions,
O battle-loving warriors,
O brave, heroic firebrands,
the Children of Conn of the Hundred Battles—
O Children of Conn, remember
Hardihood in time of battle.[10]

An anonymous poem, addressed to the Earl of Argyll on the eve of Flodden, in 1513, is another excellent example of the *brosnachadh*, this time in the larger context of Scoto–English affairs. Campbell is here addressed as the champion of the Scots against the English, and the Campbells found themselves on this occasion, uncharacteristically, on the losing side. The poem is one of the most remarkable examples extant of pre-Flodden nationalism. The following version is in verse which attempts to capture the mood of the original, although it does not reproduce its exact cadences, and in particular does not echo the a-rhythmical rhyme of the original. The translation omits a parallel from Irish legend which the poet used in stanzas 4–7, where it is recalled that Ireland was dominated by the Fomorians until Lugh came from across the sea with his war-bands and slew Balar úa Néid. The poet then asks who will succour the Gaels against the Saxons, as Lugh once did his own people, and our version resumes at this point (stanza 3 below):

> To fight the Saxons is right,
> no rising followed by flight;
> edge of sword, point of spear,
> let us ply them with good cheer.

> Against Saxons, I say to you,
> lest they rule our country too;
> fight roughly, like the Irish Gael,
> we will have no English Pale.

. . . . . .

I know one who'd fight like Lugh:
Archibald, to honour true,
Earl of the Coastland of the Gael[11]
exultant warrior, do not fail!

Send your summons east and west,
let Ireland come at your behest;
drive Saxons back across the sea,
let Scotland not divided be.

. . . . . .

Destroy the roots from which they grow—
too great their increase—and lay low
each Saxon, robbing him of life;
give the same treatment to his wife.

Burn their women, coarse, untrue,
burn their uncouth children too,
and burn down their black houses:
rid us of their grouses.

Send their ashes down the flood
when you've burnt their flesh and blood;
show no rue to living Saxon,
death-dealing salmon-hero—tax them!

Remember, cheek of raspberry hue,
that Saxons lord it over you;
keep in memory their spite
as Saxon power has grown in might.

Remember Colin, your own father,
remember Archibald, your grandfather,
remember Duncan after them,
a man who loved both hounds and men.

Remember the other Colin then,
and Archibald of Arran,
and Colin of the Heads, who won
the hero's stakes, ere he was done.

Remember these men did not yield,
for fear of Saxon in the field;
why should you make submission now
and bend before them your proud brow?

Since of the Gael there now remain
but scant survivors of the slain,
together gather all your men;
strike fear into the foe again.

Attack the Saxons in their land,
awake! MacCailein, understand,
O golden-haired one, that a fighter
profits much by sleeping lighter.[12]

Strong anti-Saxon feeling shows up elsewhere in the bardic poetry, as for example in a poem in praise of Alasdair [Colkitto] MacDonald after the battle Kilsyth (1645),[13] but the above poem is certainly a *locus classicus*.

We get a different kind of political poem, this time concerned with more domestic issues, in Fionnlagh Ruadh's elegy for Allan, of the Clanranald branch, a poem which dates from early in the sixteenth century. It is full of hostile comment on one who had committed sacrilege, and who is, according to the poet, morally depraved. It may be Allan's activities in Perthshire that are mainly commented on here, although his more domestic reputation, for incest, does not escape the poet's condemnation:

It is no wonder that he should be in torment:
it is long since Allan was gallows-ripe;
do not talk of the sexual vigour of the man
who had relations with his mother and his sister.[14]

There is extant a much more circumspect elegy for Allan, possibly by John MacMhuirich, but the existence of traditional stories about the incestuous activities of a Clanranald chief may lend some weight to Fionnlagh Ruadh's hint. The late W. J. Watson suggested that Fionnlagh Ruadh's poem may in fact be a mock-elegy, composed before Allan's death. This would explain the freedom of its accusations. The form of the mock-elegy is particularly well known in medieval Welsh poetry, but is not well attested in Gaelic.

B

A popular type of political poem, evidently forming a staple part of clan propaganda, was that which listed the allies that a chief or clan might call on. Several examples of this clan-verse occur in the surviving bardic corpus, and it is a well-defined genre in the vernacular verse of the seventeenth and eighteenth centuries. The fifteenth-century prose poem on the army and arming of John of the Isles is a comparatively early example, and there are later ones, more developed and closer to the style of the vernacular clan-verse. One such is Niall MacMhuirich's "Mór an lén-sa ar aicme Íle", where the poet lists some of the notable septs attached to the MacDonalds of Islay, producing some elegant vignettes such as that of the MacBeths, physicians and surgeons at one time to the Lords of the Isles, who are described as:

> the Clan MacBeth, accurate in their practice,
> carvers of bones and arteries.[15]

Another is the anonymous seventeenth-century (?) poem[16] addressed to the chief of the Campbells of Argyll, listing the clans that would rally to his support. It makes a strange list, including as it does MacDonalds from the north, Macleans, Clanranald, MacLeods and Mackinnons. This poem, like most of its kind in the vernacular tradition also, is competent but lacks any lyrical fire to raise its temperature.

The clans most loudly celebrated in the surviving poetry are the MacDonalds, the Campbells and the MacGregors. The two former clans were among the most powerful in late medieval times in the Highlands. The Campbells came to power partly by moving into the vacuum created by MacDonald decline, partly by aggression against the MacGregors, Macleans and other clans. It seems likely, however, that only fragments survive of their archives of bardic praise. The MacDonald archive survived rather better, perhaps because their poets had moved to the Outer Isles, where they survived into a later period. But the survival is also due to the Dean of Lismore's interest. So, entirely, is the survival of a group of poems celebrating MacGregor chiefs from the early fifteenth to the early sixteenth century, and giving a picture of war and peace which should be remembered as a corrective to the later reputation of the MacGregors after the time of their outlawry. The picture of the early fifteenth century has its warlike detail, but has a balance that is hard to find in the biased Lowland sources of the sixteenth and seventeenth centuries. Writing of the MacGregor Chief called Maol Coluim, who succeeded in 1415, the poet says:

A full battle-complement of captains
rises with him in the day of battle;
a strong thirst afflicts the golden spears
of his household in the fight.

MacGregor, beloved of poets,
clearly shows, in valour's gap,
leadership and devotion to duty
(this brings glory to all his tribe alike).

In his court with its many doors
there are numerous fair-wrought helmets and slender blades
with red gold on their hilts:
the weapons of the Lion of Loch Awe.

Harps being played in harmony
in the hero's stronghold, in the hands of minstrels;
his household go from the backgammon boards
to walk in the shade of the garden.

. . . . . .

Lamont's daughter wins
the reputation of liberality to poets;
she has enlarged her kindred's fame
by what her [generous] hand has bestowed.[17]

Maol Coluim's wife was a daughter of the Chief of the Lamonts, and it is of interest to recall that one of the two surviving medieval harps in Scotland is the Lamont Harp, said to have been brought from Argyll by a daughter of the Lamont family when she married into the family of the Robertsons of Lude in Perthshire, about the year 1464. The harps our poet writes of were probably the contemporaries of that one.

Harpers were often poets also, as we know from both the Irish and the Scottish tradition, and we have one notable survival of this in the Scottish Gaelic vernacular tradition: An Clàrsair Dall or The Blind Harper, a well-known seventeenth-century poet. The

Dean of Lismore includes two poems by a mid-fifteenth-century poet-harper, Giolla Críost Brúilingeach, who is in all probability one of a family of Galbraiths from Gigha, a family which acted as harpers to the MacDonalds of the Isles. One of Giolla Críost's poems contains a specific request for a harp. The poem is addressed to Tomaltach Mac Diarmada, lord of Moylurg in Connacht, a chief who died in 1458. The poem contains elaborate description and praise of Mac Diarmada, and his household and demesne, goes on to make the request for the harp, and ends gracefully with the traditional compliment to the lady of the house:

It is the hand that in Ireland relieves
the distress of Gael and of foreigner,
a prince among men, a smooth-soled chief,
a heart unstained, ready to give support.

. . . . . .

Red wheat grows on smooth plains
under the rule of Tomaltach, lord of Céis;
on the white-hazelled domain of Coll's descendant
each ear of corn carries its full burden.

Cows yield sweet milk in milking folds;
he has fallow land most rich in grass;
both in its smooth demesne and its hilly land
it is lovely country bearing a heavy crop.

Tomaltach, lord of all,
has fierce deerhounds on golden leashes;
in early morning there are studs of horses in the proud assembly
round the most warm lough of virtue.

. . . . . .

The most joyous court on the ridge of the world
is Mac Diarmada's fort, with its bright aspect:
the white castle with its precious stones
above the tranquil lough of Cé.

Horns and goblets and fair-wrought cups
are there in the thronging court of Lough Cé;

wine is quaffed in that capital of garnered plenty:
it is the palace of a noble king.

Numerous are the members of his household, comely and noble,
numerous his vestures and tall steeds;
spears and blades and mailcoats,
and sedate, large-kneed, stern men.

. . . . . .

I have come—good is my reason—
from Scotland to visit you, as is meet,
drawn by your fame, O white-footed son of Connacht,
O great handsome Tomaltach.

I have come to make a request of you,
from Scotland, O golden-haired one,
over the stormy sea with its clustering wave-tops,
chill and huge, the home of grilse and salmon.

A harp in special, in return for my poem,
grant me at my request, O king,
O countenance like the ripe fruit of the apple-tree,
for this is something that you happen to have.

O Son of Conchobhar of the Rock's haven,
to pay poet-bands befits you well;
the account of your handsomeness is being chronicled;
may Ireland be yours for your filling of hands.

The daughter of Walter de Burgh of Brega
is a famous lady who does not stint store;
her hair is deep-trenched, bright-locked, in tresses:
she is the choice one among Ireland's fair ladies.

Caitilín of the white palms
has a long lovely hand decked with rings;
red her lips, luscious and noble,
gleaming the rosy nails of her hands.[18]

We learn from another poem of Giolla Críost's that he got the harp: indeed it would have been surly to withhold it after that:

> Tomaltach, whose vow was not paltry,
> gave me his food and his bragget,
> and a harp because of my [song];
> that hand was the best I have found.[19]

There was nothing particularly unusual in a Scottish poet addressing a poem to an Irish patron, nor in an Irish poet paying court to a Scottish chief. The two countries formed part of the same culture-region. The region was to become attenuated in modern times, particularly after the seventeenth century, but in the age of the bardic poets it was still extensive, and it had points of great strength. In Scotland the most notable of these bastions of the Gael was the Lordship of the Isles. The premier MacDonald family had strong links with the Church hierarchy, and the one-time fount of the Christian Church in Scotland, Iona, was within their territory. The links between the Lordship on the one hand, and the Church on the other, with Ireland were very strong, and were periodically reinforced, as when a thirteenth- to fourteenth-century MacDonald chief, Aonghus Og, married an Irish Lady, who brought with her, according to tradition, a large retinue of Irishmen who founded Scottish families. This retinue was known as *tochradh nighean a' Chathanaich* or "O'Kane's daugher's dowry", and it is said to be from one of these immigrants that the MacBeth family of physicians sprang.

We find various officials retaining an Irish-type name, indicating that they had come late from Ireland: an O'Henna poet in the fifteenth century, harpers called O'Senog in the sixteenth century and, later, physicians of the name of O'Conacher in the sixteenth century also, poets of the name of Ó Muirgheasáin in the sixteenth and seventeenth centuries. An ecclesiastic called Rogellus Obrolchan was Secretary to Alexander Lord of the Isles in 1426.

As was noted earlier, the author of the eleventh-century *Duan Albanach* had probably been an Irish poet, and it is not uncommon in the twelfth and thirteenth centuries to find references, especially in the Irish Annals, to poets who hold the title "Ollamh of Ireland and Scotland". The *ollamh* was a very senior poet, a doctor of poetry as it were. The title embracing Ireland and Scotland may have been more honorific than functional, but it helps to show that the two countries were regarded as a cultural unit. In the early thirteenth century, when Muireadhach Ó Dálaigh came to Scotland, acquiring the name Muireadhach Albanach or "Scottish Murray", he addressed Gaelic poems to the Lord of Lennox, and doubtless was rewarded for them, and it would appear that he put down roots in Scotland, founding the MacMhuirich line. He had an Irish contemporary who also carried a Scottish soubriquet, Gilla Bríde Albanach, and in fact both these Hiberno–Scottish poets took part in the Fifth Crusade, in the second decade of the thirteenth century, leaving poems which comment on their Mediterranean sojourn.

The evidence of Irish poets' incursions into or connections with Scotland has not been collected, but this would make an interesting footnote to literary history. One of the most extended of such incursions was made by an Ó Dálaigh poet called Aonghus nan Aor in the sixteenth century, when he addressed satirical verses to many Scottish chiefs and lords.

There is a good deal of evidence of Scottish poets visiting Ireland and treating Irish themes in their verse. Éoin Óg Ó Muirgheasáin, in his elegy for Rory Mór MacLeod in 1626, deals in detail with Rory Mór's campaigns in Ireland in 1594 and 1595,[20] and Maol-Domhnaigh Ó Muirgheasáin wrote four poems, which still survive, during a sojourn in West Munster about the year 1642. Niall MacMhuirich contributes two poems, about the year 1690, to a bardic disputation which took place among Irish poets, regarding which clans or septs had a right to the heraldic symbol of the "red hand". It is worth noting that in both these poems there are references to the famous sixteenth-century Irish poet Tadhg Dall Ó Huiginn, who was regarded as an exemplar by later poets in Ireland and Scotland, and notably by the later MacMhuirichs. One can sense that Niall MacMhuirich feels his distance from Ireland, regarding it as a fount of bardic knowledge. Tradition reports that his family maintained their links with the Irish bardic schools until the seventeenth century.

These schools provided the rule-books of the bardic guild, and provided them quite literally. There are still extant handbooks of metre and syntax, the Metrical and Syntactical Tracts used in the bardic schools. These lay down the canons of metre and language for bardic poets, indicating what variants are permissible, what conventions must be observed. In addition to these specific conventions governing the use of "syllables, quartans, concord, correspondence, termination and union'', to quote the language of a seventeenth-century account of such a school,[21] there were many more purely literary conventions which were widely observed, and appear in bardic verse from both Ireland and Scotland. One such, or more precisely a series of such conventions, governed the ideal relationship between the chief or patron and the man of learning or the poet. It was a relationship hallowed by antiquity but tempered by practical considerations. One of the finest expressions of this complex relationship occurs in a poem to be dated between 1641 and 1645, in which the poet (probably one of the MacEwen family) addresses the Marquess of Argyle, asking him to restore the poet's patrimony, presumably those lands on Loch Melfortside that were held by the MacEwens in virtue of their bardic office:

Restore to me my father's heritage
in honour of the art [of poetry],
O branch laden with fruit,
as one might expect from the greatness of your name and the
    praise you have had.

Understand, O darling of the schools
and guiding star of poets,
since you are the lord over your kin,
that wrong inflicted by you on me is unjust.

The tribute of my ancestors from whom I am sprung,
the fervour of love, the rigour of their art;
what rent brings more lasting fame,
O chief whose hand is most resolute in warfare?

It is not gold nor other treasure
that you will get from me in special;
it is not tribute, nor gift of cattle,
but the choicest of our hard-wrought poems.

In the ancient books of men of learning,
and in the gleanings of our ever-fresh poems,
there will remain [on record] each good deed that shall be done
    to me,
O fair-judging, bright and lofty earl.[22]

It is a dignified plea, somewhat marred by the final stanza of the poem, where the Marquess is said to have the valour of Conall Cearnach and the learning of Aristotle. The late W. J. Watson thought the poem must have been written before 1645, when Argyle's conduct at the Battle of Inverlochy so clearly belied this imputed valour, but I think this is perhaps to underestimate the bardic poet's capacity for uncritical flattery.

A few years earlier, about 1636, Cathal MacMhuirich had referred to the approaching end of the system of bardic patronage:

> Now that the Clanranald have left us
> learning cannot be followed by us;
> it is time for the ollave to follow them,
> his gifts will be hidden away.[23]

Niall MacMhuirich, in his elegy for Allan of Clanranald in 1715, shows that Cathal had been too pessimistic, but echoes his mood, this time with greater justification. He recalls that Allan was a patron of the arts, interested in:

> the playing of music and the composing of poems,
> the cherishing of every artistic practice,

and he goes on to predict that now they will:

> for ever lack reciting from books
> the traditional learning of the Gael.[24]

The strong intellectual strain in these poets of the MacMhuirich family may be responsible for preventing the relationship between poet and patron from deteriorating into venality. Nor do I recall an instance from a Scottish bardic context of the cynicism which the Irish bardic poets sometimes showed when confronted with changes in the balance of power, and the appearance of an English instead of an Irish patron. Perhaps the MacEwen poet mentioned above hovers on the brink of venality. And it must have been difficult to hold in balance such disparate considerations as the demands of an ancient and rigorous artistic tradition, the practical matter of income and livelihood, and intellectual honesty.

It would not be claimed, by any student of bardic verse, that intellectual honesty was the most salient characteristic of the tradition. But convention may here be regarded as a safety-valve. There are times, for example, when it may be suspected that the honest poet used direct, lyrical praise when it was honest to do so, and resorted to the analogue or the apologue when he had no desire to be emotionally involved in his subject. It may be significant in this context that Cathal MacMhuirich uses an analogue (relating to the Clann Uisneach) in his composite elegy of *c.* 1636, an elegy which gives the impression of being a conventional exercise, and lacking true power and concentration. Again a MacMhuirich poet, probably John, includes a long and rather overworked analogue concerning Cú Chulainn, in the elegy for Allan and Ranald (who died *c.* 1509), and it has been suggested already that there were skeletons in that particular cupboard. It may be significant also that the poem of praise for the Marquess of Argyle who fled the field at Inverlochy, referred to above, includes a Cú Chulainn analogue, in addition to making extravagant comparisons to classical warriors such as Hector, Pompey and Caesar.

The analogue was not, however, used merely as a scapegoat, and if it was used in this way at all, it must have been a secondary development. Its primary function was to add variety and dramatic colouring to a poem, sometimes by bringing to a homely or familiar subject the dimensions of legend and romance, or even history. Sometimes the parallels drawn were of a kind that would be very familiar to the poet's patron, or public; sometimes they drew on more recondite knowledge, either of Gaelic story or of medieval Latin *exempla*. Fionnlagh Ruadh, praising John, Chief of Clan Gregor in the early sixteenth century, compares his house ("the palace of the poets in Scotland") with that of Aodh Mac Diarmada, the successor of that Tomaltach to whom we saw Giolla Críost addressing his request for a harp. Once, he says, Mac Diarmada found:

> an aged ill-favoured creature in his house,
> one who had slipped past the warrior-guard of his strong-
> hold.

> When she came to his house
> Mac Diarmada settled the crone
> by the ribbed side of the house,
> the cloaked spectre (or "Scald-crow") of a crone.

Without consulting the household company
a bed is spread for the witch
in the fair hostel;
she spends a year lying there without rising.

No one asked her
from what land she was;
throughout the year (she was) in his dwelling,
along with Mac Diarmada in his stronghold.

At the end of the year she arose
(it is a tale for which there is true testimony),
that crone who really lacked comeliness,
as a young, bright and lovely maiden.[25]

And the poet goes on to say that no more is a guest turned away
from MacGregor's house than the crone was from Mac Diarmada's.
It cannot be denied that this praise of MacGregor's hospitality
gains in vividness from the use of the analogue. It was a popular
one, and was used in another poem (this time an Irish one) in the
Book of the Dean.[26]

We have seen already that an Irish legendary analogue was used
in the pre-Flodden poem of incitement, and that Cú Chulainn
analogues were used in a MacMhuirich elegy and a MacEwen
panegyric. Such analogues were used in religious poetry also, as in
Maol Domhnaigh mac Mhaghnuis Mhuiligh's Mary-poem, from
the Book of the Dean, where it is of the type of *exemplum* widely
known in Latin in medieval times, and collected in Irish MSS.[27]
Giolla Críost Táilliúr, a fifteenth-century poet, has a religious
poem in the Dean's collection where he uses the apologue of the
unicorn and the man in the tree.[28] There was perhaps an element of
flourishing esoteric learning in this aspect of bardic convention.

The poets use, naturally, the common themes of their own
times, and we may take as an example of this the theme of the
Seven Deadly Sins. The most explicit treatment of this theme in
the bardic verse is in a poem included by the Dean and ascribed
to Donnchadh Óg. It may owe something to William Dunbar's
"The Dance of the Sevin Deidly Synnis", composed near the year
1500,[29] but the theme was widely known. There is a closely related
version in the late seventeenth-century Fernaig MS, ascribed
(impossibly) to Bishop John Carswell. John Stewart of Appin, in a

hymn probably of the late sixteenth century refers in passing to some of the standard sins, as does Cathal MacMhuirich in his poem "Mairg chaomhnas a cholann", on the enmity of the body and the soul.

A widely-used conventional theme of the praise-poetry is description of the house, household and demesne of the person praised. We have seen two instances already, in the poem to the MacGregor chief Maol Coluim, and in Giolla Críost's description of Mac Diarmada's house. Fionnlagh Ruadh uses this method in one of his poems in praise of John MacGregor in the early sixteenth century.

> I will vaunt, since they are within his house,
>
> . . . . . .
>
> each great smooth door within the house
> in which day and night are equally bright.
>
> . . . . . .
>
> Frequently the hounds and hosts
> of red-weaponed John perform mighty deeds;
> when the hunting party goes out from the house
> every greensward is turned to red.
>
> . . . . . .
>
> Wine is drunk by stately ladies,
> MacGregor, in your great hall:
> in your strong spacious mansion
> wax seems to blaze right to the door posts.[30]

One of the prime bardic exponents of this technique was the Irish poet Tadhg Dall, whose work dates mainly from the latter half of the sixteenth century, and he has an especially strong sense of place and appreciation of property. It was, however, central to the tradition of the bardic praise-poem to produce this kind of orchestration, and we find this being carried over into the vernacular praise-poetry of the seventeenth and eighteenth centuries. Notable exponents of this are Màiri Nighean Alasdair Ruaidh and Iain Lom in the seventeenth century.

The use of pathetic fallacy sequences may be considered in this context. These belong firmly to the tradition of the praise-poem, and, like other conventions, this one can be applied mechanically or enlivened by contact with an original mind. A case in point might be the poem by a MacEwen bard, about the year 1475, in which the following stanzas occur:

> The chick not yet hatched from the egg suffers drought
> now that MacDougall of Dunollie is dead;
> since he died (he was of the race of Conn)
> no nut has parted from the trees.
>
> A savage storm breaks the woods,
> the yawning ocean laments him;
> on the high part of the shore, because of John's death,
> flocks of birds have been able to descend from the sky and
> settle.[31]

It should be said that the first line above translates a brilliant emendation made by the late Osborn Bergin, and whether the originality was the poet's or Bergin's may be a matter for debate.

Nature is seen as being in sympathy with the fortunes of the chief in both a negative and a positive way, shrivelling and withdrawing on his death, burgeoning in the kindly warmth of a good chief's rule, so that a later poet sees the branches laden with nuts during the reign of a Campbell "lion of Loch Fyne", and the balmy heat drying up the cataracts on the burns.[32] The MacMhuirich poets use the convention freely, producing a fine range of examples. The author of the 1509 elegy for Allan and Ranald sees the produce of the land enticed away by the sea, contrasting this with the prosperity which people enjoyed when Allan was alive:

> Brilliant in the view of all was the progress
> that the land of the Hebrides made in the time of Allan;
> in his lifetime it enjoyed a spell when every produce was abundant:
> it seems to me that it was not the land that was responsible for this.[33]

Cathal MacMhuirich about the year 1636, sees the obverse of this happy condition:

small the produce that all of the lands yield,
the wave has consumed it right up to the foot of the mountains.[34]

And Niall MacMhuirich, on the death of Allan of Clanranald in
1715, says there is no warmth in the rain now, while the wind
howls, potholes are filled with water, there are no nuts on the trees,
and the salmon lie on the icy rocks in the pools. There are rather
more apocalyptic disturbances reported in an elegy of 1705, probably by an Ó Muirgheasáin poet, who refers to showers of fire, and
streams rising above the woods.[35]

Another convention which is widely observed in the praise-
poetry is the courteous address to the lady of the house. This
usually comes at or near the end of the poem. In an early sixteenth-
century poem in praise of Torquil MacLeod, chief of the Mac-
Leods of Lewis, the two final stanzas are devoted to his wife:

> Catriona, daughter of MacCailein,
> of the soft palm, of the tressed locks,
> daughter of the Earl of Argyll,
> the best lady I have found.
>
> We have found a lady who cannot be excelled,
> sprung from a great, heroic, comely line,
> MacCailein's daughter, a young shapely blossom,
> her hair curled like the *cornán*.[36]

This is another instance of the intertwining of ruling families by
intermarriage. A *locus classicus* of this situation in Ireland can be
studied in the late sixteenth-century bardic verse of Tadhg Dall,
where we see the poet moving from house to house within the
close-knit nexus of Western Irish families: Maguires, O'Donnells
and O'Neills. It was an additional stimulus to bardic mobility, and
the Scottish poets can be seen to take full advantage of it also.

Sometimes we notice the convention being observed only per-
functorily, as in a poem of Cathal MacMhuirich's. The final verse
devoted to the lady ends:

> this is a stanza for her of my lay,[37]

as though he could find nothing more to say about her. It is a
serious, and uncharacteristic, lapse of artistry for Cathal, and it
occurs in a poem which is perfunctory in other respects also.

This convention is also carried over into the vernacular verse, appearing in transitional verse, such as a sixteenth-century poem to a MacFarlane of Arrochar, as well.[38]

Yet another convention is that of the dating stanza, as in Niall MacMhuirich's elegy for Allan of Clanranald:

> Seventeen hundred years complete
> and exactly fifteen years
> from the birth of the Lord to the death of Allan,
> whosoever should make enquiry.[39]

As one further example of bardic convention, this time concerned with professional etiquette, we may recall Muireadhach Albanach's poem to one of the Lennox lords. He refers to a *dúan* or poem which he has already given to Amhlaoibh, and says that it is fitting now to give him a *laoidh* or lay. Whatever the precise distinction implied by these terms, it is clear that *laoidh* is the smaller, less weighty composition for he likens it to the after-shower or short gust of rain which often follows a heavy shower:

> there is no shower without its little shower.[40]

Bardic verse, and especially praise-poetry, was essentially a product which had to be made available on demand, when the occasion demanded it, and hence it had to rely heavily on technical competence and the application of well-understood and readily-marshalled formulae. A poem could well be constructed from these materials alone, and many were. Some of these poems, showing technical competence but no lyrical fire, can be impressive although they do not move the reader. They fit with such assurance into an established tradition, handling metrical tools with precision, or laying lapidary phrases, using syllable-counts and alliteration as guide-lines. This can occur in what is thematically a rather pedestrian poem. An anonymous poem to a Campbell chief which shows little or no originality of thought or treatment, is to some extent redeemed by this lapidary quality. It is virtually impossible to reproduce the effect of this in another language because an important part of this effect lies in the resonance that words and phrases have within a poetic tradition. The last verse of this poem might be translated, a little roughly, to give a notion of its movement, but the words have quite the wrong resonance:

From early days you learnt love
the three traits a noble needs:
to nurse anger till action,
a hard heart, and doughty deeds.[41]

The lapidary quality appears frequently in the bardic verse, showing as a classical economy in words, with syllables laid like tiles,
each in its exact place, without nudging its neighbour. One such
poem is the anonymous elegy for Sir Norman MacLeod of Bernera,
who died in 1705. It reads to me like a work of the MacMhuirich
school, and if so it would be by Niall, but this is merely a subjective
impression. A verse from this elegy may be quoted in the original
Gaelic, so that its long series of monosyllables, like earth trickling
on to a coffin-lid, can be physically observed. I shall not venture a
verse translation, but translate the sense simply:

A seal féin fuair an t-eineach,
  ag so an díle dheireadhach;
a dhrud fá chré do chadal
  rug a ré go Roghadal.[42]

(Honour had its own day,
this is the final flood,
that shut your sleep under clay,
that brought his life-span to Rodel.)

There is a tendency for the artistry to be seen as applying to the
smaller unit: the stanza is often the unit of artistic care and
deliberation rather than the complete poem. David Greene makes
the interesting suggestion that the old method of composition of
bardic verse, in a darkened room with subsequent writing down,
may "explain a certain formlessness which the modern reader at
once feels . . . every quatrain is beautifully wrought and polished
but the connection between them is less strict than our taste
demands."[43] It may be suspected that what was a feature of the
training in the bardic schools, aimed partly at strengthening the
memory, was not always observed in later life by the poets, particularly in later centuries. I would doubt if Giolla Coluim Mac
an Ollaimh, in the late fifteenth century, felt obliged to find himself a darkened room for each time he had a poem to make. His
poems, at any rate, are not formless. One of them, addressed to the

Lord of the Isles, perhaps in the 1480s, has a well-constructed plot, and includes a neat turning of the tables: the poet, cleaned out by the thiggers or beggars whom he describes in amusing detail, goes to the Lord of the Isles to replenish his stock, in return for the verses. A few verses are quoted, to give the flavour of the poem and demonstrate the turn it takes:

I will recount to you a little of the thiggers' history, when they come to ask for gear.

They are courteous, friendly, kindly, as is proper; and when they are invited to stay for friendship's sake, they take the hint very readily.

They take a fit of displeasure, rough ill-humour and peevishness; they bend and gather their eyebrows in turn: "We will never be friends to you in distress."

. . . . . .

Then I rise up, and for shame's sake—a regular bondage—I give them a full handful of what I have.

. . . . . .

I shall give you an idea of the names the thiggers go by; Sons of Roving-eyes, Sons of Fly-by-night—that gives their ancestry.

Sons of Early-risers, who on a summer's day ask for more sun; Sons of Wandering, Sons of Greed, every one of them.

. . . . . .

They have taken our cattle and our horses from our house; our best plan is to go as well to find out which of us is best equipped to make expeditions of this kind.

To the hospitable thronged house of John MacDonald, who empurples spear-points, we will go, to thig from the generous open-handed one.[44]

And so the poem goes on, becoming a praise-poem to MacDonald, and suggesting that he will replace all these horses and cows and gear. Yet the poem in no way strikes a venal note. It has a healthy irony, and suggests an easy relationship between poet and patron. Giolla Coluim's poems on the downfall of the Lordship of the Isles, in the early 1490s, substantiate this conclusion.

Giolla Coluim was almost certainly a MacMhuirich, and there can be little doub t that this was the most distinguished bardic line in Scotland. The.r best poetry holds a place of high honour in bardic poetry generally. It often has clear stylistic power. Niall MacMhuirich, almost the last of the bardic family, can conduct an argument in verse with such clarity and clean vigour that it makes an instant impression. Some of Cathal's work is densely-packed, showing strong intellectual quality, and yet he is capable of a fine controlled lyricism also. We may fittingly enough conclude this discussion of the praise-poetry with a translation of Cathal's poem *"Cóir fáilte re fear do sgéil"*, composed on the home-coming of Domhnall, son of John of Moydart, from Ireland about 1650:

It is right to welcome you with the news that you have brought from the shore: let me have a word with you privately—my pride will soar as a result.

Sweeter than harp-music is your tale, young man without wound or blemish; if the converse of your lips was true, you are like an organ being played over wine.

. . . . . .

Donald, son of John, of the wavy hair, is the dear subject of your tale, O pleasant bright one; it is natural that I should love to hear that the man has come unwounded over the sea.

His safe arrival, fit and young, causes my lively spirits to mount; he is a slender branch in a lovely garden, a tree that will not bend, therein lies my delight until I die.

To visit him I go at once; it is the rule if I follow custom; I hasten to his unniggardly company, with rising spirits.

I see him opening his eyes, he by whom my strength has been

bestowed; I recognize at a distance over the sea his countenance that is flushed with wine-red blood.

Why should I not know his ringletted hair?—I judged that he would take after his kindred: beloved one of the great daughter of the queen of Ross, whose palm is gentle and whose nails are brown and well-trimmed.

I shall recognize the words that come from his lips, and his teeth bright as pearls—teeth that are not bared sullenly at me—and his merry, cheerful, mild eyes.

I recognize, a cast-length away from me, his well-proportioned, shapely, fine eyebrows, a noble lad with whom it is difficult to contend, whose side is smooth like a splash of lime.

I would know his footstep, leaping swiftly over the dykes; the heart with the quick winning virtues has coaxed away from me unawares the lock of my will.

The grandson of Donald is my great hope, my comrade in battle, at my back, my jewel that I love, my full moon, my vigorous apple-tree.

My tree of virtues, bearing fruit, my beloved is the elegant one with the ringletted hair; the son of a prince from whom knowledge has not been concealed, my battle-belt is the vigorous white-soled one.

Our well-water that does not run dry, our chieftain who wins the victory in war, the occasion of our mirth and our spontaneous joy, our precious liquor being drunk from golden goblets.

My sword, my slim tapering spear, my choice among Gaels and Lowlanders, one who guards his love for me, the apple of my eye.

We have ever, by natural bent, been given to strife; we set great store by your zeal; I do not conceal my strength in seeing you—through you I shall get justice and fair play.[45]

Some of the finest poems in bardic language are not, however, praise-poems. Tied though the bardic poet was to this central function, and dependent for posthumous fame on the chance survival of his work in a patron's library, he still wrote verses on subjects of his own choice. There can be little doubt that most of these have perished, but enough survives to allow us to savour this other side of the bardic poet's personality.

One special class of poetry may be looked at in a little detail: the courtly-love poetry, the *dánta grádha*. Irish has a small but rich collection of such poems. Scottish Gaelic has far fewer, and a number of them are still unpublished, except in the obscurity of the Dean's original spelling. These are similar in pattern to the Irish examples: a poem on the antithesis of love and lust by the Earl of Argyll, a satirical fragment by Donnchadh Mac an Phearsúin, some poems by Iseabail Ní Mhic Cailéin, a poem which draws on legendary characters and plays on the senses of *dán* (poem, destiny) by John MacMhuirich, a poem on the theme of jealousy by a cleric Donncha MacKermont (or Donncha mac Thearlaich?), a love-poem that teases us with thoughts of personal rather than literary experience, namely Niall Mór MacMhuirich's "*Soraidh slán do'n oidhche a-réir?*" Of these we may quote the last one first, in a version which takes only one or two small liberties:

> Farewell for ever to last night;
> swift though it passed, its joy remains:
> though I were hanged for my share in it
> I'd live it over tonight again.
>
> There are two in this house tonight
> whose eyes give their secrets away:
> though they are not lip to lip
> eager is the eyes' play.
>
> The eyes' swift glances must give all
> the tale their prisoned lips would tell;
> the eyes have kept no secret here,
> lips' silence is of no avail.
>
> Those who would make my true words false,
> have sealed my lips, O languid eye;

but in your corner, out of reach,
understand what my eyes say:

"Keep the memory of this night,
let there be no change till doom;
do not let the morning in:
throw out the cold day from the room."

Mother Mary, of fostering grace,
since poets look to you for light,
save me now, and take my hand—
farewell for ever to last night.[46]

Whether or not this poem (of about the year 1600) has personal connotations, it is true that poets, both professional and amateur but more often perhaps amateur, used the bardic language and metres for personal utterance. This seems unquestionably true of the one surviving poem by Aithbhreac Inghean Corcadail, who mourns the death of her MacNeill husband, and thinks sadly but joyfully of her life with him in Gigha in the 1460's:

O Rosary that recalled my Tear

O rosary that recalled my tear,
dear was the finger in my sight,
that touched you once, beloved the heart
of him who owned you till tonight.

I grieve the death of him whose hand
you did entwine each hour of prayer;
my grief that it is lifeless now
and I no longer see it there.

My heart is sick, the day has reached
its end for us two, brief the span
that I was given to enjoy
the converse of this goodly man.

Lips whose speech made pleasant sound,
in every land beguiling all,
hawk of Islay of smooth plains,
lion of Mull of the white wall.

His memory for songs was keen,
no poet left him without fee,
nobly generous, courteous, calm,
of princely character was he.

Poets came from Dùn an Oir,
and from the Boyne, to him whose hair
was all in curls, drawn by his fame;
to each he gave a generous share.

Slim handsome hawk of Sliabh Gaoil,*
who satisfied the clergy's hopes,
salmon of Sanas of quiet stream,
dragon of Lewis of sun-drenched slopes.

Bereft of this man, all alone
I live, and take no part in play,
enjoy no kindly talk, nor mirth,
now that his smiles have gone away.

Niall Og is dead; none of his clan
can hold my interest for long;
the ladies droop, their mirth is stilled,
I cannot hope for joy in song.

Gigha of smooth soil is bereft,
no need of music Dùn Suibhne feels,
the grass grows green round the heroes' fort;
they know the sorrow of the MacNeills.

The fort that brought us mirth, each time
we made our way there; now the sight
of it is more than I can bear
as I look on it from each height.

If Thou, Son of the living God,
hast breached the cluster on the tree,
Thou hast taken from us our choicest nut,
and plucked the greatest of the three.[47]

       * In Knapdale.

The topmost nut of the bunch is plucked,
Clan Neill has newly lost its head:
often the best of the generous men
descends to the MacNeills' last bed.

His death, the finest of them all,
has sapped my strength, and cost me dear,
taking away my darling spouse,
O rosary that recalled my tear.

My heart is broken in my breast,
and will not heal till death, I fear,
now that the dark-eyed one is dead,
O rosary that recalled my tear.

May Mary Mother, the King's nurse,
guard each path I follow here,
and may Her Son watch over me,
O rosary that recalled my tear.[48]

The simplicity and emotional surge of this poem may be seen as a foretaste of the many vernacular songs by women which survive from succeeding centuries. In other ways too we can detect links in taste and in psychological make-up between the bardic poetry and the folksongs. One such may be illustrated. The interest in macabre grave-detail is strong in both types of poetry:

I saw you, in my time,
O man who does not hear me now,
when chafers/worms would not be mangling you,
when a retinue of warriors filled your stronghold.[49]

This is from an early sixteenth-century poem. The next example is from a century later:

I see the red lips turned black,
and the chalk-white teeth turned to dark bone.[50]

A poem of 1705 sees Sir Norman MacLeod of Bernera "at the mercy of the worm",[51] and a poem in mixed Classical/Vernacular language takes up the same refrain:

Remember and remember again,
remember the linen shroud and the cover,
remember how the teeth blacken,
remember the harm the body does.[52]

We shall see some of this detail recurring, reminding us usefully that though recent centuries have driven a large wedge between different parts of the Gaelic poetic tradition, and between Gael and Gael, the connections are still there to find.

The Song-makers and their Songs

THE EVIDENCE OF the past and of the present points to the central function of song in Scottish Gaelic society, and in the intimate texture of people's lives. I remember my mother, almost always singing as she went about her house-work: the washing of dishes, scouring of pans, making of beds, and dusting of furniture was lightened for her, its dullness banished in the vicarious enjoyment of an imaginative world. The Rev. Norman MacDonald recalls how in his youth in Skye (about the time of the First War) men and women could be heard singing lustily, in the fields, as they went about their work,[1]* and Frances Tolmie writes of similar customs in the early years of the nineteenth century: "On a day in harvest, more than a hundred years ago, when every sort of outdoor work was accompanied by songs of suitable rhythm, a party of reapers assembled at Ebost, in Bracadale, divided themselves into two rival bands representing the poetesses who had originally sung the words of strife, and, while working with all their might to be first at the other end of the field which they were reaping, sang this song with so much fervour that they unconsciously cut themselves with their sickles and had very sore hands at the close of day."[2] It was about this time that Wordsworth heard the Solitary Reaper "reaping and singing by herself" in a more southerly part of Scotland.[3] The song to which Frances Tolmie refers dates from the earliest years of the seventeenth century, and commemorates a famous feud between Domhnall Gorm MacDonald of Sleat and Ruairi Mór MacLeod of Harris and Dunvegan, one of these "old, unhappy, far-off things/And battles long ago" which Wordsworth surmised was the matter of the Highland songs. This was indeed one favourite kind of matter, but equally prominent was the "familiar matter of to-day/Some natural sorrow, loss or pain/That has been, and may be again".

Songs used to accompany work, especially rhythmical processes, have often been called labour-songs, but this is perhaps too solemn

* For Notes, see pp. 308–11.

a term, and may be misleading if it obscures the joy that people took in work. The highly rhythmical work-songs not only lightened the monotony of repetitive work processes but also brought to some of these a positive zest. This is most evident in the cloth-waulking songs, for waulkings became social occasions of high attraction. It is probable, however, that song was used as an accompaniment to work from time immemorial.

Song is woven into the emotional texture of life also, and is used both in celebration and as therapy. The foster-nurse celebrates the growth to maturity of her fosterling, or his heroic exploits; the jilted or bereaved girl assuages her grief in highly-wrought song. The personal keens are among the most dramatic of emotional songs, but many of the songs show a lack of inhibition which was perhaps characteristic of that "heroic" society which lasted so late in Gaelic Scotland. The keen, as well as being therapy, was also ritual, and this brings a stylized element into it. Religious song, too, has sometimes a strongly emotional drive. Rarer, but clearly represented, is song of an introspective kind, which is not actively projected, but rather leaks into the general consciousness.

The great period of this song, at any rate as it has survived, is the sixteenth to the eighteenth century, with some later outliers. This song came out of a society which was close, kin-based, rural, independent and self-sufficient in the main. It was not cut off entirely from external contact, for it had trade links with Ireland and the Low Countries, links through military service with Germany and Flanders, cultural contacts with Ireland, the Lowlands of Scotland, Italy, Spain and (perhaps mainly through Ireland) France. It was not, however, strongly attracted to external influences during the sixteenth to eighteenth centuries. Exotic references merely give colouring occasionally to the native product. We would have to go farther back, in all probability beyond the time of our surviving song-texts, to find the origins of those links with Romance folk-poetry, especially perhaps the *carole*, which Seán Ó Tuama conjectures for Irish song, suggesting that they were forged in the late Norman period.[4] One would expect influences of this kind on Gaelic Scotland to have come both more directly and via the Irish route.

The mood of the bardic verse can sometimes be seen to be carried over into the more popular verse of the sixteenth and seventeenth centuries. Inflated, romantic descriptions of a chief's style, dress or galley are cases in point, as in the late sixteenth- or early

seventeenth-century song *Tàladh Dhòmhnaill Ghuirm*, addressed
to Donald MacDonald of Sleat. This chief of Sleat died in 1617.
Although the song is called a *Tàladh* or "lullaby", and is attributed
to the chief's foster-mother, this is probably a convention, and the
song may well have been composed when he was a grown man.

Donald Gorm's Lullaby

... *Nàile nàile*
early tomorrow.
of the other woman,
west of the coast
Starvation take ye!
What ship, but Donald's
the ship of my king,
Heavy I think it,
a rudder of gold
a well of wine
a well of pure water

nàile to travel
Then asked the woman
"What ship is yon
in the sea of Canna?"
Why should I hide it?
the ship of my baby,
the ship of the Islands.
the lading that's in her;
three masts of willow,
down at her quarter,
up at her shoulder.

Nàile nàile
When the sun of my king
'tis not with five men
'tis not with nine men
a hundred to sit with you,
a hundred more *hó*
twelve hundred there
twelve hundred there
twelve hundred there

Nàile hó nàile
travels southward,
'tis not with six men,
'tis not with ten men;
a hundred to stand with you,
send sunwise the cup to you,
to make sport with you,
to drive the football with you,
in feir of war with you.

Not more are the prickles
or sheaves of oats
or wisps of old straw
than shields and swords
blue steel helmets
bows of the yew
Many the bluebonnet
and candles of wax

on the thorn-tree,
on a field in autumn,
on the side of a bothy
in the court of Donald
and arrow quivers,
and battle-axes.
hung on a peg there,
in lanterns blazing.

Might of the brightness,
be between Donald Gorm

might of the sunbeam,
and his raiment,

might of the cornshoot	in the Maytime,
might of the billows	heavy, heroic,
might of the salmon	headlong leaping,
might of Cuchulann	in full war-gear,
might of the seven bands,	the host of the Fiann,
might of sweet Oisein,	of valorous Oscar,
might of the storm	and the tearing tempest,
might of the thunder	and the hideous lightning,
might of the great sea-monster	blowing,
might of the elements	and the hosts of heaven
be between Donald Gorm	and his raiment;
each one of those	and the might of God's son.[5]

Another literary description of a seventeenth-century galley, in the song *Mhic Iarla nam Bratach Bàna* (Son of the Earl of White Banners), makes the gear and rigging no less rich and ornate:

> She had a gold rudder and two silver masts,
> ropes made of the silk of Galway,
> the thick red silk of Spain,

and adds as though to underline the point;

> It was not from Glasgow that came.[6]

We can see links with other literary models in the various kinds of love-song which form an important part of the corpus. A soldier-poet who recalls how eager the ladies of Flanders were for his attentions, begins his love-song with a conventional dream reference to his Scottish sweetheart who seems rather harder to get than the Continental ladies.[7] The strongly individual style that the poetry of *amour courtoise* took in Irish can be seen in Scottish Gaelic too, even in vernacular verses such as this example of an exchange between "him" and "her":

> He
> I would give love for love,
> fondness for fondness give,
> regard for your regard,
> for all my life and span.

> She
> If your heart were fast,
> and never prone to stray,
> I would give you love
> as Deirdre gave to Naois.[8]

Allied in rhythm and tone to the Irish *dánta grádha*, but evidently personal and sincere whereas many of these are not necessarily so, is that sixteenth-century love-song which has been attributed to Eachann Mór (Maclean) of Duart. It was addressed to the lady who became his wife, the daughter of MacDonald of Dùn Naomhaig. This is a formal love-song, literary rather than sub-literary, made in awareness of the love-song tradition which had gone before, but different from it, and different also from the detailed, itemizing type of love-song which was to gain favour later. This has simplicity and restraint:

> Restless my sleep tonight
> as I turn from side to side,
> my heart is warped in my breast,
> my mind dark and doleful indeed.
>
> In that house not far from here
> lies the tender fair-formed maid,
> chalk-white teeth and lips that sing
> sweeter-voiced than harp-strings.
>
> New season's spray, fair curling growth,
> woman whose eyes are modest, mild,
> whose cheeks are like the rowan, red,
> alight like the pictured rose.
>
> Like foam on the water, clean,
> like the swan on the eager sea,
> snow-drift-white is the gem
> of her face suffused with joy.
>
> Fair fingers on white palms,
> a breast of loveliest hue,
> the love that I gave to her
> makes a sad tale to tell.

I shall climb neither hill nor height,
my step is heavy and weak,
no joy lights up my face,
only the earth can heal.

Like the topmost grain of the ear,
like the straight young tree in the wood,
like the sun hiding the stars,
among womankind are you.[9]

Occasionally in the folksongs we find specific themes and specific workings of themes that must at one time have been known from end to end of the Gaelic area, understanding by that the larger area of Gaelic/Irish speech stretching from Cape Wrath in Scotland to Cape Clear in the south of Ireland.[10] Two well-known instances are the songs known as *"A' Bhean Eudach"* ("The Jealous Woman") and *"Dónall Óg/Fear a' Bhàta"* ("Young Donald/The Boatman") to give the usual Irish/Scottish Gaelic titles of the second song. The theme of the first song is that of the story of "Binnorie", which is found widely outwith the Gaelic area also. The "jealous woman" entices her sister to gather dulse on the rocks at low tide. The sister is trapped by the incoming tide, and drowned, and the "jealous woman" then marries her sister's husband, but after some time is heard singing this song which her sister had sung as the water rose to engulf her. This is part of her cry:

Pity tonight   my three children,
the one-year-old   the two-year-old,
the other little one   needing dandled.
Little John will have— your mother's calfie—
no suck tonight   from your mother's breast,
and if you had   it would not help you,
it will be full   not of milk but of brine.
Cold my bed   wet with brine;
lucky the bride   who takes my place,
she will meet with sense and meet with modesty,
she will have sheep,   white and hornless,
calving cows   and bulling heifers.
The boat will come   here tomorrow,
with my father aboard and my three brothers,

my goodman Macintyre   on the bow-oar,
and they will find me   drowned,
my blue coat   floating on the sea,
my silver brooch   on a rock beside me,
my rosary   in the hollow of my breast.
Hide it, hide it   from my mother
till the sun rises   tomorrow.[11]

The spread of the song *"Dónall Óg/Fear a' Bhàta"* has been investigated by Seosamh Ó Duibhginn.[12] The homogeneity here is a thematic rather than a verbal one, though there are some very close verbal resemblances also, the most striking in the stanza beginning *Thug thu 'n ear dhiom is thug thu 'n iar dhiom*:

You took the east from me, you took the west,
you took the moon from me, the sun above,
you took the heart from me, from out my breast,
you almost took my God from me, white love.[13]

It is true, of course, that lines, and sometimes whole stanzas or verse paragraphs are in a state of suspension in the tradition, and can attach themselves now to one song, now to another. A fuller comparative study of the Scottish and Irish song traditions would show that much that is common to both survived into modern times. Shakespeare, who puts the words *calmie custure me* in Pistol's mouth, presumably heard the Irish song which English sources of the sixteenth and seventeenth centuries call *"Callen o custure me"*, and the song *"Cailín ó chois tSiúire mé"* is no doubt of primary Irish origin, but we find it, in a metamorphosed form, embedded in the Scottish Gaelic tradition also.[14]

Sometimes the metre is suggestive of a much more archaic tradition than that with which ostensibly we are dealing. The split lines of the metre in *"A' Bhean Eudach"*, for example, are of an old type of which we find only the surviving remnants, I suspect, in Scottish Gaelic. In this type of song the line is broken up by vocables which have no semantic content, but which often split up close syntactic units in the line. Indeed, this syntactic cacophony seems to have attained the status of a stylistic device. It may be that these vocables, and the manner of using them, are a legacy from imported song-styles, as that of the *carole* or dance-song, imposed on an old native metrical structure.

Mental attitudes which belong to earlier times and systems are also embedded in the songs, or alternatively parts of an earlier system of society and thought survive, which give rise to some of the songs. The woman's attitude to the hunter is a case in point:

> I went to the Little Glen in autumn,
> I cast lots, and won the pick of them,
> I got the clever wise young man,
> a youth not "wanted" as an outlaw.
> You go to the hill of the joyous outcry,
> with your white sagacious hunting-hounds,
> with your terriers following after.
> That is my darling, not a wanderer,
> not a speckled-shank from the fireside,
> not a pale-face fearing cold
> . . . . . .
>
> You climb the hill with the breath coming hard,
> to gather the eggs from nests in the heather,
> and I would get my share of them
> from the breast of your linen shirt.[15]

Hunting prowess is a very common cause for compliment:

> Badger's blood on your shirt,
> and deer's blood on your coat.
>
> Blood of the speckled, spotted (deer) calf
> like cuffs above your fists.[16]

There are many songs on supernatural themes, some of them concerned with shape-shifting, and particularly with the mermaid theme, many more with the fairies, and especially their traffic with humankind. Mór (Marion), after consorting with a fairy-man, has a child, and leaves it by the fairy-mound, hiding near by. The father comes out of the mound, and sings a lullaby to his abandoned child:

> The calf of my calf (twice repeated)
> lies by the mound,
> without fire
> without comfort or shelter.

The milk-white brown-haired one (3)
bore me the boy,
though she did not
nurse him tenderly.

Mór, my beloved (3)
turn to your little boy,
and I shall give you
a fine string of trout.

You would get wine (3)
and whatever you wished.
You will get trout
from me by the loch-side.[17]

Sometimes contact with the fairy world arouses fear and horror, as in the girl who sings:

One night as I watched the fold
I began to shiver, not the shiver cold wakes.

I began to shudder, it was not the sort
of shudder that erysipelas brings.

And when I looked over my shoulder
I saw the little red-bearded man
combing and shaking out his locks.[18]

And there is a touching fragment of a song that is sometimes said to be about a fairy encounter, but such an explanation is hardly necessary:

You found me close to the cattle-fold (3)
let me home, my dear, as you found me there.

You found me close to the wall (3)
let me home, my dear, as I came.

My love is the one who comes prowling (3)
though he did not let me home as he found me.[19]

c

As might be expected in the thoroughly rural and pastoral society of earlier centuries, outdoor courting and mating is celebrated in the songs, sometimes in the form of a love-dialogue in a wood,[20] sometimes in the wistful terms of what might have been or what might still be, given the opportunity. The girl wishes she were with her young lover "on the top of a steep green mountain/With not a living soul close to us", and she says that they would consummate their union "as though we were married at the altar".[21] A similar thought appears in the song "*Mhic Fhir Shórasdail, mo rùn ort*", as in the final paragraph:

> Would that I were with the fine youth
> on top of the steep sharp mountains,
> with no living soul to see us.
> We would come modestly home,
> the red head-band would be folded away,
> and the peaked mutch would be the new fashion.[22]

The head-band or fillet was the badge of maidenhood, which the girl is anxious to put away.

A harsher, more rending cry comes through from this rejection-song:

> . . . . . .

> I gave you my love, not just any love,
> love that burnt into me like fire,
> O my God, woe to her who would give
> deep, deep love to another woman's son.

> But were you and I to meet on a moor,
> with no pillow but the holly tree,
> since it is wont to be sharp and wounding,
> I would put my arm, love, under your head.[23]

In such settings nature-references come readily to the poet's mind:

> The primrose comes in spring,
> fragrant its scent,
> your breath is fragrant, with the taste of sugar,
> it is your love-making that has deceived me.

White the swan, and white the seagull,
white the snow as it falls in February,
white the cotton-grass over the heather,
whiter than that my love's skin.[24]

This closeness to Nature is of course characteristic of much Celtic poetry, from many periods, and its capacity for fresh realization is astonishing. One further example shows how it can be combined with the most delicate kind of love-poetry:

That is how we'd go together
to cut, o-ho, the spray of pine,
that is how we'd go together.

So I'd go, we'll go together
to cut, o-ho, the spray of pine.

None beneath the sun would know
when you and I would go together.

Gladly I would kiss my sweetheart
when together we would go.[25]

The songs, however, are by no means all sad and soulful. It may be that the lighter, more humorous songs have not survived so well, for often they depend for their appeal on some facet of topicality or personality, but it is probable that they enjoyed as much popularity in earlier times as the topical and contemporary humorous songs do in Gaelic Scotland at the present time. An eighteenth-century song takes as its theme that one is never too old to try to cut a dash with the other sex. It shows the old man washing his hams, sticking his pistols in his belt, and arranging what hair he has carefully, but the young lady isn't taken in, and thinks that Rattle-bones is not much of a bargain.[26] Another popular, and still sung, song is the nonsense-song, which was supposed not to have a word of truth in it:

I saw, and well I can vouch for it,
seals delivering letters,
carrying satchel and wearing pelisse,
as wise as human beings.

I saw the crabs
dancing on the floors of carriages,
the heron with a stick
driving the sheep to the fold.[27]

At the other end of the scale, as it were, are the songs which are made of the stuff of history. The earlier of these are often on the topic of a battle or feud. Just as the earliest bardic poem of indubitably Scottish Gaelic origin is concerned with feud and approaching battle,[28] so our earliest vernacular songs survive because of similar kenspeckle connections. The poem of incitement for Harlaw (in 1411) may perhaps be called vernacular rather than bardic.[29] The stanzas ascribed to the Earl of Mar at the time of the first Battle of Inverlochy (in 1431) make another early instance,[30] and there is a long succession of songs on like themes from the sixteenth century onwards: *"La Millegàraidh"*[31] on the MacLeod–MacDonald feud *c.* 1570, *"A Mhic Iain 'ic Sheumais"* from 1601 (another episode in that feud),[32] a song from the Maclean–MacDonald feud in Islay from much the same time,[33] songs about MacGregor skirmishes in the late sixteenth and early seventeenth centuries,[34] a song about the MacDonalds at Auldearn in 1645,[35] about Highlanders who fought in Germany in the Thirty Years' War,[36] about the Jacobite Risings especially the '45,[37] and so on to modern times, with a crop of songs from the First World War, and one or two from the Second.[38]

The song to Mac Iain 'ic Sheumais, dated 1601, was composed by his foster-nurse, who nursed him back to health after his wounds at the Battle of Cairnish in North Uist. She recalls some of the other battles in which he had taken part, and goes on:

Your noble body's blood
lay on the surface of the ground.

Your fragrant body's blood
seeped through the linen.

I sucked it up
till my breath grew husky.

· · · · · ·

> Related to the King of Lewis
> is my clean, noble lion.
>
> MacLeod of Harris,
> though a friend, is a cold one.
>
> Related is my baby
> to the seed of Ailean Mac Ruairidh.[32]

The song from the Thirty Years' War begins in this way:

> I spent the night though it was long;
> I could not sleep,
> watching the brothers
> who were in the field below me.
>
> . . . . . .
>
> You acquitted yourselves well in Germany,
> your deeds there were not clumsy;
> you wear your swords slanting at your side,
> covered in a cloud of sweat;
> the helmet of steel
> becomes you on your curling hair.[36]

From the '45 there are both romantic and realist songs. One of those which presents Prince Charlie in a romantic light has this verse:

> They killed my father and both my brothers,
> destroyed my kin and pillaged my people,
> rased my country and stripped my mother,
> but my grief would ease if Charlie prospered.[37]

In stark contrast to this attitude is that of the author of what is perhaps the finest song of the '45, "*Mo rùn geal òg*". A few stanzas are translated here:

> O young Charles Stuart,
> your cause has grieved me,
> you took from me all
> in this war in your cause.

It's not cows or sheep
that I miss but my first-love,
you have left me alone
with nothing but a shift.

Alas I'm a poor soul,
full of sighs always,
I lost hope of you coming,
my heart has fallen a-bleeding;
neither fiddle nor harp
pipes, backgammon nor music,
nor young men will cheer me
since they laid you low.

Many lovely ladies,
in their silk and satin,
have envied me
for the kisses you gave me;
though I were endowed
with all Hanover's money
I'd defy the Commandments
that forbade us to marry.

. . . . . .

Thick set and broad-shouldered,
slim-waisted and shapely,
no ignorant tailor
could make you a short-coat,
or make you trews
that fitted exactly,
short-hose on your calves
white-salmon-bulging
my fair young love.[40]

These songs do not deal with historical events in a narrative
style, but there are other songs also dealing with personal emotions
to a large extent, which use narrative, sometimes tilting it in the
direction of the impressionistic style. Some of these are close in
mood to the ballads. The MacGregor songs of *c.* 1600 are impressionistic narratives, as for example "*Mi am shuidhe so 'm ònar*":

I sit here alone by the level roadway,
hoping to see, coming from Cruachan of the Mist, a fugitive
who will give me news of Clan Gregor, or of the way they went.
I have had no news of them but that they were in Strath Fillan
  yesterday,
that they were here and there about Loch Fyne, if my informants
  spoke true,
and in Dalmally, drinking wine to the health of the gentles.
Great red-haired Gregor was there, whose hand was hard behind
  his sword,
and great mirthful Gregor, the chief of our household.
O son of the laird of Strathardle, the bards used to visit you;
you would play the harp, and play backgammon willingly,
and you would make the fiddle sing, inciting women to dance.
It was a late foray you made in the Misty Glen,
you left Handsome John lying on the moor,
acting as threshold to a bog, hacked by a sword.
You lifted the dark-grey stud of horses from the windings of the
  river;
at the Dyke you took shelter on your way,
and there you left my dirk, and the baldric for my arrow-
  quiver.
This arrow from the battle field has lodged in my hide:
an arrow penetrated my thigh, a crooked ill-fashioned shaft.
May the King of the Elements save you from slim bullet and
  venomous powder,
from sparks of fire, from bullet and from arrow,
from sharp-pointed knife, and from keen edge of sword.

The company above the village on Sunday was not a talkative
  one,
and I shall not laugh merrily, when I rise or when I go to rest.
Little wonder: I am left alive when the folk of my house are
  dead.[41]

The song is shaped with much artistry: we are made aware in a
devious, ambiguous way of what happened, but the climax is held
until the final lines.

A still more impressionistic style is used in the song "Cairistìona".
Its exact circumstances are unknown, but it may be addressed to a
chief's daughter, perhaps a daughter of one of the Macdonalds of

Islay, and on stylistic grounds it reads like a seventeenth-century song, or possibly a sixteenth:

> *Cairistìona*
>
> Will you not answer, Cairistìona?
> Will you not answer, my dear love,
> if you answered I would hear you.
> I fostered you and gave you suck,
> I spent a year in the King's Court with you,
> why not say it, I spent three.
>
> . . . . . .
>
> I see ships on the Sound of Islay,
> many a ship and boat and galley,
> sailing the Sound as the tide rises,
> coming for Cairistìona,
> not for your wedding to the king,
> to lay you low in the ground,
> in the coffin whose boards are fast and closed.[42]

We find the impressionistic style still in later songs, such as the eighteenth-century love-keen "'*S dubh a choisich mi 'n oidhche*". It is combined here with prosaic, sober detail:

> I walked through the black night, to visit the lovely maiden,
> I walked more than nine miles, in country that was strange to
>   me,
> and when I reached her home, nothing was as it should be:
> there was no heed for lovers, and no love for drinkers,
> the women were sewing and the girls were sorrowful,
> and my most faithful love was lying in the room,
> lying under the window where she could not hear my talk,
> lying on a board in her cold frozen shift.
>
> I knew your qualities, you were neither capricious nor haughty,
> you had sense and wisdom, understanding and knowledge.
> Your hair was like the flower that grows in the barley,
> when you put a comb in it the sheen of gold could be seen.
> You were lovely and virtuous, steadfast, serious.

Creator of the world, keep me sane,
keep my sense and my wisdom, until you come for me.[43]

The eighteenth century song "*A Mhic Dhùghaill 'ic Ruairidh*" is
one of several songs on the theme of a love-affair ended by violence,
the girl's family taking sides against her lover, and (to put it at its
mildest) not escaping the suspicion of being involved in his death.
The action which the song describes is obscure in parts, and only
part of the song is quoted:

> I am displeased with my sister,
> with her yellow, flowing hair,
> I have no cause to thank my mother,
> I was young when she pinned lies on me,
> and my thousand blessings on my father:
> he would not hear ill of me.
>
> . . . . . .
>
> It was when he was climbing the dyke
> that my love first cried out,
> it was coming down the slope
> you got the bruising that wounded you.
> The blood of your fragrant breast
> was seeping through your shirt,
> and though, my love, I drank some of it
> your wounds did not heal.[44]

We have already come across the blood-drinking motif, and it
occurs in other instances as well, one of the many instances of
archaic thought and practice that are commemorated in the
songs.

Topical events are chronicled sometimes in a light-hearted way,
although there seem to be fewer such songs, or fewer that have
survived from earlier times. A song about "The Minister and the
Bailie" was very popular in the late nineteenth and early twentieth
century. A very neat version of it is included in MacDiarmid's
MS Collection of 1770. The song was probably of fairly recent
composition at that time, and gives some insight into some of the
oppressions that new systems in Church and State had brought on
the Highlanders:

The Minister and the Bailie,
the Bailie and the Minister,
hard though the law of the Bailie is
God save us from the Minister.

If I give a kiss to a maiden
and someone tells the Minister,
I have to pay through the nose
and give my gold to the Minister.

Not satisfied with fines like that
they put me on a pedestal
before the congregation
where I confess my dreadfulness.[45]

The Gaelic version is not quite such doggerel as my translation, but the song is meant primarily to amuse, although it has its bite also. The writer goes on to tell how the Minister lectures him in Church, and he finds this hard to bear, for the rumour is that the Minister certainly was, and probably is, rather fond of the girls. The Bailie for his part makes his exactions of rent, taking a beef-cow if the rent is ten marks short. The poet concludes by hoping that the King sends an order to check the Bailie, and that Death takes care of the Minister.

Many of the songs had a functional aspect which was of primary importance at one time. The tradition seems, however, to have been flexible and adaptable, so that songs used for one work-process could be taken over (perhaps with some modification in rhythm and tempo) for another. Eighteenth- and nineteenth-century commentators make a distinction between the *iorram* or rowing-song and the *òran luadhaidh* or waulking-song, but many of the former seem to have been used as an accompaniment to waulking.[46] It may be that the waulking-song tradition, surviving late as it did in the Western Isles (and it is scarcely dead yet), gathered to itself many songs that did not originally belong to it. At any rate the waulking-song repertoire in modern times was a very large one. That it is also a fairly old tradition may be gathered partly from the dating of the songs themselves (this taking us back at least to the first half of the seventeenth century) and partly from the regional variations in overall style, and particularly tempo, which are reflected in the modern singing of these songs. Some of the songs

were of a "framework" type, with for example boy-and-girl coup-
ling formulae, and so by definition fresh composition continued.
There is, however, some evidence that the tradition was slewed in
the direction of conflated versions of songs, perhaps in the
eighteenth century, that great age of literary meddling.

Leaving these theoretical considerations aside, it is worth noting
that the functional use of song—for lullaby, dandling, toddling
song, for match-making, grinding with the quern, milking, reaping,
spinning, weaving, waulking, rowing—gave a marked if indirect
stimulus to composition, and greatly aided retention of the songs
in the folk memory, so that generally speaking they are better preserved in modern times than less functional compositions, even
when these were also sung. Since we are concerned here with the
poetry of the songs, there is perhaps no special need to discuss the
work-songs in isolation, since their isolation, if it could be so described, was of a functional and rhythmical nature rather than of a
poetic one. It seems quite clear that poets might choose to compose
in the tradition of the waulking-song without being immediately
or physically involved in it as a work tradition: that, in other
words, it was, or remained, a literary as well as a practical
tradition.

It was in the waulking-song repertoire that one of the most
remarkable—perhaps indeed the most remarkable—of early Scottish Gaelic songs was preserved: the song *"Seathan Mac Rìgh
Eireann"* ("Seathan Son of the King of Ireland"), described by one
tradition-bearer as "the queen of waulking-songs". We have various shorter versions of this song, and one magnificent text which may
well be a conflated text, but which nevertheless carries much conviction. This latter is the text presented to posterity by Alexander
Carmichael, the great nineteenth-century collector, and printed
in 1954 in vol 5 of his *Carmina Gadelica*. It might be argued that
this song of close on 200 lines is not all the work of one person, that
its formulaic construction permits of unobtrusive addition, that it
is the result of some sort of team-work over the centuries. Without
being able to adjudicate such an argument, I find it hard to understand what is meant by team-work of this kind, and in particular
find it hard to imagine a motivation for it. There are some kinds of
song where it is easy to find a communal motivation: the match-
making songs and the nonsense-songs are cases in point. And it is
equally easy to accept that there can be a widespread mimetic skill
which allows people, many people, to compose variants of songs, in

such a way that the priority of one over the other cannot be easily established. But the case of "Seathan" is different. It might well be accepted that there are lines here and there which did not belong to the original text, that the individual formulae could be imitated in this way, but I would not willingly go beyond that. For the song has a highly distinctive emotional drive which unifies it and I would judge that we see in it the unity imposed by one artist's imagination. The song has never been dated. Its style and language, to my mind, argue more strongly for a sixteenth-century than for a seventeenth-century origin, and if that were so it would suggest that the metrical pattern of the song is a still older one, for here we have an assured and mellow use made of the pattern, with its rhyming paragraphs of varying length, modulating the movement of thought and emotion. The full translation of Carmichael's version is given here:

Seathan Son of the King of Ireland

Woe to him who heard of it and did not tell it,
   Hu ru na hur i bhi o
woe to him who heard of it and did not tell it,
   Na bhi hao bho hao bhi o an
that my darling was in Minginish;
if thou wert, my love, thou hadst returned long since:
I would send a great ship to seek him there,
with a famed crew, fresh and bright and expert,
young men and lads would be there,
he would visit here when he returned,
I would spend a festal day dallying with him,
I would sit on a knoll and engage in sweet converse,
I would curl thy hair as I did oft-times,
I would lie in thy arms and keep the dew from thee,
I would wash a fine-spun shirt full white for thee,
so long as any water remained in the pool,
and I would dry it on a moorland branch.

But Seathan to-night is a corse,
a sad tale to the men of Scotland,
a grievous tale to his followers,
a joyous tale to his pursuers,
to the son of the Hag of the Three Thorns.

Dear Seathan of the tranquil eyes,
oft didst thou redden the hillocks:
it was not with the blood of cattle or horses,
or the blood of the swift deer,
or the blood of the roe in a nook of the corn-field,
but the blood of thine enemy bent on strangling thee.

When I thought thou wast giving chase,
thou wast dead in the conflict,
borne on the shoulders of the young men,
and on the point of being buried.

When I thought thou wast in Galway (?),
thou wast dead without breath,
borne on the shoulders of scornful (?) men,
and as cold as the mountain snow.

My love thy right hand, though now cold,
oft did I have it, seldom was it away from me,
oft did I have a present from it,
and never with aught that was mean,
it was not with stick or cudgel,
it was not with abuse or quarrelling,
but with green satin and fine silk,
with the noblest of gifts.

O brown-haired Seathan, calf of my love,
I would go far away with thee, my love,
I would go with thee through the branchy wood
where the birds are wont to warble,
I would cross the Irish Sea with thee
where the swelling ocean surges,
I would cross the Sea of Greece with thee,
the haunt of swarthy corsairs.

I and Seathan traversing mountains,
I was weak, but Seathan was strong,
I could endure but little clothing,
a russet coat to the middle of my thigh,
a kerchief of fine pure-white linen,
as I fared with my darling Seathan.

O Seathan, Seathan, bereft of life,
own son to my king from Tyrconnel,
oft have I lain beneath thy cloak;
if I did, it was not in a homestead,
but in a green hollow in a tree-sheltered field,
under the slope of the rugged blue peaks,
the wind from the mountains sweeping over us,
the wind from the glens with a sough taking
its fill of the first burgeoning of spring.

Many a glen and ben we traversed,
I was in Islay and in Uist with thee,
I was in Sleat of the yellow-haired women with thee,
I was in Iona of the nuns with thee,
I was in the land of birds and eggs with thee,
I was in Ireland, I was in Latium with thee,
I traversed Brittany and Burgundy,
I traversed the Continent and the Mearns with thee,
I traversed the Boyne, I traversed Munster with thee,
I heard Mass in Cill Chumha with thee,
I heard the music of the fairy-mansions with thee,
I drank a draught from the well of wandering with thee,
I was the day before yesterday and last year with thee,
I was from cape to cape with thee,
I was in Kildonan of the pines with thee,
I was three years on the hills with thee.

I kept watch for a day in the treetops with thee,
I kept watch for two days in the sea wrack with thee,
I kept watch for a night on a sea rock with thee,
I kept watch, my love, and I did not regret it,
wrapped in a corner of thy tartan plaid,
the spindrift ever breaking over us,
water that is very pure, cool and wholesome.

My love is Seathan of the tranquil eyes,
I would lie with thee on an uneasy bed,
a bed of heather with my side on stones;
dearer Seathan in a coil of heather rope
than a king's son on bed of linen;
dearer Seathan behind a dyke

than a king's son in silks on deal flooring,
though he should have a restful bed
which had been well-planed by wrights,
and protected by power of druids;
dearer Seathan in the birch wood
than to be in Magh Meall with Airril,
though he had satin and silk under his feet,
and pillows lustrous with red gold.

If Seathan were seen as he arose
in shade of hill on a May morning,
a short kilt to the middle of his thigh,
a narrow black belt about his tunic,
his foster-mother's love, his wife's darling,
the sight seven times dearest to his own mother,
a secret lover he is to me.

O brown-haired Seathan thou gentle hero,
small is the place in which I would put thee,
I would put thee on the very top of my head,
I would put thee between my breasts,
between Bride and her soft kerchief,
between a young maiden and her snood,
between a fair virgin and her silken mantle,
between myself and my shirt of linen.

But Seathan is in the lonely chamber,
without drinking of cups or goblets,
without drinking of wine from splendid silver tankards,
without drinking of ale with his cronies and gentlemen,
without drinking to music, without kiss from seductive woman,
without music of harp, without listening to melody,
but strait bands on his shoulders,
and looped bands on the bier poles.

I am a sister of Aodh and yellow-haired Brian,
I am a kinswoman of Fionn son of Cumhall,
I am the wife of brown-haired Seathan, the wanderer,
but alas! for those who said I was a joyous wife,
I am a poor, sad, mournful, sorrowful wife,
full of anguish and grief and woe.

My father put me in a distressing place
on that night he made a wedding-feast for me,
alas, O King! that it were not my lyke-wake,
that the linen shroud had not been cut for me,
that the pine planks had not been polished for me,
that the loops had not been tied on me,
that I had not been hidden in the mould,
for fear I should be alive on earth.
There is many a table where I shall be slighted,
where my teeth shall no more chew bread,
where my spoon shall no more draw,
where my knife shall no more cut,
where my fancy shall no more linger.

If Seathan could be but redeemed
the ransom could be got like rushes,
silver could be got like ashes,
gold could be got on the fringe of meadows,
wine could be got like spring water,
beer could be got like a cool verdant stream;
there would not be a goat in rock or stony upland,
there would not be a young she-goat in meadow,
there would not be a sheep on rocky shelf or mountain top,
there would not be cattle on plain or in fold,
there would not be pig or cow in pastures;
the salmon would come from the seas,
the trout would come from the river-banks,
the geldings would come from the rushes;
there would not be a black or white-shouldered cow
high or low in the fold,
at the edge of township or in stall,
that I would not send, my love, to redeem thee,
even to my green plaid,
though that should take the one cow from me,
and it was not the one black cow of my fold,
but herds of white-shouldered cattle,
of white-headed, white-backed, red-eared cattle.

But Seathan is to-night in the upper town,
neither gold nor tears will win him,
neither drink nor music will tempt him,

neither slaughter nor violence will bring him from his doom,
neither tumult nor force will wake him from his slumber;
and my heart is broken and distraught,
my tears flow like a well,
uneasily I sleep on a pillow,
for thou hast no one who pities thee
save me, running to and fro.

O Seathan dear! O Seathan dear!
I would not give thee to law or king,
I would not give thee to the gentle Mary,
I would not give thee to the Holy Rood,
I would not give thee to Jesus Christ,
I would not, for fear I would not get thee myself.

O Seathan, my brightness of the sun!
alas! despite me death has seized thee,
and that has left me sad and tearful,
lamenting bitterly that thou art gone;
and if all the clerics say is true,
that there is a Hell and a Heaven,
my share of Heaven—it is my welcome to death—
for a night with my darling,
with my spouse, brown-haired Seathan.[47]

This song is unique in its tremendous build-up of detail, and its skilful use of incantation. The incremental repetition is used as a passionate incantation. Despite the continuous, almost devastating play on the emotions there is a remarkable degree of control. Emotion here is very highly-wrought, becoming exotic in its colouring. The elaboration of the various aspects of the theme is carried much further here than is usual in Gaelic folksongs. But the difference between "*Seathan Mac Rìgh Eireann*" and many other Gaelic laments or keens is a difference of degree rather than one of kind. The author gives a multiplicity of examples within each category: the places she visited with Seathan, the places in which she spent the day or the night with him, the things death had deprived him of, the items that would go to his ransom. All of these categories could be paralleled in other songs; it is the combination of them all, their elaboration, and the intensity of the song, that are unparalleled.

On a psychological level, we see song being used here as therapy, and clearly this is a highly important aspect. A specialized case of this is the jealousy-song, sung by a woman. There are a number of examples of this type of song; I choose one from Carmichael's collection again, though the song seems to fall into two distinct parts: (1) the jealousy-song, and (2) a keen for Donald of Clanranald (*ob.* 1686). Here are the venomous lines of the jealousy section:

> Would, O God, that she would come,
> with her hand wounded and her leg broken,
> seeking a leech at the side of every bed,
> and no leech in the land but me;
> by my hand, I would take courage,
> I would bend bone and draw blood;
> when I closed your coffin lid
> I would put earth on the bank of your tomb.[48]

A more unusual instance is the song addressed to the Minister of Kilninver included in the eighteenth-century anthology, Gillies' Collection. The girl says:

> By the river-side your welcome was kindly,
> the sun shone so bright that it blinded my modesty,
> there was nothing hidden, my love, that you did not see,
> from the top of my head to the soles of my feet;
> I appeared before you like my original mother.[49]

There is a more jocular, light-hearted therapy in songs like the following one:

> I will not marry a little old man,
> an old man I won't take at all,
> he will be late in rising,
> slow to put his clothes on,
> slow, slow dressing.[50]

No doubt there is more joke than therapy here; in other instances the fatal step has been taken before the song is made.

Song was also used as ritual. The clearest case is that of the death-keen. It is not very long since keening was practised in Gaelic

Scotland, and it survived strongly in the nineteenth century. There
are some fine examples, the oldest being that known as Macintosh's
Lament or *"Bealach a' ghàrraidh"*, with its cry of pain:

> I was a kerched woman, a maiden
> a kerched woman, a maiden,
> a kerched woman, a maiden,
> and a widow all in that one hour.[51]

Many of the keens have the metrical characteristic of rhyming
paragraphs, or alternatively of the same end-rhyme sustained
throughout the song. We noticed the rhyming paragraph technique
in the Seathan lament, and it is used also in the finest of Irish
keens *"Caoineadh Airt Uí Laoghaire"*, a song dating from about
1773, the year of Art's death.[52] The variant form of metre, with
sustained rhyme, is used, for example, in *"Cumha Bhràithrean"*
("Lament for Brothers"), a Skye song. A few verses may be
quoted:

> I am suffering sorrow, black melancholy in my face,
> it is not my sweetheart I mourn, though he should stay away
>   from me,
> but I mourn my brothers, who are mouldering in the sea.
>
> . . . . . .
>
> I am distressed by the thought of your curly hair being waulked
>   in the seaweed.
>
> . . . . . .
>
> Your bed is deserted in that room up there,
> I shall not go to make it; you, my beloved, are far from me.[53]

Dating from much the same time as the Irish keen mentioned
above, is the song *"Ailein Duinn, shiùbhlainn leat"* ("Brown-haired
Allan, I would go with you"), composed by Ann Campbell of
Scalpay, Harris, to Allan Morison, who was drowned at sea, having
according to tradition set out to marry her. This is not a keen in
the ritualistic sense, since the body has not been recovered, but it
is in the keen tradition, and again uses the verse-paragraph style.

The song contains a number of the motifs we have already met with, combining ancient beliefs with everyday detail in a moving way. Only the second half of the song is quoted here:

> It is a sad tale I have tonight,
> not of the death of the cattle in want,
> but of the wetness of your shirt,
> and of the porpoises tearing at you.
> Though I had a foldful of cattle
> I would care little for it now,
> I would not wish a change of spouse,
> better to be with you on the mountain-top.
> Brown-haired Allan,
> I heard that you had been drowned,
> would that I were beside you,
> on whatever rock or bank you come ashore,
> in whatever heap of seaweed the high tide leaves you.
> I would drink a drink, whatever my kin say,
> not of the red wine of Spain
> but of your breast's blood, I would prefer that.
> May God give payment to your soul
> for what I had of your private talk,
> for what I had of your goods without purchase,
> lengths of speckled silk,
> though I shall never live to use them.
> My prayer to God on His throne
> that I should not go in earth or shroud,
> in a hole in the ground or a secret place,
> but in the place you went, Allan.[54]

We have already noticed song used as ritual in a different sort of way, in a celebratory way, as in the songs composed by foster-mothers or nurses to heroic figures such as Dòmhnall Mac Iain 'ic Sheumais *c.* 1601 or Dòmhnall Gorm of Sleat about that time also. Song is of course also used as ritual in a specific religious sense, but after discussing the keens it will be convenient to look first at how the songs deal with the facts and furniture of death.

The prevalence of death-songs in various parts of the verse tradition, in elegies, laments, songs of war by bardic and vernacular poets, has led to some specialization and concentration on the topic of the coffin and the grave. The interest in observation (common to many poets) and in detail (characteristic of much Celtic art) has accentuated this preoccupation until it at times comes close to the macabre. Even in these circumstances it often has great literary merit; it induces the shock of recognition, the spark leaping between mind and matter, that can be regarded as one of the touchstones of poetry. This is especially so when the observation is fresh. One does not feel it to the same degree in lines like:

> The rook calls early
> round your house on Sunday.

The effects used here are fairly conventional, and so too in the following lines:

> Your fiddle untuned,
> the strings have gone slack.

> Your great house is unthatched,
> a sight gloomy to see.[55]

References to the shroud are frequent and fairly conventional:

> Your sisters stay over there,
> with little thought of coming over
> since they sewed the shroud over your mouth.[56]

The references to shroud and lying-in-coffin are more developed in the song *"Coisich a rùin"*:

> My young brown-haired sweetheart is home,
> the back of your head on an oak plank;
> no need for a shirt in your house,
> but plenty of need for a shroud,
> for great numbers of white candles.[57]

Observation of the coffin, and its making, features prominently:

> Putting you in earth,
> where I cannot see your eye,
> putting you away with the backs of hammers.

> In a white narrow confining coffin,
> closely planed,
> no comfort under your head but a plank.[58]

Another poet recalls equally sharply the construction of the coffin:

> In a narrow confining coffin,
> (with its planks) shaped and dove-tailed.[59]

Intensity of grief finds its expression in intensity of observation: the poet uses the precise technical term for the dove-tailing of planks.

In a song commemorating a famous love-affair of the eighteenth century, that between Dalness's son and the daughter of Fear Thìr na Dris, the following words are attributed to the girl:

> Alas that I were not,
> unknown to you, behind you,
> when the slab was lifted
> and the earth broken.
> I would ask for no coffin
> but that my side should be close to you;
> this news has driven my wits from me,
> that it is to Death you made your accounting.[60]

Imagination does not stop short at the time of interment. With that interest in colour contrast that is common in Celtic poetry, one girl thinks of her lover, now dead, with his

> . . . very white body
> being ravaged by beetles.[61]

The piper who has been spirited away to the Cave of Gold does not expect to return soon:

> My side under me, my flesh rotting,
> a beetle/worm in my eye (2)
> before I return, before I arrive
> from the Cave of Gold, the Cave of Gold.[62]

And there is the startling and lovely poetic conceit in these lines:

Would that I were buried to the eyes
in the earth where my love is.

I would kiss your chiselled lips,
tearing down the pale shroud.[63]

There is more picturesque detail, here perhaps with less intensity
of emotion, in the song on a gentleman drowned that includes
these lines:

Your silken garters
are in shreds round your legs.

Your bonny blue bonnet
floats aloft on the wide sea.

Your fine-spun shirt of Holland cloth
Is being ripped by the seals.

The seagull has your head,
the eel has your side.[64]

There are some religious songs that have the poetic quality of
folksong, but the majority, if one omits for the present the chants
and incantations of *Carmina Gadelica*, tend to concentrate on a
didactic purpose. But Anna NicEalair's "Ditty" reads at first sight
like a love-song, and has the direct simple quality of evangelical
religion: it is a love-song to Christ:

It was in the poor bothy of sorrow
that I got to know you first,
and I brought you to my mother's house,
and looked after you there for a time.

It is your love, my love,
it is your love that drew me;
it is your love, my dear,
that wakened me in the morning.

. . . . . .

You gave me your love
in the shade of the juniper[65] tree,

and the companionship of your affection
in the garden of the apples.

Sweeter your love to me than wine—
yes, than wine at its strongest,
and when you gave to me your love
my body melted away.

. . . . . .

And you went up to a high spot
to prepare a place for my soul;
and you say you will come again
to fulfil your promise.[66]

Gaelic poetry, broadly speaking, is not strongly introspective.
Even so introspective a poet as Uilleam Ros is drawn by the tradition towards an extroverted verse, although admittedly it may be,
in the main, his introspective verse that suffered the greatest
destruction, or least saw the world while he was alive. I think the
same is probably true of the songs. If there were fewer inhibitions
in the Gaelic society of the sixteenth to eighteenth centuries than
now—which seems to me almost axiomatic, but it has not been
demonstrated—this might partly account for the relative lack of
introspection, but perhaps it has something to do also with the
notion that the poet is an observer, a chronicler, a technician who
has learnt the rules and practises his craft for the benefit of society.
Even if he puts his verse to therapeutic uses he must not opt out of
society. This leads to an externalizing even of personal emotions,
and in some of the saddest and most harrowing situations the
songster seems to observe her own predicament rather than become submerged by it. The possessive "her" is used deliberately,
for many of the songs are evidently the work of women. This
detachment prevents the songs becoming sentimental, and there
are very few sentimental songs in Gaelic until we come to the
nineteenth century, the break-down of the old Gaelic society, and
the adoption of mixed cultural values.

It is commoner, then, in the songs to find an extroverted attitude
to life, including love, such as we have in the (probably) seventeenth-century song "*Bothan àirigh am Bràigh Raithneach*" ("A
Shieling Bothy in Brae Rannoch"):

My love and my treasure
went yesterday to Glen Garry.

He whose hair is like gold
and whose kiss tastes like honey.

. . . . . .

You're the one who best suits
hose with light boots and laces.

Coat of dark nap from London
and crowns go to buy it.

When you go to the fair
you bring my gear home with you:

My belt and my comb
and my slender snood ribbon.[67]

So it goes on, all very much in this strain, light, fresh and happy.
We may take as another example the rumbustious smugglers'
song, "*Mo thruaighe léir thu 'ille bhuidhe*":

The yellow boat at anchorage
in Belfast in Ireland.

With cutters and with gauger-men
annoying us conjointly.

With lead and English powder
going thumping at her oak-planks.

We were in the western sea with you
before the sun was rising.

Our *Roe-deer* was as water tight
as a flask of wine with wax on it.[68]

What could be more fitting than the simile in the final stanza?
We have seen an example of jealousy expressed in a forthright

way,[69] and this seems to be the more usual fashion. There are signs of a more tentative, soul-searching approach in the lovely song *"Thig trì nithean gun iarraidh"* ("Three things come without seeking"):

Three things come without seeking,
jealousy, terror and love.
Nor is it shame to be counted
among those whom such agonies grieve,
since so many great ladies
have suffered the crime that I have,
being exiled by passion.
They gave but they did not receive.

You who are climbing the defile
bear my love to the glen of the north:
take this vow to my sweetheart:
"I am his while I live on the earth.
I will marry no other
nor allow such news to go forth.
Till, my dear, you've denied me,
I'll distrust the words of their mouth."

You, of the blue eyes beguiling,
(from the glen where the mist would arise)
your eyebrows showed courteous mildness
like the moor-cotton dewed from the skies:
when you aimed as you lay on your elbow
the stag would be caught by surprise:
my love, if you lived in my dwelling,
no-one could mock or despise.

My dear, if I saw you arriving
and knew that it really was you,
my heart's blood ascending
would break like the sun into view:
and I'll give you my promise
each hair that was grey would renew
its greyness to yellow
like the flowers that the waters pursue.

It was not for your riches
and not for your numerous herd:
it was not for a weakling
that my heart was troubled and stirred:
but the son of a noble
who conquered a land with his sword:
we'd suffer no hunger
for many would furnish our board.

If you're never returning,
I'll know an exchange has been made,
that being more wealthy
another has suited your trade.
I'd not give my courage,
my wisdom, the love you betrayed,
for a field of bright cattle,
and a girl without sense at their head.

And though you've disowned me
I've no dark dishonour to hide:
my fame is unsullied;
I've never lain down at your side.
For a man who'd crowned monarchs
I suffer more pangs from my pride
than to rear him young bastards.
I'd strangle my love till it died.

Yet gentler the insult
if her love were higher than mine:
but a slatternly scullion
whom even the cows would disdain:
when the spring comes with tempest
and the cattle are lost in the glen
she'll be lying in child-bed,
the house without rudder or rein.[70]

To take another example, this time falling clearly into neither of
the categories mentioned, there is this stanza from a fairly modern
variant of an older song, "*Mo nighean donn nam meall-shuilean*"
("My brown-haired girl with the alluring eyes"):

> There is a custom in this place,
> it was this year I noticed it,
> no lad I know of ever wed
> the first girl he had courted there.[71]

This is not far from bathos, but far enough to allow it to be memorable for other reasons. There is a hint of mocking detachment which helps to preserve that ambiguity which is one of the conditions of poetry—or if that is too dogmatic, a condition of one important kind of poetry.

The "cry from the heart" is often considered to be one of the touchstones of excellence in folksong. It can take many forms, from near-bathos to subtle delicacy of expression. A few examples are quoted as a reminder of that range. The first is from a North Uist song of the late sixteenth century, referring to the onslaught by Uisdean Mac Gille-easbaig Chléirich of Skye on the MacVicars of North Uist, in the course of which five MacVicar brothers were killed. The song is partly spoken by a sister; then the mother takes up the strain:

> Quiet, girl without sense or reason!
> They are sons of mine though they're your brothers,
> it was from within my womb they dropped,
> it was in my lap that they found comfort,
> it was my linen shift they wetted,
> it was the milk of my breasts they swallowed.
>
> I built the wall and filled the corn-yard,
> not with the clean dry barley,
> nor with white oats used for meal,
> but with the young men of my clan.[72]

The first of these stanzas in particular has the rending cry that one associates with sixteenth- to seventeen-century Gaelic song.

In another of the lovers' family tragedies, this time with a supposed fairy background, the girl whose fairy lover has been killed by her brothers sings:

> Sorer than the ant's bite,
> my brothers have killed my first love.

> My own brothers are coming
> on their horses, nimble, swift,
> may sharp knives pierce their hearts
> and their bodies' blood flow in flood.

But in a touching reversal of her anger she goes on:

> The curse I laid upon my brothers,
> in the passion that was in my heart,
> let it lie on the brindled meadows,
> and on the deer of yonder glen.[73]

Often the situation is less dramatic than in the two last instances quoted, and it is fair to give an illustration from a song in a lower key. Here, characteristically enough, the cry comes in isolated lines and couplets, and the emotion is often linked with ordinary, everyday matters:

> I gave you love and may not deny it,
> such love as sister never gave to brother,
> nor yet a woman to her three-month baby,
> nor cow to calf on a summer shieling.

> It was love I gave you, it was not hatred,
> and all my kin are now surly with me.
> Pity who asked and who had refusal
> of a warm drink from cold flagstones.

> The weight on the welts of my boots is heavy
> as I go to Kirkton to church on Sunday,
> in hope of seeing there the gallant,
> the brown-haired lad I was pledged to marry.[74]

Another of the touchstones of excellence in song, as in poetry generally, is the isolated line or passage, the peak in a song or poem, the moment at which perception, or imagination, or wit, or irony, or the manipulation of sound, is being deployed at its most intense level. It is axiomatic that there should be such peaks, and it is right that they should influence our taste and judgement. I am not at all sure that I would think so highly of Dorothy Brown's song[75] to Alasdair Mac Colla (the younger Colkitto), were it not for the line *Dòrn geal mu'n dean an t-òr sniomhain*, though I think less highly of the translation, "White fist round which gold entwines"! There are instances like this where the differing genius of two languages defies all attempts at equivalence. This is another axiom.

It should perhaps be recalled that in that same song there occurs a striking image. Dorothy Brown thinks of those who would come to help her hero:

> Many a man with gun and sword,
> green wadded shirt and coloured plaid,
> would rise with you from both sides of the river,
> as thick as the floss from the blackthorn.[75]

The poets, as always, draw on their own experience for their imagery, and an important part of it is in Nature as it lies around them. A girl addresses these lines to her sweetheart:

> You are the man   I love best
> of all who walked   on corn or grass,
> of all who lay   on right side or left,
> or put a shoe   on to a foot.
> My honey in satchel   my honey of bees,
> my flowers you are,   between fields,
> my music, music   my fiddle music
> and my harp music   high and low.[76]

The imagery in the next quotation is more darkly coloured by the imagination. The lines occur in that lament for Donald of Clan-ranald (who died in 1686) already referred to:

> There is no sleep for me; I lie awake,
> I cannot make merry nor be sportive;
> I have seen your wood being stripped,
> the rider of the black horse in the van,
> the rider of the sable steed,
> the rider of the prancing, well-shod charger,
> with his golden spurs and his boots that would not crack.[77]

In the song *"Craobh nan Ubhal"* ("The Apple Tree"), an Islay song, perhaps of the sixteenth century, there is something magical about the subject of the song, MacKay of the Rhinns:

A versatile man is Mackay
he can make silk of May wool,
he can make wine of mountain water,
he can make butter of the pure-white foam.[78]

Perhaps it is this magic, or perhaps it is the emotion of the woman
who loves him, working on her imagination, that tilts the imagery
of the poem to symbolism, the ancient and deeply imagined symbolism of the apple and the apple-tree. The song was fairly widely
known. I first learnt it from my mother, in Lewis, but the fullest
versions, though these are still fragmentary, were collected by
Alexander Carmichael. Here are two fragments relating to the
apple symbolism:

O apple tree, may God be with you,
may the moon and the sun be with you,
may the wind of the east and the west be with you,
may the great Creator of the elements be with you,
may all that ever came be with you,
may great Somerled and his band be with you.[79]

The reference is presumably to the Scoto–Norse ancestor of the
MacDonalds, the twelfth-century Somerled. In another version
are these lines:

When you go to the wood to strip it,
recognize the tree which is mine there,
the tree of softest, sweetest apples,
the branching, pear-like, apple-laden tree,
its roots growing and its top bending.[80]

I do not profess to understand this song adequately. I think the
imagery may have sexual connotations, but it may be that the texts
are now too fragmentary for a full understanding of them.

One final instance of the use of imagery may be given, this time
a more sustained example, from the eighteenth-century song "*Eala
nan Cuantan*" ("The Swan of the Seas"). Only a part of the song is
quoted:

As I rest in bed on my elbow
I get neither sleep nor rest,

seeing the swan of the seas
always being taken from me;
though I had encircled her with my net,
and was edging her towards the shore,
my hook is unbaited,
ah! my song is vain.

. . . . . .

You were the grouse in the grove,
on a bush, the earliest to cry,
you were my music at sleeping-time
and at waking-time in the morning;
in the many-windowed room,
my love, I could hear your voice clearly,
and in the clustering wood
I often held you in my arms.

. . . . . .

You were the flower in the garden,
sweet its scent in my nostrils,
you were the tree that grew,
bending hither and thither with the strong wind;
but an entangling gust came,
destroying the intertwining of twigs,
and at the next onset
it broke its way through as it wanted.

At the next onset
it broke its way through as it wanted:
I am like a tree stripped of fruit in a garden,
like a drunkard, drinking hard,
like a soldier without a sword,
or a blacksmith without a hammer,
or a hunter without a gun,
a hound that has lost its scent.

Slippery the grip on the salmon's tail,
or on the hind-leg of the deer,
or on the fins of the porpoise—
my grip was most slippery of all.

To grasp the side of the ship
were just as easy a thing to do
as to grasp the hand of the blackhearted girl
who deceived me for seven years.

Pity him who set his heart
on the deer-skin with its hair,
though you might catch it by the antler
do not set your heart on its hide;
nor lay up expectation
for the seal at the water's edge,
nor for the cunning little fox,
though your hound were near it.[81]

The imagery here carries a great emotional surge, and is symbolic of that surge, comprising as it does so many images of moving, darting, elusive things.

Some of the songs are clearly much more satisfying than others in terms of structure or "plot". The habit of slotting in stock passages, or literary stereos, whether it was a habit of song-composers or (as I tend to believe) mainly of tradition-bearers, is often destructive of a song's unity. As far as song collections go it is a characteristic of the later (and island) collections rather than the earlier (and mainland) ones, though it is not suggested that this is an absolute distinction. These stereos are large-scale clichés, similar in function and in effect to clichés of word or phrase, except that the stereos have the additional potential effect of disrupting a song's unity. The song "The Swan of the Seas" does have unity, however, and I end this chapter with another example.

I paid dear for the fishing

I paid dear for the fishing,
this year has destroyed me,
I lost the swimmer of kyles—
never called for a ferry!
At Stoc Beul an Athain
the hero was drowned;
I would never have thought
such a fate would befall you,
that you would be drowned

on this side of Doomsday.
Your jaunty new plaid
floats high on the sea,
your silken garters
are in shreds round your legs,
your fine Holland shirt
is being ripped by the rocks,
your brown braided belt
is rumpled and warped,
the King of the green waves
by the side of your bed.
You were a fine cow-herd
in wide and lush glen,
a strong mountain walker,
soldier eager for action.
The rook calls early
round your house on Sunday,
your fiddle untuned,
the strings have gone slack;
your great house is unthatched,
a sight gloomy to see.
Your sister lacks brother
and your mother lacks son,
your young wife lacks a spouse
and I lack my fosterling.[82]

3

Poetry in Transition

BARDIC VERSE AND song-verse in a sense represent two extremes of the poetic tradition. It will be clear that these extremes are not of art but (at least in a loose sense) of artist-organization. Bardic verse implies bardic schools, at least somewhere in the background, whereas song-verse can flourish, and has flourished, in a population that is not far removed from illiteracy. These stark antitheses need to be qualified in various ways. Illiteracy in a literal sense can co-exist with a high degree of "oral literacy", and this phenomenon has been strikingly present in the Gaelic area. Highly literate poets can write in the song-tradition, and a variant of the bardic tradition can be found in the work of poets who were probably not literate in a literal sense. The sixteenth and seventeenth (and to some extent the eighteenth) centuries show Gaelic poetry in a period of transition, and we find at this time in particular poetry that belongs to the bardic tradition structurally but not thematically, or thematically but not structurally. Or we find (and this is another way of making the same point) a type of verse that had been practised by professional poets now the province of amateurs, or discover a record of what existed, not in the MSS. of chiefs and their bards but in the memory of the tenantry.

It may be that these variants would have appeared naturally in a thoroughly stable society, but in fact we find them jostling each other in a period of great uncertainty and change: that period which embraces the Reformation, the less closely defined *Linn nan Creach*, or "Age of Forays" (the traditional name for the age when centralized government had not properly succeeded in winning control over the Highland area), the Montrose Wars, and the breakdown of a widespread system of bardic patronage. The period may be loosely defined as 1500–1700.

It would be surprising, however, if the changes and variants we shall consider had their origins mainly in this period. At any rate, a different conclusion is suggested by what we know of the history of one large and popular class of verse: that of the heroic ballads.

These fall mainly into the class of Ossianic ballads, and they have enjoyed a long popularity: some extant ballads probably go back to *c.* A.D. 1100, while there are still one or two of them sung traditionally in the Western Isles. The earlier part of this history can be reconstructed only from Irish sources. Gerard Murphy, in his Introduction to *Duanaire Finn*, vol III,[1]* refers to a poem, probably of the tenth century, ascribed to Cinaed Húa Hartacáin, which is concerned with the death of Finn/Fionn, and refers further to the existence of both popular oral and literary matter as early as this time. Murphy saw the rise of the Ossianic balladry as a phenomenon of the eleventh and early twelfth centuries, part of the movement which produced West European balladry generally. He dates, on linguistic grounds, four of the ballads to *c.* 1100, six to *c.* 1150, four to *c.* 1175, seventeen to *c.* 1200, five to *c.* 1250, ten to *c.* 1300, seventeen to *c.* 1400–*c.* 1500, and six to *c.* 1500–*c.* 1600. These datings refer only to ballads included in the early seventeenth-centry collection *Duanaire Finn*. The Irish and Scottish bodies of heroic ballads are closely connected, though by no means identical. Only a handful of the ballads in *Duanaire Finn* are included in the Scottish collection, a century earlier, in the Book of the Dean of Lismore, and both there and in later Scottish collections there are ballads which are known only in a Scottish context, together with some which are ascribed to known Scottish poets. The later history of these ballads in Scotland shows a gradual process of assimilation taking place in their language: by the eighteenth century, although the basic syllabic metrical outline remains, the language is no longer Classical Common Gaelic but vernacular Scottish Gaelic, with a liberal sprinkling of archaisms and a detritus of Common Gaelic morphological remains, such as the negatives *ní* and *níor* and the termination—(*e*)*adar* of the 3rd plural past tense. The legends, which originated in a folk context, and were taken up by professional writers in a variety of ways, appearing as ballads, as sagas, and in such an ambitious compendium as the twelfth-/ thirteenth-century Irish *Acallamh na Senórach*, eventually are seen to have reverted to the folk and their vernacular. But I do not mean to suggest that the process was a dramatic one of a humble literary damsel being swept into high society and eventually returned in a shop-soiled condition. We must envisage the ballads, and their themes as having had a continuous existence over many centuries, and the ballads as being gradually assimilated to the folk idiom.

* For Notes, see pp. 311–12.

Their language was in any case less esoteric, their syntax less involved, their style plainer than that of the poetry of panegyric, and the probability is that they were always comprehensible and popular in a way the panegyrics could scarcely have been.

The story-line of the ballads would have done much to ensure that popularity, and in many cases the plot has a clear outline, even when the elaboration seems excessive to a later sensibility. This is the case with the ballad which describes how Caoilte ransomed Fionn, who had been taken prisoner by Cormac, by bringing in a pair of each wild creature to be found in the land. This catalogue-formula is of course capable of much elaboration. The ballad appears in *Duanaire Finn*, and is dated by Gerard Murphy *c.* 1175. A much longer version (of 292 lines) appears in the Book of the Dean of Lismore, from which a few stanzas may be translated, to suggest the flavour of the ballad. Cormac speaks first (stanza 27):

> "If you get for me before day
> a couple of every creature,
> you would win your lord thereby,
> in keeping the bargain justly."

> I clinched the mad bargain
> with Cormac son of Art Einfhear,
> that he should let the king go free
> if he got the wild creatures.

The catalogue begins almost immediately, and continues in concentrated form for twenty-three stanzas, e.g.:

> I brought back two fierce *geilts*[2]
> and two tall taloned griffins,
> two ravens from the Wood of Two Peaks,
> two ducks from Loch Saighleann.

> Two foxes of Sliabh Cuilinn,
> two wild stags from Boireann,
> two swans from Fiodh Ghabhráin Dhuinn,
> two woodcocks of Fiodh Fordhruim.

. . . . . .

> Two young cormorants from Dublin,
> two wolf-hounds from Crota Cliach,
> two gannets from Tráigh Dhá Bhan,
> two young roes from Luachair Dheadhadh.[3]

It can be seen, incidentally, that this ballad is securely located in Ireland, although one of the fuller versions survived in a Scottish anthology.

There are ballads which have links with widely-distributed stories, e.g. The Lay of the Smithy showing connections with the Vulcan/Weyland/Volund story, and others which show a special affinity with Norse lore, and which must have the origins of their popularity in the mixed Gaelic–Norse society of the ninth to thirteenth centuries. It is to these two classes that the most popular surviving ballads of the present day belong ("*Duan na Ceàrdaich*" or "The Lay of the Smithy", and "*Duan na Muilgheartaich*", "The Lay of the Sea-hag (or Sea-monster)").

The ballad of the Magic Cloak has close connections with the story of the chastity-testing cloak which appears in Arthurian literature, having perhaps been carried from Wales to Brittany. The relationship of the Gaelic ballad (which appears in the Book of the Dean and in Duanaire Finn,[4] as well as in other later versions) to the English ballad "The Boy and the Mantle",[5] and to the Arthurian mantle story has been much debated. The Dean's version relates how, at a feast in Almhain, the wives of Fionn, Diarmaid, Ossian, Oscar and two other warriors all began to boast of their own purity and chastity. At this point they were joined by a woman who wore a cloak made from a single continuous thread, and it appears that the characteristic of the cloak is that it will cover completely only women who have been entirely faithful to their husbands. One of the husbands foolishly accepts the implied challenge, and asks his wife to try on the cloak:

> Then Conan's wife took the cloak
> and angrily threw it on;
> her faults were easy to read:
> her white bosom was quite bare.

> When Conan Maol saw the cloak
> rumpling up about her side
> he seized his venomous spear
> and killed the maiden outright.

The wife of Diarmad beloved
took the cloak from Conan's wife;
it fitted her no better,
curling up about her breasts.

Oscar's wife then took her turn
to try on the long smooth cloak;
though the fair cloak's skirt was long
it did not hide her button.

Maighinis[6] without deceit
took the cloak and put it on;
quickly the cloak rumpled up
and curled all around her ears.

Mac Reithe, fully expecting the worst, asks for the cloak to be
handed to his wife, and she puts it on:

Mac Reithe's wife bared her side,
put on the very fine cloak:
it covered all, hand and foot,
right to her little toe's fork.

"The one secret kiss I got
from Diarmad, O Duibhne's son—
except for that unique kiss
the cloak would have reached the ground."

The reader is thereby encouraged to compute the extent of the
other wives' lapses. The owner of the cloak at this point prepares
to leave, with the parting shot that the only fault she had committed was to lie with Fionn himself. Fionn curses her as she goes,
but seems philosophical about the whole episode.

The literary sophistication of the ballad is clear enough, and
indeed many of the heroic ballads must be the sophisticated product of practising poets, tailored to the needs of a cultured rather
than a learned circle. Some of the ballads are much more directly
concerned with heroic action than that of the Magic Cloak, but
there is not much reason to suppose that they were the work of
poets other than professional ones, including in that class the
several gradations to which the Laws and later writings refer.

There are good and bad poets among them, and the bad ones, I suppose, indulge more freely in that formulaic padding which lists names and places, stories and episodes, at times blurring effectively the plot of the ballad. At the other end of the scale is the artistic restraint of *Is fada anocht i nOil Finn*,[7] a literary occasional piece which reconstructs the legendary situation in which Ossian finds himself the last survivor of the Fian:

> The night in Elphin goes slow,
> slowly too last night went by;
> although I felt today long,
> longer still was yesterday.
>
> Each day that comes wearies me;
> this is not how we once were,
> no fighting now and no raids,
> no learning of agile feats.
>
> No meetings, music or harps,
> no cattle gifts, horsemen's deeds,
> no paying the poets with gold,
> no chess, no feasting or drink.
>
> No love for courting or hunt—
> two ploys to which I was prone—
> no battle-array or fight,
> alas, a poor way to end.
>
> No catching of hind or deer,
> not how I wanted to be,
> no talk of dogs and their feats:
> the night in Elphin goes slow.
>
> No war-gear ever again,
> nor playing of games we loved,
> nor heroes swimming the loch:
> the night in Elphin is long.
>
> Alas for my worldly plight,
> I'm wretched, O God, as I am,
> alone, and gathering stones:
> the night in Elphin is long.

The last of the famous Fian,
great Ossian, the son of Fionn,
listening to baying of bells:
the night in Elphin is long.

Find out, O Patrick, from God
word of the place I'll be in;
may my soul be saved from harm:
it's a long night in Elphin.

The ballads still enjoyed a widespread popularity in the eighteenth and nineteenth centuries, as is clear from the numerous collections made from Sutherland to Argyll and from Perthshire to the Western Isles. In the eighteenth century in particular, Perthshire and Argyll were rich sources, and perhaps it was natural that what fresh creation there was in literature of this kind should be found there. The amusing parody called "*Laoidh an Tàilleir*" ("The Tailor's Lay")[8] makes the tailor go to Almhain to ply his trade among the members of the Fian. Fionn wants him to make a pair of velvet breeches, not too tight around the hams, as he needs to run vigorously. Conan is still acting the part of trouble-maker in the Fian. Diarmaid, finding that the tailor comes from Glen Lochay, asks for his kinsmen there (the MacDiarmids). The poem was evidently composed between the '15 and the '45 Risings, and the Fian express their regret that they had not been called in to give a hand:

"A curse on you, devil's company,
why did you not send word to us?
We on our own would have flushed out
the English, driving them beyond Newcastle."

Composition of Ossianic verse on a large scale took place later in the eighteenth century, following on the success of James Macpherson's translation and adaptations. Translations into Gaelic were made of Macpherson's work, which was founded (though tenuously at times) on the ballads, and a school of fabricators of Ossianic verse came into being in Perthshire and Argyllshire.[9] A prime example of such work is the Rev. John Smith's collection entitled *Sean Dàna* ("Ancient Lays"), which shows a great familiarity with the Ossianic "matter", but whose style belies the claim that these are genuine traditional poems.

I have suggested that the heroic ballads made concessions, in language and style, to popular taste, or in some cases to a cultured rather than a learned taste. They may also at one time have been the stock-in-trade of a particular class of poet quite distinct from the *filidh*, or learned poet. We have seen that the history of composing such ballads is a long one. It would not be surprising to find other classes of verse being practised outwith the ambit of the *filidh*, but still distinct from popular vernacular verse. One would similarly expect the tradition of such verse to be older than has normally been assumed, for the more styles of poetry in Gaelic are examined the less likely does a theory of sudden innovation appear.

There is in fact a well-defined class of verse in Gaelic which has been called semi-bardic verse.[10] The description is a loose one, which must serve to include a considerable gradation of styles and linguistic canons. We would be justified in regarding some of the heroic ballads as being semi-bardic in language and style, and the term includes also verse whose language is basically vernacular Scottish Gaelic, but whose style and metre slew it in the direction of bardic verse. It may well be significant that such a verse anthology as the Turner MS. (an Argyllshire collection of *c.* 1745), includes a mixture of heroic ballads and semi-bardic panegyric.[11] When we come on a sizeable number of so-called semi-bardic poems in the first half of the seventeenth century, they have the air of a poetry very secure in its own tradition. This is a vernacularized but strongly literary version of bardic verse, using the basic bardic metres (but not with classical strictness), familar with some at least of the bardic thought-patterns, somewhat archaic in its vocabulary and morphology (but in a selective sense), yet comprehensible to those who did not have bardic schooling.

Perhaps we shall never know how old that tradition was in Scotland, but it seems likely now that it was at least over a hundred years old by the middle of the seventeenth century. My guess would be that it was considerably older than that. It is basically the same tradition we find in the sixteenth century poem "*An Duanag Ullamh*", which W. J. Watson dated 1555–8.[12] Watson, however, made a highly selective use of sources in arriving at this dating, and sometime between 1516 and 1525 seems much more likely.[13] The style of the poem is mellow, suggesting that there may be a long tradition behind it then also, but firm evidence is lacking. It is thought that the poem was composed by Maclean of

Duart's bard, and it is addressed to an Earl of Argyll. Long afterwards, in 1685, we find a lament for the then Earl of Argyll, in the same metre as "*An Duanag Ullamh*". This later poem is by An t-Aos-dàna MacShithich, *aos-dàna* having become a description of a particular class of poet: it is more honorific than *bàrd*, and less so than *filidh*, and by the seventeenth century at least was used of the second rank of poets in professional service. It may be that these were the poets who had earlier on built up the semi-bardic tradition, using their own range of modified bardic metres, and a modified linguistic canon, and attracting to their tradition amateurs who were always (as far as the evidence goes) persons of social status in the hierarchy of the times, usually lairds or heads of clans, or septs, sometimes also clergymen. By the late seventeenth century, however, the title *aos-dàna* does not imply the use of semi-bardic styles. The corpus of surviving poetry of this type is not large. The main poets concerned were An Cléireach Beag ("the Little Clerk", Laird of Coll), Fear na Pàirce or MacCulloch of Park (a Ross-shire laird and clergyman), John Stewart of Appin (a clergyman-laird also), Gille Caluim Garbh, Laird of Raasay, Donnchadh Mac-Raoiridh, Bard to the MacDonalds of Sleat, and Alasdair and Murdoch Mackenzie, successive chiefs of the Achilty sept of the Mackenzies. The first three were sixteenth-century poets, the latter four seventeenth-century.

An Cléireach Beag is said to have composed verse in both Latin and Gaelic, but his main surviving poem is "*Caismeachd Ailein nan Sop*", a vaunting of the noted pirate, Allan Maclean, of the Duart family. The tradition is that An Cléireach Beag, who is miscast as a praiser of pirates, composed the poem *c.* 1537 to regain his own freedom from Allan's clutches. He refers to Allan as "a powerful gallant who wets goblets/with your spiced, potent liquor", and describes his galley, decked with breastplates and red English bows and well-planed masts.[14]

We have already noticed the group of MacGregor poems dating from the late sixteenth and early seventeenth century, a group particularly associated with the outlawed MacGregors. But the earliest poem dealing with this period of turbulence has its roots clearly in the more stable society of an earlier period, and is transitional in both metre and mood. According to the Chronicle of the Vicar of Fortingall, Gregor MacGregor of Glenstrae was beheaded at Belloch, or Taymouth Castle, in 1570. The lament composed by his young widow has survived. Its metre is somewhat irregular, but is based on one of the syllabic metres, *séadna*, and the song can be regarded as being transitional between the modes of bardic verse and of folksong. It is as though a folksong theme had been imposed on a literary metrical pattern, and that pattern in its turn had imposed on the statement of the poem a deliberation, a grave undemonstrative movement, which is in marked contrast to the emotional surge of many of the earlier lovesongs. The incremental repetition is itself given a greater deliberation by the quatrain-pattern of the metre. But the direct statement, and the passion, of the folksongs survive in it also:

> Early on Lammas morning
> I was daffing with my love,
> but before midday came
> my heart was sorely grieved.

The chorus is addressed to her orphaned child:

> Ochan ochan ochan uiridh,
> sore is my heart, my love.
> Ochan ochan ochan uiridh
> Your father hears not our moan.

> A curse on gentles and friends
> who have rent me thus with pain,
> who caught my darling unawares
> and made him captive by guile.

> . . . . . .

> They placed his head on a block of oak,
> and spilt his blood on the ground;
> had I but had a cup then
> I'd have drunk my fill of it.

> . . . . . .

> I came to the lawn of Taymouth
> and found there no peace;
> I left no hair of my head unpulled,
> and left no skin on my hands.

......

Would that Finlaig were aflame
and great Taymouth ablaze,
and that fair Gregor with the white palms
were fondled by my two hands.

I have no apples left now
though all the others have;
my apple, fragrant and shapely,
lies low on the ground.

Far better to be with Gregor
roaming heather and wood,
than tied to the wrinkled Baron of Dull
in a house of lime and stone.

Far better to be with Gregor
driving the cows to the glen,
than tied to the wrinkled Baron of Dull
and drinking wine and ale.

Far better to be with Gregor
under tattered sealskin cloak,
than tied to the wrinkled Baron of Dull
wearing satin and silk.[15]

Another well-known poem from roughly the same period may be referred to here, although it is not entirely clear how it fits into the semi-bardic category. This is *"Oran na Comhachaig"*, sometimes called "The Owl of Strone". It is more probably a group of poems, on related Lochaber and personal themes, by a poet called Dòmhnall Mac Fhionnlaigh nan Dàn (Donald son-of-Finlay of the Lays). It was probably composed about 1585,[16] and its themes, as categorized by Professor Rankin, are a dialogue with an Owl, praise of hunting, praise of various Chiefs of Keppoch, farewell to well-loved places, and old age. Metrically it is a mélange of classical or *dán díreach* metres, not strictly adhered to, and some of its themes and devices (such as the dialogue with the Owl, and the treatment of old age) are strongly traditional, with well-known parallels in Irish and Welsh literature. In all, some eighty-seven quatrains are attached to the poem in its variant versions but here only a few stanzas which recreate the excitement of the hunt are quoted:

> The Rock that I loved to visit,
> the Rock the hunters swirled around,
> where the sound voice of the deerhound was sweet
> as the herd was driven through a narrow pen.
>
> Sweet-tongued the eagles on its slopes,
> sweet its cuckoos and its swan,
> a hundred times sweeter than these the cry
> of the fine-speckled, spotted calf of the deer.
>
> . . . . . .
>
> I have heard the music of my choice
> the cry of the great hound as he comes,
> a stag twisting his course through a glen,
> hounds darting in and back.

A delight in Nature appears also in some of the religious verse of this semi-bardic type, which we have from the late sixteenth century. This shows in the work of John Stewart of Appin. Two of his poems are included in the Fernaig MS., one being a poem in a distinctly classical mode, contrasting the final states of the blessed and the damned:

> In fact the two are far apart:
> salt bitterness and fine-flavoured wine;
> woe to him who had the chance of choosing:
> a blind man could make his choice there.[17]

The other deals with man's main enemies: the world/worldliness, greed and the flesh. Man's worldly sojourn is brief:

> Like dew on a calm day,
> or snow that lies fine and white,
> the growth of leaves on the tree:
> men stay here but a space.

The most fragrant rose, or lily,
the plum, or the red cherry,
their bloom doesn't last long:
so too with the people's mirth.[18]

Fear na Pàirce, or MacCulloch of Park (near Dingwall) deals more in straightforward homiletics, and his use of language is rather flat and perfunctory. It is curious in his case to contrast the occasional touches of Classical Common Gaelic with the use of unnecessary English loanwords such as "garden" or "ransom", both stylistic tendencies being indications of this writer's reading.

The crossing of two worlds appears again in the fragments that survive of the poetry of Donnchadh MacRaoiridh, who is thought to have been bard to MacDonald of Sleat in the early decades of the seventeenth century. Two of his poems are of a religious nature, and another two are elegiac, with Mackenzie references. He may have owed a clan allegiance to the Seaforth chiefs, and had connections with their Western Ross territories, where MacRyrie survived as a surname long after this poet's time. The two religious poems are said to have been composed on his death-bed, one of them on the day he died. This latter has a classical simplicity:

Take me with you, Son of God;
with You I would wish to stay
keep closely on your path
my heart and thought and love.

My constant penitent prayer
is always to be with you;
forgive the sin we have done
we shall do no more again.

Another request we make—
it is in your power to give—
that the soul should be with you
while the body of clay goes in earth.

May the soul reach the throne of the blessed,
together with those that are there,
since You know well how I am
take me soon along with You, take.[19]

I have reproduced the "closure" or *dùnadh* by which the classical bards often brought their poems to an end on the word with which it had begun.

Perhaps, however, continuity and change, backward and forward links, are best illustrated by the work of two Mackenzie poets, father and son, whose work falls in the early and middle years of the seventeenth century. Both were in succession head of the Achilty sept of the Mackenzies, and both acted as representatives of Seaforth, the Mackenzie chief, in his recently acquired Lewis possessions. The father was Alasdair Mac Mhurchaidh, and a mere handful of his poems has survived. Three of these are on religious themes, the conflict of flesh and spirit taking a prominent place in them. One ("*B'éibhinn mo shuain an raoir*") gives, in the form of a dream, pictures of Heaven and Hell, but this poem lacks the unity and restraint of "*Ta cogadh oirnn do ghnàth*", with its simply and classically stated Christian faith, and its resort to a lay imagery that was no doubt congenial to this captain of his sept:

> There is always conflict here
> through my love for You, O God:
> my spirit governing me
> when the rein holds back the flesh.
>
> The subtle weapons you gave,
> belief and prayer and love,
> to use them as it were right
> trust the Holy Ghost alone.
>
> The One who strengthened the arms,
> was wounded sore in the fight,
> our tender affection goes
> to Him, His side gashed by spear.
>
> They placed a crown on his head,
> nails fast through His tender palms
> to deliver us from death—
> a miracle—cause of grief.
>
> Let us leave ill-will and guile,
> anger and bodily pride;
> let us render every day
> our thanks to Him though He fell.

My Captain will win the fight,
host's leader who stems pursuit;
my faith will be my defence
as good Peter and Paul said.

My Captain will win the fight
whenever His tryst comes up:
the shedding of my King's blood
protects and sustains my soul.

All Adam's seed have been blind,
unseeing of joy beyond:
short is our visiting here
and that death will come is sure.

Since the war must end in death
I would shun it on no count:
our total joy is beyond;
the world we have here is false.

Binding

My soul to Christ as all the apostles wrote,
my soul again by baptism from the Church,
the bread and the wine and the silver in which they come
lessen my fear that my soul will suffer pain.[20]

In the binding or summing-up verse the seven-syllable line gives
way to a longer one with a freer swinging rhythm, a technical
touch well attested in Irish verse, but appearing in only a very
small number of Scottish instances.

The religious resignation of his other poems is somewhat belied
by "*Is tùrsach dhuinne ri port*", where he laments his old age and
inactivity, together with friends and patrons now dead. He recalls
his love of the sea and of wine and women (regretting that he is now
too old to enjoy the latter, or perhaps too old for them to enjoy
him), and it is in this less than respectable context that he turns to
the "holy book".[21]

Religious themes, including that of the flesh/spirit conflict,
figure in the work of Alasdair's son, Murchadh Mór Mac Mhic
Mhurchaidh, and in two poems jostle with political themes. These

are poems on the betrayal and exile of Charles II, where he condemns the deceit of those who greedily drank toasts to the King while plotting his downfall.[22] A poem on the theme of *vanitas vanitatum* has something of the chiselled quality of good bardic verse. This is how it begins:

> Vain are your tresses, thick tumbling down,
> vain are your goblets, your cups made of staves,
> vain are your breast-knots, and useless your gems,
> all things are vain at the hour when death comes.
>
> Vain are your castles, embattled with flags,
> vain are your houses, lime-washed every day,
> vain, though you like it, your sport with the dames,
> all things are vain at the hour when death comes.[23]

Murchadh Mór composed an elegy for Dòmhnall Gorm Og, chief of the MacDonalds of Sleat, who died in 1643. This poem draws heavily on the mood and style of bardic verse, of which it is as it were, a vernacularized version. Again, I quote only the opening stanzas, to indicate this flavour:

> You bring news, wind from the south,
> more bitter than gall is your loud sough,
> it's no peaceful sound you bring
> from the Minch, my destroying.
>
> The tale that came over the sea—
> I could wish, God, delay to the ferry—
> that the bright, brisk Chief was dead,
> the Isles' peaceable King-Head.
>
> The Hebrides' battle post,
> key to noble verses' riposte,
> that stock of Conn's seed lies flat:
> fine champion in combat.
>
> True lion at battle's breast,
> from stock highest and noblest,
> mild though proud at music's fête,
> guileless at time of banquet.[24]

The metre of the original is *Deibhidhe*, that great favourite of the bardic poets. I have tried to reproduce a hint of its asymmetrical end-rhyme, especially as in the last stanza above. Murchadh Mór observed only some of the rules, omitting alliteration for example. This poem also has a *Ceangal* or binding stanza.

It may be significant—for the time always comes in a poetic succession or tradition when the new is more stimulating than the old—that Murchadh Mór's best poem is in the three-line stanza which had a great vogue in the seventeenth century, offering as it did fast-moving compulsive rhythms and a more popular melody. This poem is "*An Làir Dhonn*" ("The Brown Mare"), in which he gives a spirited and pleasantly whimsical description of his boat, and recollects his life in Lewis. He contrasts the boat with his present form of transport, a filly, and says:

> It needed no chaff,
> or straw or mash,
> but the clash of the waves on its prow.

He recalls, in vivid incisive vignettes the deer-hunting, flaying, seal-hunting, fishing, drinking, and musical entertainment of his Lewis days, giving a picture part of whose detail can still be recognized by those familiar with that remarkable island.[25] This was probably one of Murchadh Mór's later poems, dating perhaps from *c.* 1670.

The inexorable revolution in Gaelic poetry had established itself fairly firmly by this time, and survivals and recreations of the older moods and styles become rarer. They crop up, certainly, as in the Aos-dàna MacShithich's Lament for the Earl of Argyle in 1685,[26] or in the Rev. John Maclean's praise-poem to Edward Lhuyd in 1707,[27] Niall MacMhuirich, as we shall see,[28] bears witness in 1715 to being a master of both bardic and vernacular styles, both still distinct in his case. Metrical echoes of bardic days haunt even later poetry and song, and poets such as Eachann MacLeòid and Alasdair Mac Mhaighstir Alasdair show themselves to be very conscious of elements in the old tradition. The period of transition is therefore a very long one, hardly short of 250 years, which may excuse the length of this interchapter.

4

Clan and Politics

BY THE SEVENTEENTH century Gaelic Scotland was already engaged in various confrontations which were beginning to establish
the pattern of a beleaguered minority community and culture within Scotland. This was scarcely as yet a linguistic minority, or at
any rate what imbalance there was linguistically was not severe,[1]*
but the relative isolation and autonomy which the Gaelic regions
had enjoyed was breaking down. The forfeiture of the Lordship
of the Isles in the last decade of the fifteenth century was one of
the earlier signals of the new order. The Statutes of Iona in 1609,
and succeeding Privy Council enactments, helped to sap the power
of the clan system by a policy of denationalizing of the clan leaders:
ensuring that they were schooled in the Lowlands, and through
English. (The further development, that of schooling potential
chiefs and lairds in the caste-schools of England, came without
benefit of legislation.) Religious differences, exacerbated by the
civil war of the mid-seventeenth century, helped to reinforce older
clan divisions and undermine racial or linguistic unity. The dynastic struggles of Scoto–English and German royalty were a further
pathetic source of disunity in Gaelic Scotland. It is against this
somewhat tawdry background that we observe the surviving work
of Gaelic poets of clan and politics in the seventeenth and early
eighteenth centuries. Sometimes they are involved, usually in a
peripheral way, in national politics, sometimes they appear to be
playing the game that might have delighted the enemies of their
race (as where Iain Lom whips up the hatred of the MacDonalds
against their fellow Gaels, the Campbells). At other times they are
seen as still immersed in the age-old history and legend of their
own race, enjoying, for example, the euphoria of simply being
Macleans or MacDonalds.

These outworn rivalries and preoccupations may sometimes
make it difficult for the modern reader to achieve empathy with
the seventeenth-century poet. There is another barrier to be

* For Notes, see pp. 312–14.

considered, in the case of a number of the poets of the time. It is in this period that we first become acutely aware of the spread of a discursive style of poem-making, which missed the virtues both of the logically structured poem and of the poem which is organized round a series of themes or images, but is held taut by an emotional spring. The bardic poets sometimes show this discursiveness, but more frequently an overall plan can be discerned in their poems. A suggested explanation has already been referred to: that the practice of composing in the dark, without resort to writing until afterwards, may have encouraged a degree of formlessness. This may well be true of all but the clearest-headed of poets.

The same explanation, with a difference, may serve for the discursive style of some verse of the seventeenth century and later. No doubt composition in the dark died with the bardic schools, but the darkness of illiteracy descended over the land of the Gael for a time after the native system of learning withered. and before a new system, based on schools of various kinds, had time to spread. Both in the seventeenth and the eighteenth centuries, and in isolated instances later than that, we have examples of poets of note who could not write their own verses, or read their own language. Outstanding examples are Màiri Nighean Alasdair Ruaidh from the seventeenth century, and Donnchadh Bàn and Rob Donn from the eighteenth. And we may look for some explanation of the discursive style not only in the personal situation of the poet, but in the oral situation in which he operated, if it is agreed that this situation denied him in some measure the clarity of presentation that can be a virtue of a written tradition. These suggestions are hedged with qualifications, for it is clear that the criticism of formlessness cannot be made against all non-literate poets, and it would be rash to assume that other factors were not at work also.

The preponderantly oral setting in which poetry was appreciated for a time by its public no doubt leads to other conventions which seem awkward or strange in a reading context. One such is the convention, which still persists among twentieth-century "village" poets, of signalling the last stanza of a poem by some such phrase as "I shall bring to an end these few verses . . .", a signal which serves the same purpose for the listener as the sight of blank paper does for the reader of a poem.

Despite these strictures and qualifications, the Gaelic poetry of the seventeenth century has much of interest to offer, and has a

strong individuality stamped on it, at its best. It would be misleading to suggest too strongly that it has a homogeneous character.
We have already seen how the bardic and folk traditions live
through the century, and how the semi-bardic style achieves a
limited flowering. In addition to these styles we can see several
others emerging, or continuing, in the poetry of this time. Centuries are not, of course, natural or logical frameworks for poetic
styles or traditions, and are used thus retrospectively only for purposes of rough definition. The seventeenth century spills over into
the eighteenth, and the eighteenth is anticipated long before the
year 1700. The year 1715 perhaps gives a more natural point of
division, and probably it would be true to say that 1640–1720 (in
round figures) represents the time at which the verse of clan and
politics flourished most vigorously. This excludes the most exuber-
ant of all Gaelic political propagandists, Alasdair Mac Mhaighstir
Alasdair, but as we shall see he belongs whole-heartedly to that
eighteenth century which overlaps the seventeenth only in some
respects. On the other hand, it seems both convenient and logical
to consider such a poet as Mairearad Nighean Lachlainn along
with these notable seventeenth- to eighteenth-century women,
Màiri Nighean Alasdair Ruaidh and Sìleas na Ceapaich, although
some of Mairearad's poems post-date the '45 Rising. Having thus
tried to establish an undogmatic critical stance, and left room for
some proper flexibility, it remains to look at the various styles of
verse from this period, to discuss briefly the most significant poets,
and to try to achieve in the process a balanced view of what poetry
was about at this time.

As we saw, poets such as the Mackenzies of Achilty were writing
verse with some political overtones in the middle years of the
seventeenth century. The poet, however, who was most deeply
absorbed in political themes at this time, and throughout the
remainder of the century, was John MacDonald, or Iain Lom. The
adjective *lom* has various senses, but surely it was applied to him
because of his gift for the cutting, scathing phrase. Enough of his
poetry has survived (close on three thousand lines) to establish
clearly its characteristics, and to plot his career in a little detail.
The historical background to his work has been filled in with much
detail in Dr Mackenzie's edition of the poems.[2] Iain Lom's earliest
extant poems date from the early and middle 1640s. One is addressed to Sir Donald MacDonald of Sleat. This is a formal poem,
much closer in spirit to the bardic than to the folk-poetry tradition.

Here Iain Lom seems to be casting himself in the role of a Mac-
Donald laureate. He may have already taken on the role of clan
poet to the Keppoch MacDonalds, and felt it appropriate to pay his
respects, and his compliments, to MacDonald of Sleat, regarded
by then as the senior MacDonald chief. Iain Lom's verse is already
very assured, though he could scarely have been twenty years of
age at the time. This poem, however, is sparse in imagery, and we
may suspect that the poet's imagination, and his emotions, were
not greatly stirred by the subject. There is, at any rate, a distinct
difference between it and the Lament for Aonghas Mac Raghnaill
Oig, the young Keppoch chief who was killed in a skirmish at
Sròn a' Chlachain, above Killin in Perthshire, probably in 1646.[3]
The mood of the poem is personal and subjective, and its method
impressionistic. The poem is an expression of personal grief, not
an official tribute.

Lament for Angus son of Young Ranald of Keppoch

> Lord, low is my spirit,
> though courage must bear it—
> whoever will hear of my losses.
>
> Since death, that brisk caller,
> kills my friends of high valour,
> what pleasure to me in Lochaber?
>
> Lonely, unfriended,
> on each side I am wounded.
> Death's arrows descend on my comrades.
>
> I'm a goose that is plucked
> without feather or brood,
> or like Ossian condemned by Saint Patrick.
>
> Or a tree that is stripped,
> without apple or nut.
> the sap and the bark having left it.
>
> That raid to Loch Tay
> has darkened my way:
> Angus lay dead by its waters.

When we climbed the high hill
we left many a skull
of these masterly marksmen we slaughtered.

Though my father was slain
it's not he whom I mourn,
but you, sworded deep in the kidneys.

What wrung tears from my eyes
was the gap in your side
as you lay in the house of Cor Charmaig.

For I loved your gay face
(branched with blood and with race)
both ruthless and graceful in warfare.[4]

Already, so early in his career, we see here Iain Lom's characteristic directness of utterance, allied to economy of language, and his liking for hard, clear imagery. This skill and economy in the use of language and in the selection of telling detail, can be seen, highly developed, in his famous poem on the Battle of Inverlochy, fought on Sunday, 2nd February, 1645. There are no superfluous lines in this poem: every line makes its point briefly and sharply. The core of the poem consists of a succession of vignettes of the battle and its aftermath. The description is worthy of a skilled war-correspondent in our journalistic age, but it has a controlled venom, an unholy exultation, that would rarely be met with in the modern press. The exultation takes two forms: he exults over the defeat of his clan's enemies, the Campbells, and in the valour and victory of the MacDonalds, and especially their leaders, Iain Mùideartach (John of Moydart) and Alasdair mac Colla. This is a carefully planned, functional poem. Some of its highlights are given in the translation: the poem runs to ninety-two lines.

The Battle of Inverlochy

I climbed early on Sunday morning
to the brae above Inverlochy Castle;
I saw the army taking up position,
and victory lay with Clan Donald.

As you climbed the spur of Cùl Eachaidh,
I recognized your high mettle;
though my country had been left ablaze
what has happened now repays the score.

Though the earldom of Brae Lochaber
were for seven years now as it is,
unsown, unharrowed and fallow,
we are repaid with good interest.

. . . . . .

Many a well-saddled, armoured man,
as good as the Campbells have alive,
could not escape with his boots dry,
but learned to swim at Nevis Foot.

. . . . . .

On the day they thought all would go well
the heroes chased them over frozen ground:
many a great sallow-skinned sloucher
lay on the surface of Ach an Todhair.

Those who climbed the Mound of the Watch
could see newly-lopped paws ill-salted,
the film of death on their lifeless eyes,
after the slashing they had from sword-blades.

. . . . . .

Alasdair of sharp, biting blades,
if you had the heroes of Mull with you,
you would have stopped those who got away,
as the dulse-eating rabble took to their heels.

Alasdair, son of handsome Colla,
skilled hand at cleaving castles,
you put to flight the Lowland pale-face:
what kale they had taken came out again.

> You remember the place called the Tawny Field?
> It got a fine dose of manure;
> not the dung of sheep or goats,
> but Campbell blood well congealed.

> To Hell with you if I care for your plight,
> as I listen to your children's distress,
> lamenting the band that went to battle,
> the howling of the women of Argyll.[5]

Besides having at call an impressionistic style and a style which shows sharp and pungent control over both matter and form, Iain Lom uses a sinuous, highly allusive style. This is used for the development and deployment of an argument, particularly of a political or religico–philosophical argument. There was a tradition that he was intended for the priesthood, and had embarked on studies to that end. I know of no factual evidence for this tradition, but it is not hard to imagine him flexing his mind on theological argument; nor would it be difficult to think of him as an apt student of politics and intrigue. The movement of his thought, at any rate, is often flexible rather than undisciplined, oblique and sinuous rather than disconnected. It may be, of course, that the circumstances in which his poems have come down to us—by oral tradition between his life-time and the mid-eighteenth century—have disturbed their sequence in some cases, but I tend to think that flexibility and obliquity were habits of his mind. Sometimes it is tempting to see in certain poems a disconcerting duality of theme, akin as it were to the formlessness referred to earlier, but again it is usually possible, and preferable, to interpret this as obliquity which is of his essence.

In what is at first sight a lament for the Marquis of Huntly, who was executed in March 1649, Iain Lom develops an argument addressed to the King, Charles II. It is worth quoting at least on grounds of style:

> But, young Charles Stuart,
> it is a sorry slumber you take;
> since you have long been listless
> it is right to waken you from your sleep;
> if it is your intention
> ever to claim your kingdom

do not let it slip, in an evil hour,
if there is any hardihood in your spirit.

Worth more to you than the third of an army
is to have right on your side,
to avenge your father
on those devilish evil-doers.
But if they sense that you are vain,
that there is a touch of flatulence in your talk,
let not your soft tin sword
be in a fair sheath that is gilded.

Do you not pity your loyal subjects,
in every parish church and kirkton (?),
trussed up in hempen ropes,
consigned there by the English;
standing at the clergy's threshold
like unbaptized rebels,
because they supported your claim to the throne
which belonged to your race by heredity?

A little later in this poem, Iain Lom makes a scathing contrast between the Parliamentary Navy and the royal fleet, now being allowed to decay:

> The troughs for urine
> hoist sail on the open sea;
> decaying are the ships of oak
> on whose hatches wine was drunk,
> they are cast on shoals
> away from their wonted ports;
> but if this deluge lasts
> woe to him who has lived to see it.[6]

Some of Iain Lom's political poems conduct their argument in strongly figurative language that is hard now to match to the factual episodes of his time. His poetry seems almost always to rest on a factual basis, and its main interest, as poetry, lies in the methods he chooses to play with the facts, to disguise, deploy or heighten them, to create patterns with them, using dexterity of language, a robust swingeing argumentative movement, colourful figures, and a rich and scathing invective. One aspect of the truth about his work might be summed up by saying that he uses intellectual tactics to deal with topics that are only potentially intellectual: that he seldom develops fully the potential of an argument about the divine right of kings, or the murder of a chief which is to him an equivalent of regicide, but that his style is shot through with the shrapnel of intellectual brilliance.

Some of his poetry has a density of texture which distinguishes it from the mass of seventeenth-century verse. Where poetic texture is thin, where a few ideas are spread over a large area of composition, the intervening spaces are often filled out by padding, frequently padding of a formulaic nature. The conventional heroic and other virtues are ascribed to the subject, as they had been ascribed to a long line of his predecessors. Such passages do not have an independent life, although this lack of life may sometimes be disguised by linguistic or metrical skill. When this happens, we are usually dealing with an inferior poet, for good poetry implies concentration of a high order. This concentration can be achieved through either emotional or intellectual intensity. In Iain Lom's case both kinds of intensity are being brought to bear. Thus, for example, in his poem *"Murt na Ceapaich"* ("The Keppoch Murder"), the theme allows him to combine his emotional and intellectual reactions to authority, loyalty, religious principle and justice. And his personal involvement in all these issues is sufficiently intense to produce a figurative heightening which comes from intensity of emotional and intellectual passion. It is a longish poem, of some 200 lines, and only selected passages are included here. The poem is one of a series concerned with the murder of the young Chief of Keppoch and his brother just before Michaelmas in 1663, and Iain Lom's campaign to avenge these murders. The theme straddled, as it were, two worlds: the clan world, itself based on the ancient structure of the kin-based society, with its own legal sanctions; and the feudal and Christian world, in which appeals could be made to the doctrine of divine right of kings and to the sanctions of the Church.

The Keppoch Murder

Few my reasons for laughter,
walking westerly roads,
I see sowed and harrowed

Inverlair's level land,
and in wilderness Keppoch
with no work taking place;
may God witness, brothers,
the storm broke heavy on us.

We long remember the Friday
that cast us ever in gloom;
as Michaelmas neared us
it was not cattle we killed;
what has left us dejected,
butts of fun at each cross,
is that when clans come together
we're dispersed on the hill.

On Saturday, early,
calamity struck,
I stood above the white bodies
whose blood seeped from their cloaks;
my hands were all patterned
after staunching your wounds;
placing you in your coffins
has weakened my strength.

. . . . . .

Dearly loved the fresh bodies
on which knife-stabs lay thick,
on the floor lying stretched,
being lowered into a vault,
beneath the tread of Sìol Dùghaill,
the spoilers of breasts;
the set of dirks made your skin
like the skin of a sieve.

. . . . . .

The world has seen many murders
since his brother killed Abel,
but this deed's true fellow
were the killing of Adam,

for these impious men killed
the head of their house;
but vengeance rests still
with Holy God or his Son.

We set a peace-tree before us
for protection and guard,
and we should not confront it
as long as we live;
if we ourselves have destroyed it,
that brought ill in its train,
an axe will fall from the Heavens
cutting branches and limbs.

Some sins enjoy respite,
not revealed in a trice,
adultery, whoredom,
theft, gluttony, drink;
but murder, abhorrent,
is too loathsome and vile:
God is by it so angered
He'll not delay his revenge.[7]

The poem goes on to urge the chiefs of the leading septs of the Clan Donald to do, as it were, God's work for Him. The poem becomes more functional at this point, losing its emotional intensity, although it does not at any point become flabby.

Iain Lom continued to comment on matters of clan, and Highland, and Scottish interest, and we have extant poems on the Battle of Killiecrankie and on the accession of William of Orange and Mary (this latter marked by bitter vituperation). The last poem to be ascribed to him is on the theme of the Union of the Parliaments of Scotland and England, an infamous event which took place in 1707. Dr Mackenzie quotes a contemporary comment: "While there was great rejoicing in England, in many parishes in Scotland 1st May was observed as a day of fasting and humiliation."[8] Iain Lom evidently believed implicitly that bribery played a part in the whole transaction and he gives a lively description of the almost physical manifestations of avarice in some of the Scottish Lowland "nobles":

Lord Dupplin, without delay
the vent to your throat opened,
a turbulence rose in your heart
when you heard the gold coming;
you swallowed the hiccoughs of avarice,
your lungs inflated and swelled,
control over your gullet was relaxed,
and the traces of your arse were unloosed.[9]

Dupplin's dubious ancestry is hilariously described, and other prominent traffickers of the time, such as Queensberry, are given the notoriety of a stanza. Iain Lom, at eighty-three or whatever age he was in 1707, was what the Lowlanders might have described as "a coorse chiel". It is of some interest that both he, and that most intellectual of eighteenth-century Gaelic poets, Alasdair Mac Mhaighstir Alasdair, should have had so well-developed a predilection for bawdy invective. It is of some interest also, whether it is of significance I do not know, that they were both Catholics.

At any rate Iain Lom's work, though it is uneven, and has its share of flat or conventional passages, covers a very interesting range of styles, is intellectually stimulating to anyone who takes the trouble to reconstruct the context in which it was composed, and still carries for all to see the marks of linguistic exuberance and (most clearly on the verbal level) creative energy.

An older contemporary of Iain Lom, a little of whose work has survived, was Eachann Bacach. All his extant verse seems to belong in date to the middle years of the seventeenth century, mostly about 1647 to 1651. All the poems have a strong Maclean connection, and he seems to have held office as a family-poet to the Chief of Duart, in Mull. He is one of a group of seventeenth-century poets to whom the title *aos-dàna* is, rather loosely, attached, apparently implying some official status, but clearly distinguished from that of the professional classical bards.[10] There are strong similarities between their work and that of poets such as Iain Lom, who do not happen to be given the title of *aos-dàna*, and probably the label is not a particularly useful one.

All Eachann Bacach's poems are concerned with the praise of Macleans. This praise sometimes takes the form of description of the chief's weapons, e.g. Sir Lachlan (*a.* 1648) carries a bow, gun, sword and shield, though perhaps not all at the same time! Sometimes the chief's allies are enumerated, as in two poems addressed to Sir Lachlan. In a more personal poem addressed to the same chief,[11] the mood is a "heroic" one; the warlike and plundering aspects of the chief's activities are underlined and to these are added pictures of hunting, and of household pursuits. Towards the end there is a premonition of disaster for the chief and his clan, suggesting composition about the year 1647, when Argyll took him prisoner. The last three extant poems ascribed to Eachann Bacach are concerned with the next Chief, Sir Hector, and the disastrous Battle of Inverkeithing, fought in 1651, a battle in which Sir Hector and huge numbers of his clansmen were killed. The rashness and the courage of Sir Hector are vividly suggested in a stanza from one of Eachann Bacach's laments for him:

> Cromwell came against you,
> your heart swelled with rage
> you leapt into the fight with sword shining.[12]

Undoubtedly, however, the finest of Eachann Bacach's surviving poems is *"A' Chnò Shamhna"* ("The Hallowe'en Nut"), his elegy for Sir Lachlan Maclean who died in April, 1648. It is a densely textured poem, with many elements of traditional elegy. In a number of ways it invites comparison with the work of the bardic poets: in its initial use of history and legend, its tree imagery, and perhaps in the use of extended images, especially in the second stanza and the final two stanzas. But the overall tone of the poem is different from that of bardic verse. It has the incantatory style that we find in some of the folksongs, particularly in the keens, and this repetition and incantation suggest mutual influence between the two kinds of song. It is noticeable too that, syntactically, periods are more extended than is normal in bardic verse or in folksong; the period or sentence has a broad sweep, often extending throughout a stanza. The stanzas are well-moulded, each having an individual life of its own. Also, there appears to be a logical development in the sequence of ideas or topics: this is most strikingly illustrated by the final two stanzas, with their extended and consistent imagery. There is, indeed, something quite modern about Eachann Bacach's use of imagery here. The poem has a wide range of reference, and an imaginative life, moving in a darting but incisive way from legend to nature imagery, to imagery of the grave, reminiscence, and description. It uses verse paragraphs of five to eight lines, each line having two strong stresses, with parallel-phrase

structure, building up sub-themes within paragraphs, and with
an extra stress, carrying a consistent rhyme throughout the poem,
in the final line of each stanza.

The metre is a variant of *ochtfhoclach*, which is attested from
the twelfth century at least, and is no doubt older than that. There
is nothing experimental about this metre. It is handled with assurance by the poet, and has every appearance of having a long tradition behind it. Presumably it comes into *prominence* in the seventeenth century in Gaelic Scotland because it was earlier associated
with poetry by "lesser breeds" of poets—*aos-dàna* rather than
filidh—and with the decline in influence of the *filidh* it at last got a
hearing. In the translation I can hope to confirm only some of these
assertions that are made about the Gaelic text:[13]

The Hallowe'en Nut

Your stock went back to King Pharaoh,
who was able to fable it,
MacMhuirich or Ferguson?
A tree that lasted an age,
that put roots down in Scotland,
a branch helped at Harlaw,
your co-name, our treasure, still lives.[14]

It was no sapling or plantling,
last year's nut that you grew from,
no flower planted in Maytime,
but growth of leaves and of branches—
this top twig that has left us:
send, Christ, more in the place of the dead.

Hard the hurt of this season,
dark the gloom that grows on us,
too narrow your dwelling
in the staves of the coffin:
we think long of the laying of boards.

In winter-house lies your chest,
uncracked the Hallowe'en nut;
Hebridean men's mettle,
great the hurt to your clan

that armour gave you no fright,
most esteemed in the camp of Montrose.

. . . . . .

Your foe got no purchase
when he threw down the gauntlet:
you were always the winner;
your coming was welcome
to the rent-payer's home;
not whey-like your colour
when pride entered into your pores.

. . . . . .

Well, I've seen the day,
when you joined in the hunt,
the rough slope did not stop you;
no yew-bow was fashioned
that could daunt you or stress you:
you could draw to the limit
while the timber stayed supple
and send the tail-feathers at speed.

A neat skinful placed
in the old badger quiver,
jagged heads from the smithy,
not an inch but was buried
from the head to the butt,
powered by hemp-string from Flanders;
no quarry was safe
when you aimed that arrow at will.

It was not my post-Easter Monday
when the dart of death struck you;
you have left your friends wretched,
hum of bees round the ruins
of a nest that's been plundered,
or spring lambs without mother
whose bleating lasts long round the fold.

Good was your dispensing
in the big house at evening:
pot-still whisky being poured
into goblets of silver,
while the harp was being tuned to sing.

Our fresh rose has been plucked,
our leader and crowner,
the first on the highway;
many days are recounted
that your own country's nobles
spent in love and joy with you:
I came to your court
before I could crawl on the floor.

I knew well of Sir Lachlan
that one of his pleasures
was to drink wine with women
who were lovely and gentle,
in a great house, with music,
and joy as the cups went their rounds.

When the dusk began closing
the harp would be plundered,
no music was hoarded,
the fingers disclosed it,
the hands did not weary
till the time came for sleeping in peace.

The gamblers, quick-moving,
shot the dice at backgammon,
the chessmen were rattling,
at cards, calling and trumping,
Spanish dollars and testoons
were being paid without anger at all.

All spoke well of your virtues:
love and fear of the Saviour,
a spouse with reason to love you,
most alert and most handsome,
as warrior, unquestioned:

there was reading from Scripture
in your hall before men left the board.

Though frequent rain's gusting
you kept for your son upright
your fair sail untattered;
your yard-man stood by you
since Christ was your gear-man
He gave the sheet-rope in your hand.

If you take, son, this rudder,
your traditional chiefship
will incline you to prayer;
let the Trinity crew her:
put the Father at first there,
let the Son be the helmsman,
Holy Ghost take her in to the roads.

The name most frequently linked with that of Iain Lom is
Màiri Nighean Alasdair Ruaidh (Mary MacLeod), though the link
probably owes more to romantic associations than to critical assess-
ment. The story of her banishment from the house of the Chief of
the MacLeods is alluded to in her verse, and seems to have caught
the imagination of succeeding generations. There is, further, the
fact that both poets used the so-called strophic metres, and in
particular the three-line stanza which became very popular in the
seventeenth century. At one time people seemed to believe that
these two poets had foregathered to invent this stanza, but we now
know that it was in existence before they were born. Màiri Nighean
Alasdair Ruaidh's surviving work runs only to some 1,200 lines,
and if this is a fair sample we can conclude that her work and her
mind were very different to Iain Lom's, lacking his range and
subtlety as well as his power.

What her poetry has *par excellence* is music and rhythm, and
these characteristics are strongly marked in her earliest datable
poem, "*Marbhrann do Fhear na Comraich*" ("Elegy for the Laird
of Applecross"), which presumably dates from the year 1646. Her
style uses as a salient element a succession of parallel statements
which give a powerful build-up to her total emotional statement.
The technique is clearly that which we find in songs like "*Cumha
Sheathain*",[15] although it occurs in these songs in a different

metrical context, yet one which has some strong similarities to the
strophic paragraphs which Màiri Nighean Alasdair Ruaidh uses
here. The emotional build-up depends greatly on the rhythmical
beat, and to a lesser extent on the vowel-music. Together they
constitute what we tend to think of (perhaps not quite accurately)
as Mary MacLeod's music. The translation does not attempt to
recapture the vowel-music, but seeks to salvage at least a general
impression of the rhythm.

From *Elegy for the Laird of Applecross*

. . . . . .

My joy yesterday stopped;
my dear knight went off;
I put the harp in its box;
the smith refused me a key,
and no doctor can cure
me, my honour is gone—you are dead.

The tree has fallen its length,
the grain has showered to the earth;
you have wounded the clan
whose chieftain you were,
guarding them every day,
I'm destroyed, death has taken its bite.

. . . . . .

I found my handsome young dear
without the music he loved,
joiners fitting the boards,
women plucking the grass,
no board-games or song;
sad to hear all the pain of my tale.

When the throng came about
then the parting was sore,
as bees hum in a bank
when their honey is lost;
sad and wretched their load,
the corpse of the brave host's leader.[16]

The stanza in that poem is consistently one of six lines, but in the "*Marbhrann do Iain Garbh* . . ." ("Elegy for MacLeod of Raasay")[17] the stanza varies between five and eight lines, as in the poem by Eachann Bacach quoted already.[18] Sometimes, but not always, the longer stanza is used to develop a sub-theme more fully, and one might think that this was its logical *raison d'être.*

A number of her poems are rather formal, with set pieces about ancestry, heroic qualities, and the tributes to spouses which are often placed as afterthoughts to panegyrics by bardic poets also. She praises MacLeod's hall, as Tadhg Dall Ó Huiginn in Ireland praised the houses of his patrons, although there is nothing in Tadhg Dall to match the simple felicity of this reminiscence of Dunvegan. Referring to Rory Mór, the famous MacLeod Chief who died in 1626, when Màiri Nighean Alasdair Ruaidh was perhaps a teenager, she says:

> In his great house
> I have been joyful,
>
> Dancing merry
> on a wide floor,
>
> The fiddle-playing
> to put me to sleep,
>
> The pipe-playing
> to wake me in the morning.
>
> Bear my greeting
> To Dunvegan.[19]

The late poem, "*Cumha do Mhacleòid*" ("Lament for MacLeod"),[20] composed in 1699, is rather formal again, and, perhaps because of its low temperature, goes into a passage of clan-verse. By this time the eight-line stanza was being used for the more formal praise-poetry. Perhaps she found the metrical form inhibiting. At any rate, it turned out that the Chief was not dead after all, and she composed "*An Crònan*" (The Croon")[21] in variable strophic para-graphs, recapturing in places the emotional surge often associated with this metre. She captures this again in the Elegy for Sir Norman MacLeod, who died in 1705:

Beneath boards in a coffin
is the prop of wisdom,
esteemed, liberal
with feasts and gifts,
with fame unbroken:
earth under flag on my treasure.[22]

There is, however, much repetition from poem to poem of basic ideas and phrases, and one can scarcely escape the conclusion that this poet's reputation has been greatly inflated. She wears the narrow strait-jacket of the bardic panegyrist without his learning, his occasional wit, and his metrical virtuosity, bringing to her work, however, the positive virtues of musical phrasing, not infrequent verbal felicities, and occasional images of some vividness.

Not much survives of the verse of Catrìona NicGillEathain (Catherine Maclean), a poet who lived in the island of Coll, and was composing in the latter part of the seventeenth century. She composes elegy with fluency, using mainly an eight-line stanza. Her style is strongly influenced by folksong, but she shows occasional fluency in handling bardic conventions which have been adopted by the folk poets. Sometimes a conventional image is brought alive again by some striking addition:

There was a shaft in my kidneys
thrust in right to the feathers.[23]

There is much talk in seventeenth-century verse of the feather dressing of arrows and of gashed kidneys, so that one experiences a start of appreciation to see this new combination of motifs. The lines come from her lament for her husband, a good, unpretentious folk-type elegy. Her style generally is low-key, and her language does not have an inner life: it is not alive and growing in her mind.

There are two women poets, in the latter part of the seventeenth and the first half of the eighteenth century, whose work survives in some bulk, and shows strong and individual quality. It is probable that both were born in the 1660s, and they both survived, and were composing vigorously, well into the eighteenth century. Probably the older of the two was Sìleas na Ceapaich (Julia or Giles or Cicely MacDonald of Keppoch) who was married to Alexander Gordon by 1685. The majority of her dateable songs in fact belong to the first quarter of the eighteenth century. Her surviving work shows a good variety of interests and styles. There is a strong political interest, a somewhat more subdued clan interest, a moral vein and a (late?) religious vein. She uses folk styles at times, but composes also formal laments. There is some structural firmness in her poems, and like Iain Lom she can conduct sinuous poetical argument. There is not much sign of humour, and not very much in the way of highly memorable lines or passages. One can sense her secure, cultured background, and see the evidence of a long literary tradition behind her work.

She shares Iain Lom's opinions about the place bribery played in bringing about the Union of the Parliaments, but lacks his mobility of scornful invective. In the poem probably composed in 1714, and with an incitatory purpose in the months before the '15, she appeals to the outraged national sentiment of these post-Union years:

> Scotland, arise in concert
> before the English cut your throats,
> since they took your credit from you,
> and your goods too for gold
> though your pocket's empty now.[24]

Probably the best example of her sinuous, colourful, figurative style of argument is in another political poem of this time, *"Do dh' Arm Rìgh Sheumais"* ("To King James' Army"), probably composed towards the end of 1715.[25] She castigates the Jacobite Army for its lack of activity after Sheriffmuir, resembling the leaders to the dog of Aesop's fable that "drops his meat for the reflection".[26] This is the verse in question:

> Water rises beneath you,
> you must quickly awaken,
> long is your sleep without worry;
> if you don't turn your cloak
> your throat will be slit,
> long is your sleep without waking;
> like the foraging dog,
> with collop in jaw:
> when he saw its reflection
> he started to catch it;
> when he lost what he had

he was hungry thereafter;
long is your sleep without worry.[26a]

The poets of her time usually combine clan with wider national interests, in varying degrees according to their predilections and temperaments. Sileas' work includes one example of a dignified, elegant elegy to a clan chief, her elegy for Glengarry (*"Alasdair á Gleann Garadh"*). She had already had experience of elegy-making, for her husband and for her daughter, and these show more of the quality of the folk lament as in these lines about her daughter Anna:

> I would rejoice to see your face,
> blue lively eyes, and cheeks like rowan;
> I gave you breast, and knee, and side:
> and all that work was well worth while.[27]

She makes an oblique reference, perhaps, to her own bereavements at the beginning of her lament for Glengarry, and again in the second-last stanza, but the formality of the present occasion forbids her be more specific. It may be, however, that her family grief heightens the tone of her formal lament. The opening stanza, and the final five are quoted. There are nine stanzas in all:

Alasdair of Glengarry

> Alasdair of Glengarry
> you brought tears to my eyes today;
> no wonder that I am wounded,
> and that my wounds open up again;
> no wonder that my sighs are heavy,
> misfortune falls heavy on my kin;
> Death often cuts and takes from us
> the choicest and the tallest oaks.
>
> . . . . . .
>
> You were the red torch to burn them,
> you would cleave them to the heels,
> you were a hero in the battle,
> a champion who never flinched;

a fresh-run salmon in the water,
an eagle in the highest flock,
lion excelling every creature,
broad-chested, strong-antlered stag.

A loch that could not be emptied,
a well liberal in health,
Ben Nevis towering over mountains,
a rock that could not be scaled;
topmost stone of the castle,
broad pave-stone of the street,
precious jewel of virtues
noble stone of the ring.

The yew above every wood,
the oak, steadfast and strong,
you were the holly, the blackthorn,
the apple rough-barked in bloom;
you were not akin to the aspen,
the alder made no claim on you,
there was none of the lime-tree in you,
you were the darling of lovely dames.

You were the spouse of a precious wife,
I'm sad that she has lost you now;
though I must not compare myself with her
I too have borne a bitter fate;
let every wife who lacks a spouse
pray that God's Son take his place,
since He is able to give her help
in the grief and distress that come on her.

I pray that your soul may be saved,
now that your resting is in the clay;
I pray joy for those behind you
in your home and in your lands:
may I see your son in your place,
in wealth and responsibility:
Alasdair of Glengarry,
you brought tears to my eyes today.[28]

It was probably in her latter years, after her husband's death in 1720, that Sìleas turned afresh to that religious consolation which she offers to Glengarry's widow. Several hymns are ascribed to her, and these suggest wider reading in the literature of piety, as well as good knowledge of earlier Gaelic literature. A reference in one to the Seven Deadly Sins,[29] and especially the arrow references, suggest that she knew some of the earlier Gaelic verse on this theme. In *"Laoidh na h-Oidhche"* ("The Night Hymn") there is a somewhat macabre passage where the poet counsels that we think of our beds as graves, of the deal-boards (of which fashionable beds were made at the time) as the boards of the coffin, of our night-shirts as shrouds, and of the bedclothes as the clay of the grave.[30] One may suspect that there is an element here of following the fashion. In *"Laoidh Mhoire Mhaighdean"* ("Hymn to the Virgin Mary"), in which the Gospel story is versified, in simple style, there is a surprisingly free use of English loanwords, suggesting English hymns and scriptures in the background, and indeed the Gaelic scriptures were not available at this time. The most ambitious of her religious poems is *"An Eaglais"* ("The Church"), a poem which owes a good deal to medieval models, however these were mediated to Sìleas. The construction of the Church is related in allegorical terms, in what is a carefully worked-out, fluent ordering of dogma.[31] In addition, from a period of her life that cannot easily be pin-pointed, though it was probably late, we have a poem giving worldly advice to marriageable maidens (this is neatly and pithily expressed), and a song against sexual licence, which has a little plain speaking, but is moral rather than bawdy, though earlier critics, on a cursory glance, had been censorious of it. Probably one of her later songs (composed as her Editor conjectures between 1721 and 1727),[32] was the Lament for Blind Lachlan (*"Cumha Lachlainn Daill"*). He was one of the latter-day Scottish harpers. This is not great poetry, but it has some felicitous lines, and goes easily. A translation which ventures, perhaps unwisely, into rhyme, is given:

Lament for Lachlan Mackinnon, the Harper

> Goodbye to the music of the harp,
> Death's mark is on you, Lachlan, now;
> I must not yearn to hear your lore,
> nor evermore to see your brow.

When I was young and but a child
your music held me in its thrall,
and though I left you and came north
you often visited my hall.

My heart would leap each time I saw
your form approaching, for I knew
that you would tell me all I asked
about old friends, with answers true.
When we met, our talk turned first
to Sleat; in your deliberate way
you spoke of Donald and his wife,
and told me all there was to say.

You brought me news, concisely told,
of old friends living there; and then
spoke of the great Clanranald, and
gave tidings of my friends again.
You told me of my Knoydart kin,
of Morar and Glengarry too,
brought news from Brae Lochaber of
each town and household that I knew.

Marion and Janet, though they live
in far Argyll, sent news by you;
you brought me gossip from Glencoe—
I love to hear of what they do.
Sad is the tale they bring me now:
my story-teller's gone away,
none can replace his ready tongue,
his quicksilver is turned to clay.

Since you will never come again
dark sorrow broods over my mirth;
Death's swift call brought to my eyes
a flood of tears—a bitter birth.
I loved you well, and dearly loved
the music that your sweet harp made;
no surly company we kept
when I sat by you as you played.

When you took your harp, and tuned
it, quietly sitting close to me,
no dolt could understand my song,
nor all your tripping grace-notes see:
sweetly your fingers stroked its side
when I asked you, and you played
laments for Mary and Archibald,
the Bishop, and Clanranald's Maid.

Stately Melody, Lament,
Salute or Song—I'll never hear
any of these but tears will fall,
sadly recalling you, my dear.
Although blindness closed your eyes,
you were blind in no other way:
your lips could find the talk of love,
your supple hands saw how to play.

Hard that your harp is stripped from you,
bitter the way that things have gone,
sad to think I shall never see
you here, nor hope you may return.
May God show mercy unto you
and clothe you in angels' attire:
and since you loved music on earth
may your soul sing in the saints' choir.

In life you asked for no reward
save what the nobles gave you; then
you spent your fee right merrily,
bringing joy to your fellow-men.
But what good does it do to lament
the death of so many men of mark?
Much though I loved it in my youth,
Goodbye to the music of the harp.[33]

The final woman poet of this group being considered is Mairearad Nighean Lachainn. There has been some debate as to whether she was a Maclean or a MacDonald. In fact she seems to have been both, a MacDonald in her maiden state, as the internal evidence of her poetry suggests, but married to a Maclean, and with a Maclean mother.[34] Her surviving verse is almost exclusively concerned with Maclean personalities, and with Mull, and she seems to have become known as a poet only in middle life. She was born probably in the mid-1660s, and lived until the middle of the eighteenth century.

Despite the outward narrowness of her range, I am inclined to think she was the most talented of the group of women poets. Her opinions have a strong individuality, and one can sense in her language the texture of freshly-hewn units. She has a facility also in that style of sinuous argument that is a characteristic of some seventeenth-century verse. Her verse is interesting metrically also: not because it is innovatory, but rather because it is so vital and buoyant in spite of its basically conservative patterns. In the late poem *"Oran do dh'Ailein MacGill-Eathain, Fear Bhròlais"* ("Song to Allan Maclean, Laird of Brolas") she uses basically that metre with its salient characteristic of rhyming paragraphs, which Dorothy Brown had used a hundred years earlier in her song to Alasdair Mac Colla,[35] and an earlier panegyrist had used in a song to that John MacDonald who was killed in Mull in 1586.[36] She uses various lengths of strophic paragraph, of four, five, six and eight lines,[37] and she uses the eight-line stanza, which we saw coming into vogue in the latter part of the seventeenth century, using it with great assurance, particularly in the very late poem ascribed to her, her elegy for Sir Hector Maclean, who died in Rome in 1751.

The surviving evidence suggests that she saw herself as a clan panegyrist rather than a private person who composed verse: that she was in this respect closer akin to Màiri Nighean Alasdair Ruaidh than to Sìleas na Ceapaich. It may be that the primary sources for her verse have helped to cast her in that role. At any rate, she was no mere uncritical panegyrist, but a sophisticated observer of current affairs. Yet she can play on the traditional strings with consummate ease, as in the *"Cumha do Lachainn MacGill-Eathain"*, ("Lament for Lachlan Maclean"), which seems to be an early song. She concludes it with a stirring passage of name-dropping, not in the snobbish sense, but in the context of a kin-based society, where kin-bonds and pride of ancestry are natural, almost the stuff of small-talk, but very important small-talk.

> My beloved is related
> to Maclean of the breastplates,

to whom warriors would gather,
and to that Earl of Antrim,
famed rider of coursers in Ireland.

. . . . . .

There for the telling
is your kinship to Moidart,
to MacNeill from his towers,
with his vigorous clansmen,
my love's close in kin to Sir James.

. . . . . .

Great-grandson to Allan
who took the ship from MacCailein,
on a bright moonlit night,
with its lading of cattle
that reached no spring fold with their lowing.[38]

In her elegiac strophes in particular she makes effective use of
these sudden changes of subject within the stanza which are a
characteristic device of the composers of laments, juxtaposing
factual and emotional statements, and in this way providing the
aesthetic jolt that is achieved in painting or ceramics or (meta-
phorically speaking as in poetry) in music by change of texture.
The longer paragraph of the seven-line strophic stanza is an
effective vehicle for this style:

O man who purchased the wine
and was able to pour,
worthy wielder of bow
and shafts with fine polished tips,
alas! Mary, my loss,
I was there on the shore
when they brought you to holy Iona.[39]

There are many more examples of this style in her verse. In what is
one of her best-known poems, *"Gaoir nam Ban Muileach"* ("The
Mull Women's Cry of Woe"), we find again this variety of textures
within the stanza, and overall an easy range of reference and

assurance of opinion. The poem is a lament for Sir John Maclean of Duart, who died in 1716. His career had many similarities to that of Allan of Clanranald, praised by Niall MacMhuirich and others. They were born within two or three years of each other, lived for a time in France, and both fought at Sheriffmuir. Maclean took ill in Perth, shortly after the battle, and died in the following March. I quote only two stanzas from the poem:

> I was suddenly startled:
> joiners sawing your coffin,
> your being laid under flagstones
> in hiding, unnoticed;
> the West has been broken,
> the heir's not come to wisdom,
> this year brought destruction,
> sore our loss from Mar's sudden rising.

> . . . . . .

> Alas, the leader of champions,
> who knew no shame in the battle,
> lost in our time of hardship;
> though our cattle be lifted
> your flag will not flutter,
> we will not hear your war-song;
> an evil eye spied you
> from Perth on that day as you marched.[40]

In the post-Culloden elegy[41] for Sir Hector Maclean, there is some strong anti-English feeling. The poet wishes that Duke William and his host should all be drowned off the Point of Ardnamurchan. But more interesting, and more subtle politically is the contrast drawn between the Macleans and the Campbells in *"Oran do Shir Iain MacGill-Eathain"* ("A Song to Sir John Maclean"). The Macleans are depicted as loyal royalists, and the Campbells as deceitful and ingenious schemers. The poem is to be dated to the reign of Queen Anne, but is composed against the backcloth of legal sharp practice by which the Campbells had undermined the power of the Macleans in the previous half-century.[42]

The Clan Maclean were treasured,
and had dignity of mind,
their heads are high no longer now,
the law has brought them down;
alas for those whose loyalty
is paid to king or prince.

Ingenious guile pays better,
as your spiteful foemen found:
you would be strong and numerous
with your affairs all prospering,
if you were cautious, prudent,
and knew the time to turn.[43]

Another Mull poet who was almost a full contemporary of
Mairearad Nighean Lachainn was Iain Mac Ailein (John Maclean).
He belonged to the Ardgour branch of the Macleans. Like Eachann
Bacach he is given the title of *Aos-dàna*, and may have acted as a
family bard to Maclean of Duart. He carries over some of the
legendary lore of the old bards into vernacular verse, and is much
concerned with the older values in society. He is not, in the main,
an innovating poet, and on the whole his language lacks creative-
ness. He is capable, however, of making social criticisms, can
use verse in both humorous and moral causes, and gives an early
instance of that style of verse which is later associated with the
village-bards. His work has survived in some quantity, because of
his relatively late survival (post-1745) and his proximity to Dr
Hector Maclean, whose MS. anthology was in progress by 1738.
These circumstances, rather than a rush of innovation, explain why
we find him ostensibly so near the fountain-head of village-verse,
which is presumably much older than his time.

In the rôle of family bard John Maclean composed poems of
welcome and laments. The chief he was most prominently associated with was Sir John Maclean, who returned from his temporary
French exile in 1703. The poem *"Nan tigeadh Sir Iain"* ("Were
Sir John to come")[44] was apparently composed on hearing that the
chief had come to England. The language of this poem is lively and
spontaneous: it achieves that spontaneous combustion which is a
mark of the style of Iain Lom's political verse. The impression he
gives is that the clan Maclean, since the days of Killiecrankie some
fourteen years previously, have led a cowed existence, like wethers

crowding round the sheep-fold, while plundering neighbours (the Campbells?) treat them with as much contempt as the lackey who helps a gentleman to draw on his shoes. He hopes, with the impending return of the chief, for better things.

There are hints, throughout the poetry of the 1690s and early 1700s, of change and Anglicization, and the threat to the old order. The Chief of Clanranald, Allan who lost his life at Sheriffmuir, is praised for not giving all his attention to material things, but he also, like the generation of leaders who had been involved in Killiecrankie and its aftermath, had had a taste of foreign luxury. The poets, whether vernacular ones like Iain Mac Ailein and An Clarsair Dall, or bardic ones like Niall MacMhuirich, set the older ideals before their chiefs, and offer them some pointed advice. Iain Mac Ailein in "*An Sùgradh*" ("The Mirth-making") is perhaps tackling the same problem in a different way, recalling the old order in the chief's residence in Aros, and giving an account of his own poetic circuit of the houses of friendly Chiefs:

> When the makers of mirth came
> they would not hide them away;
> they made them joyously welcome
> close to their high-ceilinged rooms.
> They showed regard to the songs,
> and the bards had their joy of it;
> and the travellers from Ireland
> did well at their liberal hands.
>
> When winter had gone away
> and the warm summer had come,
> we would go overseas
> to visit our dearest friends.
> They would reach Sir James's
> in Sleat—he was closest at hand—
> and spend a pleasant time there
> with stories and drinks round the board.[45]

The board is perhaps the *clàr Lochlainneach* (The Norse platter) on which food was piled in the middle of the table. The poet goes on to refer to other chiefs who kept open house, e.g. John of Talisker and Allan of Clanranald. Other poems are concerned more specifically with visits to MacLeod of Talisker, whose house was a favourite resort of Gaelic poets especially in the 1690s.

Where Iain Mac Ailein is at his most original is in his adaptations of old Gaelic legend and in his humorous verse. In prose and verse he gives an account of the coming of the Milesians (the ancestors of the Gaels) and their meeting with the Tuatha Dé Danann.[46] Some of the latter had disguised themselves as strong drinks, in order to get the better of the Milesians, and several Socttish "brands" are named, such as "Glasgow Whisky" and "Tiree". The account leads into a verse, one where the powers of whisky are analysed: the eighteenth-century poets were to take up this refrain. Another pair of prose and verse compositions is on the theme of *"Cath Alphuirt"* ("The Battle of Alphort"), where the opposition to the Tuatha Dé Danann is organized by Sir Colin Campbell of Ardkinglass, Sheriff-depute of Argyll. Most of the characters in this piece are again of an allegorical nature.

In other poems he satirizes those who have become new-fangled in dress and in their tastes in food, and (perhaps with a personal involvement) he criticizes families who pay little attention to their own old-folk, and the chief who relegates the old man to the kitchen. In this latter very self-possessed poem[47] he also criticizes foreign customs and tastes:

> . . . . . .
> What has brought you these new debts
> is your liking for the Lowlands,
> the little pot beside the hearth
> with the honey-tasting brew in it,
> spending what your father used
> to keep an armed household.

Presumably he means to include more than the tea-pot in the sweeping condemnation of the final two lines!

A conversation, as though between two sisters, gives a fluent verse argument concerning the religious and the secular life,[48] and we see the poet's gentle humour in verses addressed to a young girl who had praised him.[49] The poem consists of a succession of verses of this type:

> O modest maiden, so proud of form,
> although your cheeks are as crimson red,
> I care as little for your love, and hate you,
> as the fireside cat hates to hunt the mouse.

Iain Mac Ailein's poems have not been definitively edited as yet: when they are they will throw a useful light on the progress of Gaelic poetry and society in the first few decades of the eighteenth century, showing both in transition again.

The Skye poet Lachlann Mac Theàrlaich Oig (Lachlan Mackinnon) has some points of similarity to Iain Mac Ailein. A close contemporary, he composed a good elegy for John MacLeod of Talisker (*c.* 1700), and wrote humorous verse which is occasionally broad. He is the author of a love-poem, *"Oran do Nighean Fhir Gheambail"* ("A song to the Laird of Geambail's Daughter")[50] in which a catalogue of the lady's charms is given. His best-known poem *"Latha Siubhal Sléibhe"* ("One day as I walked the hill"),[51] in praise of famous and generous Skye chiefs, a continuation as it were of the matter we saw used by one of the Mackenzie of Achilty bards, has some originality of plot. Not much of this poet's verse has survived, perhaps unfortunately, to judge from the cryptic verse he is said to have written in the Bible of his second wife, whom he married as a widow:

> The world is divided,
> there are two destinies:
> a destiny for happiness
> and the Devil's destiny.[52]

Also contemporary with Iain Mac Ailein was Iain Dubh Mac Iain 'ic Ailein (John MacDonald), who was a competent poet—he is another of the poets referred to as *aos-dàna*—with little or no innovating freshness, but a "central" poet for his own time and tradition. A folk-style strophic lament, to be dated about 1686, is ascribed to him,[53] but most of his extant poems are dated in the years before and after Sheriffmuir (1715). Two poems, which may be earlier, illustrate well the bead-string type of poem structure, in which each stanza is worked separately. The *"Oran do Mhac Mhic Ailein"* ("Song to Clanranald"),[54] one of these two poems, is rather formal panegyric, with a mechanical use of adjectives, and *"Oran nam Fineachan Gaidhealach"* ("Song of the Highland Clans")[55] consists of a long series of rollicking verses about each clan that would come as allies of the MacDonalds. This is all rather tedious. There is some vivid realistic writing, however, in his *"Bruadar mu Chor na Rìoghachd"* ("A Dream about the State of the Kingdom")[56] dated 1715, as these verses may confirm:

I saw, as I was sleeping,
a kind of vision,
it gave me such a fright
that I scarce recovered;
I looked up to the skies
in alarm and consternation:
Mar was in that turmoil
clad in bright steel armour.

. . . . . .

Common in their camp
sounds of clarions and pipes,
beating on the drum
enhancing their courage;
when every commander
got his orders for action
they then began to march
not for peace but for battle.

The voice spoke words to me:
"Though what you see is fearsome
they will never harm you
till you deserve their ill-will.
Do not even privately
ask for the one you seek
until you see the borrowed sow
being rent apart by deer-hounds."

I saw, as I was sleeping,
for that long time enough,
siege set to our towns,
and many quietly captured,
the cannon volleys
smashing limbs before us,
the cries of weans and mothers
and their men in prison.

The "borrowed sow" is of an order of description which the Jacobite poets loved to apply to Queen Anne. The poet, on the other hand, pays in another poem a most graceful tribute to Penelope, wife of Allan the Chief of Clanranald, comparing her to the wife of Ulysses.[57]

A special interest attaches to the work of Roderick Morison (An Clàrsair Dall/The Blind Harper) who is the most famous example in Gaelic Scotland of a person who was both a poet and a harper. He comes late in the line of harpers, who became obsolete in Gaelic society soon after the mid-eighteenth century. There is no certainty that any of his harp compositions have survived. He lived from *c.* 1656 to 1713 or 1714, and became established in Dunvegan, in close association with the household of the MacLeod chief, in the early 1680s. Sometime after the Revolution of 1688 this close association was broken, possibly because of the poet's Jacobite sympathies,[58] and the poet had closer ties thereafter with John MacLeod of Talisker, whom we have already met as a patron of poets.

Only a small number of poems by Roderick Morison has survived and of these only two, or at most three, are truly memorable. Of the others, "*Oran do Iain Breac MacLeòid*" "(A Song to John Breac MacLeod"),[59] addressed to his first MacLeod patron, is panegyric with a swing. It goes merrily, in keeping with the connotations of convivial times spent together. But the overall impression is light-weight. "*Féill nan Crann*" ("The Harp-key Fair")[60] is rather trivial, relying overmuch on a forced joke, though it livens up towards the end, where the *double entendre* is exploited more sharply. "*A' Cheud Di-luain de'n Ràithe*" ("The First Monday of the Quarter") has strong similarities of style with popular "village" verse of a later date, and provides another indication[61] that such verse had been in existence for some time, though it is late in breaking the surface. Here the popular verse is interspersed with passages of a more formal and bardic nature. "*Cumha do Fhear Thalasgair*" ("Lament for the Laird of Talisker")[62] has two memorable stanzas in a poem which is otherwise not remarkable. "*Creach na Ciadain*" ("Wednesday's Plundering")[63] is an interesting blend of the song and the bardic traditions, with its repeating final lines linking the stanzas. The first section, which is the elegiac part, has much imagery, some of it conventional, some individual. It has emotional drive, which is often associated with such use of imagery. Also, it has a fluid development of the argument of the poem, a sinuous movement which is not unlike Iain Lom's. The latter part, addressed to Iain Breac's sister, and to his son Ruaidhri, is more calculated "political" verse, and rather breaks the mood of the earlier part of the poem. Some verses from that earlier part are quoted:

. . . . . .

> This Wednesday's plundering,
> wounding, weak as by fever,
> has banished my health—
> my like is scarce in the region;
> my cry like the blackbird
> sadly mourning her fledglings;
> wonted joys have departed,
> a husk has lodged in my tooth.
>
> A husk has lodged in my tooth,
> and this year has thrown me,
> leaving under my shirt
> hurt that no leech can succour;
> for me there's no healing,
> no smooth road to soundness;
> my Easter Day dinner
> put an end to my pleasure.

. . . . . .

> This marching I heard
> has brought on my weeping,
> bruised blood under my ribs
> ever seeps through my vitals;
> week seems longer than year
> since you went over the water
> with liberality's fount
> in a linen shroud's winding.
>
> In a linen shroud's winding
> I left the strength of the weakly,
> goal of all men of song
> and wealth of the seanachies,
> and learned poets' treasure—
> your death puts their life in question;

                         since you went in the cist
                         I'm no object of envy.

   An Clàrsair Dall's best-known poem is the "*Oran do Mhacleòid
Dhùn Bheagain*" ("Song to MacLeod of Dunvegan"),[64] often
referred to as "*Oran Mór MhicLeòid*". The central motif of the
earlier part of the poem is that Echo is dejected in the hall where
music once sounded. This idea is skilfully developed, as for example in the third stanza:

                    Over Echo lies gloom
                    in the hall where music was played,
                    in the haunt of the bards,
                    reft of joy, banquet, esteem,
                    merriment, love,
                    swift circling of drinking-horns,
                    feasting, plenty for poets,
                    conversation or words of love.

But even more effective is the latter part of the poem, which is
strongly political, with its very direct criticism and satire of the
spendthrift absentee chief. There was a tradition of criticism,
though it was too often muted, in the work of the bardic poets, and
we have seen the changing conditions of the later seventeenth and
the early eighteenth century edging other poets towards similar
criticisms, but it may be doubted if any of them go as far as An
Clàrsair Dall. His language has in large measure been stripped of its
native dialectic tones by the mode of its transmission, but it may
not be altogether fanciful to think that in the sentiments and the
manner of this poem we hear the independent and fearless voice of
the Lewisman. Accusing the chief of the MacLeods in no uncertain
terms of living a life of luxury and self-indulgence, at the expense
of his tenantry, he says that after a spell at Court among the
southern strangers the next step is to go to France, and live there
on the security of bonds. This passage ends with the telling figure:

                    Now the boil starts to swell
                    on the back-thigh, with pain at its root.

He goes on to recount, contemptuously, what each item of vain-
glorious expenditure means in terms of rent and kind: seven

gatherings (of rent?) are borrowed to pay for a well-shod loudly whinnying horse, "a lordly saddle under their bottoms", and preferably a golden bridle. Giving a wealth of detail of this kind, he then pictures the chief returning home, and ordering a levy of cattle to be made, while his factotum William Martin sallies forth, aping his master's dress and manners.

> William Martin goes out,
> conceitedly set on his horse,
> as important—he thinks—
> as the liberal lord we had;
> he never touches a plough,
> or soils his hand with a spade,
> finely dressed like a duke,
> though his father could only delve.

The sad transformation of the clan chief to a foreign cockatoo is well portrayed. Of course all the detail of later times could not be included: the loud discourteous talk in foreign accents, the offensive flaunting of Highland dress, the appalling ignorance of Gaelic language and literature, the loathsome sycophancy and the laughable parades at Highland Games, nor did An Clàrsair Dall see the later development of the *nouveau riche* who were to win a (relatively) cheap stake in this ersatz society. But he saw enough to see the danger. He was lucky to have seen no more.

One of the main sources for "instant" political comment in Gaelic verse at this time is the Fernaig Manuscript, an anthology compiled about the time of the Revolution of 1688. The compiler, Duncan Macrae (Donnchadh nam Pìos), and his friends in southwest Ross-shire had strong Jacobite opinions and Episcopalian sympathies. The political comment is one-sided, as is not unusual. In the case of poems contributed by Macrae himself, religion and politics are well mixed. In a poem on the exile of James VII, in 1688, he makes his transition from the political to the religious viewpoint as follows:

> We change as the current changes;
> James yesterday, the Prince today;
> I'm certain, from the news I've had
> Better the old than the newcomer.[65]

An anonymous poem on the Battle of Killiecrankie[66] has several points of interest ranging from realist comment on the battle including verbatim snatches of English, to political summing-up:

> There were plenty of bodies
> then moving, and wounded,
> heads, hats and hair,
> earless men without talk;
> the cries that were heard
> were "Alace!" and "Woe is me!",
> "Quarters for Jesus"—
> this was their constant talk.

And with reference to William and Mary:

> Though religion's their veil
> they've rejected the Bible,
> Achitophel lives
> in Mary for certain;
> they've abandoned friendship
> and *Caritas* also,
> and abhorrently broken
> the injunction Christ gave them.

Part of the political summing-up goes thus:

> I think, and great is my fear,
> regarding what's happening,
> that Britain will suffer,
> there'll be bruised blood in Ireland;
> James and Mary will share
> the bone that is shattered,
> and the Frenchman will have
> while you quarrel, the marrow.

Some of this political verse has a fairly rumbustious style of argument, but is probably affected also by the pulpit style, as well as by contemporary political verse in English. The subject has not been properly studied as yet. It could hardly be claimed, at any rate, that it is of great significance as poetry.

In one sense the political verse of the Fernaig MS. could perhaps be regarded as an isolated pocket, the product of one man and his close circle, but we have seen that certain kinds of wider political involvement show clearly in the work of many Gaelic poets at this time, frequently in conjunction with an involvement in domestic clan politics. There were many occasions when the two could scarcely be separated. The escalation to large-scale confrontation which is seen particularly in the '45 Rising was to involve some poets very prominently in the eighteenth century, providing an important overlap with the poetry we have been looking at. But the old, traditional "heroic-type" society which the more conservative of the poets in the seventeenth and early eighteenth century are so concerned to praise and preserve, was already becoming an anachronism by 1745, and the poets of that era and after reflect a different set of tensions and connections, and in the social turmoil of their age are driven to innovate. Niall Mac-Mhuirich, composing two poems in vernacular Scottish Gaelic[67] on the wounding and death of Clanranald in 1715, was showing that he belonged, and had to belong, to two worlds, but the style he chose in his gesture was symbolized, as it were, by the strophic paragraph which we saw already enjoying a long popularity in the seventeenth century. The post-1745 innovators had to make rather different gestures. The clans, and their significance in politics, were become a dead letter.

5

Poetry of the Eighteenth Century

GAELIC POETRY IN the eighteenth century reflects clearly the changes that had taken place, and were taking place, in society. That there is a relationship, whether of accord or of reaction or rebellion, between poetry and society, almost goes without saying, but at certain periods the correspondence between changes in society and in poetry strikes us forcibly, and seldom more so than in the present instance. The poetry is in part marked also by that characteristic which we have seen was a strong one in Gaelic—literary conservatism—so that we find the firm evidence of tradition in the work of even the most innovatory poets, and on the other hand find the old ways followed by conservative poets well into the nineteenth century. These are fairly minor qualifications; the central fact is clear: Gaelic poetry breathes a new air in the eighteenth century, and shows a new vigour.

There were changes and influences of a negative kind, especially those associated with the decline in native clan leadership. The notion, and ideal, of patriarchal leader, accompanied by a traditional panoply, had been in decline for some three centuries, and had indeed gone far enough to justify some attempts at artificial revival in the mid-eighteenth century and after. Sir James Mac-Donald of Sleat made John MacCodrum his bard, in a vain romantic attempt to call back an age that had gone. The patron-employer belonged firmly to the past, and his disappearance made certain types of verse superfluous. He was succeeded, it is true, by what we might term the patron-ideal, and verses continued to be addressed to him as a figurehead, by poets whose concept of poetry required some such target. Donnchadh Bàn, as we shall see, feels this need at times. Gradually, as more and more of the chiefs deserted their race and culture, the credibility gap widened, and the praise-poetry withered.

The changes and influences of a more positive kind are the more interesting ones, and these seem on the whole to be of a literary nature, resulting from contacts with other literatures. Variety of literary contact and experience was seriously curtailed by those events and trends which had cut Gaelic Scotland off from Ireland in the sixteenth and seventeenth centuries, and in the same or a similar process, from Latin learning. It was not until the native learning had been almost entirely supplanted, and recourse had to the Lowland Scotland system, and especially the Universities, that contacts were established afresh with other literatures. By this time English literature begins to be a source of influence and of specific models.

It is in the context of these ideas concerning tradition and innovation, the detritus of an old system and the stimulus of external contacts, together with the break-up of the old social system and the painful building of a new one, that we must consider the poetry of Alasdair Mac Mhaighstir Alasdair (Alexander MacDonald), one of the greatest, and certainly the most innovatory, of the eighteenth-century poets. His work comes fairly early in the century, and his innovations have left a deep mark on eighteenth-century Gaelic poetry as a whole.

Alasdair Mac Mhaighstir Alasdair was born *c.* 1690. His father, Maighstir Alasdair, was minister of Islandfinnan in Moidart, and came of notable MacDonald stock, being a grandson of Ranald MacDonald of Benbecula and Mary, daugher of Angus MacDonald of Dùn-naomhaig (Dunnyveg). The poet could therefore claim close connections with the main line of the MacDonalds. The famous Flora MacDonald was his first cousin.[1]* According to tradition he was a student at Glasgow University, but did not complete his course, possibly because of domestic complications. He married a daughter of MacDonald of Dalness; she was of a family that had strong literary interests. Whether the poet was originally intended for the Church or the Law, he eventually became a schoolmaster, but we know nothing of his career until 1729, when he was teacher of a Charity School at Islandfinnan. He appears on record spasmodically as a teacher, at various centres in the west, until 1745, when he "voluntarily deserted" from his post, but already in 1744 his son Ranald had acted as his substitute in the school. He had "deserted" to take up a commission in the Jacobite army of Prince Charles Edward.

By 1745 Mac Mhaighstir Alasdair was a man of middle age, perhaps fifty-five. In the next decade or so he was to compose a series of exhortatory, political poems, and bitter satires, flowing

* For Notes, see pp. 314–16.

from a total involvement with the Jacobite cause. The mainspring
of this, however, was not a narrow dynastic loyalty to the House of
Stuart, but a dream of Gaelic independence. There are signs that
his nationalism was a Scottish as well as a Gaelic one. The union of
the Parliaments had taken place in his youth, perhaps in his student
days, and left its mark on his thought and attitudes. His poetry, at
any rate, is the most overtly nationalist in Gaelic in the eighteenth
century. But this political poetry is the work of his middle years
and middle period, and the earlier poetry is of quite a different
nature.

Probably, however, his poem "In Praise of the Ancient Gaelic
Language", which has a strong flavour of Gaelic nationalism, is a
relatively early one. The poem is in a sense a *brosnachadh catha*, a
battle incitement, but the battle is on behalf of Gaelic. If we accept
this premise, the poem can be seen to be well planned and successful. Its enthusiasm is communicated, and the element of exaggeration is best understood in a propagandist context. We can see
that the poet is concerned to emphasize the larger Scottish relevance of the language and as a humorous bonus to make still
larger claims for it:

> It lived still
> its glory shall not fade
> in spite of guile
> and strangers' bitter hate.
> Scotland spoke it,
> and Lowland carles did too,
> our nobles, princes,
> dukes of high degree.
> In King's Council
> when the court gave its decision
> knotty problems
> were solved with Gaelic precision.
>
> . . . . . .
>
> Adam spoke it,
> even in Paradise,
> and Eve's Gaelic
> flowed in its lovely wise.[2]

Gaelic poets have seldom been concerned to give any sort of
poetic credo to their public, and it is a measure of Mac Mhaighstir

Alasdair's consciousness of his role as a poet that he does this, at least to some degree, in his *"Guidhe no Urnaigh an Ughdair do'n Cheòlraidh"* ("Entreaty or Prayer of the Author to the Muses"). Like the poem on Gaelic, this has a carefully ordered structure and development. Each of the Muses is addressed in turn, and asked for help in one special particular. The Celtic artist's desire for completeness or exhaustiveness can perhaps be seen in this, but the points made are mostly relevant enough. After this piecemeal consideration of the gifts the poet needs, he goes on to consider the type of end-product he wants, and to reflecting on his own shortcomings as a poet. There is a strong implied criticism of a certain type of Gaelic verse which was already too common, and was to become more so:

> . . . work of rattling sound
> and empty of sense.

And he feels, apparently, that he is not learned enough in his craft, implying probably that he lacked the training of the professional poets. He had in fact taken the trouble to learn to write in the Gaelic script, and seems to have had a knowledge of some Gaelic bardic verse, but he seems to have been impressed by the technical knowledge and skill of the professional poets. He may well have known the last two practising poets of the MacMhuirich dynasty. The poem as a whole is very much an exercise, and the last lines suggest that he is not over-serious, but there is a core of serious intention, especially in the final passage:

> My vigour and range are small enough,
> though ambition's great,
> to build a wall on so large a base,
> lacking chiselled stones;
> I have no polished words, though I tear my will
> I am empty of skill;
> a thing of no substance is art that's unschooled,
> though the subject were sweet.
> My pen is blunt, my lips not sharp,
> my brain does not praise,
> my paper and ink are full of defects,
> a sad lack that.[3]

Mac Mhaighstir Alasdair's stance as an innovator, and his profound influence on succeeding poets, and on his contemporaries, can be seen vividly in his descriptive verse, in topographical or "Nature" poetry. Three surviving poems in particular, of this kind, belong to the pre-1745 period, and are probably to be dated between 1738 and 1745, and perhaps more narrowly *c.* 1743. These are his songs to Summer and Winter, and his poem "*Allt an t-Siùcair*" ("Sugar Brook"). It has been shown that "*Oran a' Gheamhraidh*" ("Song to Winter") was most probably composed in 1743, as the detailed references to the solstice suggest;[4] a comparison with the song to Summer suggests strongly that it had been written earlier, and the poet lived in the region he describes in "*Allt an t-Siùcair*" from 1741 to 1745. If he wrote songs about Spring and Autumn they have not survived. Several of the eighteenth-century poets took up these subjects and are influenced by Mac Mhaighstir Alasdair's style and practice, though only one of them, the much later Ewen MacLachlan, has a surviving quartet of seasonal poems to his name.

Alasdair Mac Mhaighstir Alasdair's seasonal poems are the earliest examples in Gaelic, although there was of course much natural description in earlier Gaelic verse, including seasonal vignettes in sixteenth-century verse. Mac Mhaighstir Alasdair may well have been familiar with this earlier tradition. It is, however, no coincidence that James Thomson's *Seasons* had been published between 1726 and 1730. Perhaps it was several years later that these poems came into Mac Mhaighstir Alasdair's hands. Thomson, like Vergil to whom in this respect he compares himself,[5] had experienced a deep delight in Nature, and each poet felt an urge to relate Nature to man, and to man's ethics. Not so Mac Mhaighstir Alasdair. He seldom or never moves from the particular to the general, nor does he use Nature to illustrate aspects of man. He does not even relate the works of Nature to a divine principle, nor attempt to show in them any general principles. We can see this difference in approach, for example, in passages where Mac Mhaighstir Alasdair and James Thomson write of birds:

(1) Mac Mhaighstir Alasdair:

> These are tunes cleanest cut,
> with most elegant divisions,
> your chanter's note-spread at milking
> sent my mind gaily lilting . . .[6]

(2) James Thomson:

> The blackbird whistles from the thorny brake,
> The mellow bullfinch answers from the grove,
>
> . . . . . .
>
> 'Tis love creates their melody, and all
> This waste of music is the voice of love,
> That even to birds and beasts the tender arts
> Of pleasing teaches.[7]

For the Gaelic poet the experience or scene he is recording is all-important and sufficient; for Thomson it shares the interest with some reflection which it arouses.

We can see a difference in method, and a complete independence of thought, in the two poets' description of bees, to take another instance. Thomson's has some artificiality, and a hint of pompousness:

> Around, athwart,
> Through the soft air, the busy nations fly,
> Cling to the bud, and with inserted tube,
> Suck its pure essence, its ethereal soul.
> And oft with bolder wing they soaring dare
> The purple heath, or where the wild thyme grows,
> And yellow load them with the luscious spoil.[8]

Mac Mhaighstir Alasdair has less Border Twilight in his description, and a more direct and unmixed observation:

> Honey-sucking of striped bees,
> with their fierce crooning hum,
> among the clustered, brindled flowers,
> the sunny blossoms on the trees;
> brown viscous drops through straws
> fall from your grasses' breasts;
> they have no livelihood or food
> but the roses' pleasant scent.[9]

This is not to say that Mac Mhaighstir Alasdair is never guilty of admitting artificialities and mannerisms into his Nature poetry.

F

Sometimes his eye wanders from the object, and he writes also without much feeling behind the words, borrowing what he must have considered a fashionable and elegant formula of classical terminology. Some of these stylized elements in his Nature poems can be seen to derive, quite directly, from the poetry of Allan Ramsay, whose *Tea-Table Miscellany* had begun to appear in 1724. There is, indeed, clearer evidence of direct influence in these cases, but a strong case could be made for concluding that Mac Mhaighstir Alasdair knew Thomson's *Seasons*, borrowed the general idea, and ideas for sub-themes from it, but had a mind and a method of his own, which was in accord with his own literary tradition.

Of the two seasonal poems the "Song to Summer" is clearly the more original and the more striking. Winter is seen largely as the antithesis of summer, which argues that the poem was written soon after that to Summer. There are some stanzas where the positive qualities of the season are observed, but the poem in general is more laboured than the "Song to Summer". This latter gives a wonderfully vital impression of teeming activity. It is full of movement, sound and colour. Even the adjectival exuberance comes off here. The metre and style are very highly-wrought, the sharp consonantal cut-off of the salient words giving a sense of great precision to the metre, reminiscent of a pipe-tune cleanly played. In an important sense the poem is a pattern in sound, with the emphasis on the consonants (perhaps this is a more intellectual music than the music of vowels). Nature is here described as much in sonic as in visual terms. Unfortunately there is no hope of reproducing all this sound and sense: an approximation must suffice:

> The lithe brisk fresh-water salmon,
> lively, leaping the stones;
> bunched, white-bellied, scaly,
> fin-tail-flashing, red-spot;
> speckled skin's brilliant hue
> lit with flashes of silver;
> with curved gob at the ready
> catching insects with guile.
>
> May, with soft showers and sunshine,
> meadows, grass-fields I love,
> milky, whey-white and creamy,
> frothing, whisked up in pails,

time for crowdie and milk-curds,
time for firkins and kits,
lambs, goat-kids and roe-deer,
bucks—a rich time for flocks.

. . . . . .

Now the cock leaves the budding
thick blossom of trees,
for the heights of the heath-hills,
with hen short-beaked and brindled;
he's a right courtly wooer
on purple cushions of heather,
and she answers him hoarsely:
"Pi-hu-hù, you vain thing!"

Short-winged cock of the woodlands
with your dark sable cloak,
black and white are commingled
in your feathers most finely;
throat well-groomed and shining,
green and sleek, often bending,
beak that never drips slaver
but melodious notes.

A clean, elegant twittering
with sweetest notes on a knoll
warbling seemly and gentle
on a pleasant May evening:
a group white-skirted, red-breasted,
with strong but finely-arched brows,
white-tailed and high-chested,
sun-burnished, brown-backed.[10]

Only five of the nineteen stanzas are given in translation; the last
three are in fact the final stanzas of the poem, which ends sharply
on the note of meticulous if amused description.

Though the "Song to Winter" does not have the same brilliance,
it has its highlights too. The month he describes in the following
stanza is in truth an eighteenth-century Scottish one:

Month of broth, steaming high, and of feasts,
greedy, spendthrift, voracious of pork,
full of porridge, and sowens and kail,
pots and beards that revel in fat;
though we thatch our bodies without
against air that makes merciless holes,
a dram is needed for lining the chest,
to kindle a bonfire within.[11]

Similar techniques are used in the poem which is usually referred
to as "*Allt an t-Siùcair*" ("Sugar Brook"), although this is something of a misnomer, and was not the poet's own title. He called it
"A Song for a certain village called Coire-Mhuilinn, in Ardnamurchan, and for a burn that flows through that village, namely
Sugar Burn", and the poem in fact describes the surrounding
countryside, the corrie, the bay, and so on, giving an idyllic picture
of plenty. There is some telling selection of detail (as always in this
poet's work) as well as some exhaustive treatment of particular
aspects. And even in the "exhaustive" passages, language is firmly
controlled: each epithet adds to the description. The poem ends
with five stanzas in praise of the corrie, and these may have inspired
Donnchadh Bàn's choice of subject in his poem "*Coire a' Cheathaich*" ("The Misty Corrie"), which is similar in method and style,
though stamped with the younger poet's own individuality also. A
short quotation may serve to suggest the mood and style of "*Allt
an t-Siùcair*":

Nature's work of graving
is done neatly on your banks,
wild garlic growing freely,
fair nut-gall up above;
shamrock, daisy, red-berry,
freckling your meadow's floor,
like stars through frost the twinkling
of the fresh and lovely flowers.

Trees with their tops like scarlet
with rowan berries there;
and golden nuts in clusters
bursting above your head;
blackcurrants and raspberries

bend their own branches down:
smooth, ripe, sweet and fragrant,
moisture dried off by the sun.[12]

It is typical of the careful, detailed observation of this poetry that
there is a comment, in the final line quoted, on the way in which
the evaporation of surface moisture on these soft-fruits, in the
warm sun, perfects their flavour. Detailed observation is of the
essence of this poetry, but at its best it has a loving, fondling
quality also.

This Nature poetry is marked, often, by verve, exuberance and
fecundity of language, and these qualities show elsewhere in Mac
Mhaighstir Alasdair's work, for example in the Jacobite verse, with
its strongly evangelical flavour—a secular evangel of course—
which he produced in his middle period, and also in the series of
satires which seem to have followed that flow of exhortatory
Jacobite poems. It is reported that he went about the Highlands in
1745, stirring up enthusiasm in the Prince's cause, and this is confirmed in the verse exchange between himself and the Mull Herds-
man.[13] The latter goes on to suggest that Mac Mhaighstir Alasdair's
conversion to the Church of Rome, which must have taken place
at this time, was more of a political than a religious nature. Whatever the truth of this—and it is hard to see the poet in a religious
light—there is an almost religious fervour in some of his political
verse, the fervour from which the fanatic draws his energy and
power. This fervour sings in his "Song to the Prince":

> Last night I saw in a vision
> Red Charles coming over ocean,
> with his pipes and his war-song
> and his banners of scarlet.
>
> As I woke in the morning early,
> great was my joy and my gladness,
> since I heard of the Prince's coming
> to the land of Clanranald.
>
> Topmost grain of all kings,
> may you come home safe, Charlie;
> the true blood, undefiled,
> flows in your most modest cheeks.

But before the end of the song his fervour has found another out-
let, and appears as hatred of Butcher Cumberland:

> And if I had my desire
> the Duke would be in sad plight:
> the butcher who butchered the meat
> would have hemp round his throat.

> And I would make a gift of the Maiden
> as an heirloom to his brother;
> but may you come and reach us well,
> you are welcome here, Charlie.[14]

Much more stirring is the *"Oran nam Fineachan Gaidhealach"*
("Song of the Highland Clans"), which is a lively battle-incitement
which has a conscious debt to the Harlaw Brosnachadh.[15] Propos-
ing, in the first stanza, a toast to James Stuart, he says:

> But if there's any fear in your guts
> do not defile the divine cup.[16]

He goes on to list the clans that would rally to the Prince's cause,
including some who did not rise in the event. Here is the stanza
referring to the MacDonalds of Glencoe:

> The warriors of Glencoe will come
> eager to join your camp,
> like heath-fire on the hill-slopes
> fed by the winds of March;
> like tight-reined horses' riders
> that attack without delay,
> as ready as dry powder
> when it's touched by the spark.[17]

He imagines, with a ferocity that had been equalled only by Iain
Lom, the destruction of his enemies in battle:

> A great many will be stripping
> the corpses on the field;
> ravens hoarsely calling,
> flapping wings and hovering;

> kites and vultures ravening
> as they eat and drink their fill;
> ah! faint and sad at sun-rise
> the groans from the slaughter-field.[18]

The series of exhortatory poems did not come to an end when the action of the '45 began. We find, in 1746, the evangelical fervour if anything accentuated, and subtle, singing metres being used to cast a persuasive spell over the mind, to help the fluent, eloquent verse-argument by bringing mesmeric qualities of rhythm to bear:

> Slender the string, O George,
> you played on the three kingdoms;
> guileful the Act and cloak
> with which they made you King;
> there are fifty men and more
> closer in blood and claim
> in Europe than you are;
> remote and weak and devious
> is the female line you came from,
> at the outside of the tree.[19]

And the series continued after the Rising was over, while there still seemed hope of another.

The same verve and exuberance appear again in the series of satires, as of the Oban poetess (who had apparently composed a poem critical of Prince Charles) and of the Campbells. One of the satires of the Oban lady in particular is very fluent and colloquial, drawing generously on Biblical lore and making free use of contemporary historical references.[20] The series of Campbell satires pours scorn on that clan very effectively, suggesting that they were far better trencher-men than fighters, and emphasizing their greed in general, and desire for wealth. He considers in *"Aoir do na Caimbeulaich"* ("Satire of the Campbells") the feast they will make for the Maiden, recalling that it is close on one hundred years since they last fed the Maiden, clearly a reference to the beheading of the Marquis of Argyll in 1661. This helps to date the poem: it is also of interest as showing Mac Mhaighstir Alasdair's bookish knowledge of history, for dates do not figure in traditional lore.

He ends this poem with a scathing variant of grave-poetry:

When you get your charters
to your beds that are narrow,
your wills all in order,
and your carcase for beetles,
you will see sums of silver
are exceedingly vain.
The world altogether
and the wealth that is in it,
you must leave these behind you,
save for three planks around you,
and a cold, narrow shroud
sewn under your chin.
The poorest of beggars
who asks for his alms
is as rich in his lands,
with as copious a wardrobe.
That rabble fared ill,
lost before and behind;
till a camel goes through
the eye of a needle,
no joy will ensue
from treachery so vile
as poured on us in floods.[21]

In another satire on the Campbells[22] he paints them as warriors such as that prince of Irish gluttons, MacConglinne, would dream of. There is an element of bitter humour in this, as also in his Ragman's Roll of the Campbells whose conduct during the Rising displeased him: this latter poem is called "*An Airce*" ("The Ark"), and is very interesting from the historical point of view if not from the poetic. He has other scathing poems where the element of bawdiness is much in the ascendant, as the lewd mock-elegy for the poetess known as the Aigeannach,[23] and "*Mìomholadh Mòraig*" ("The Dispraise of Morag").[24]

There was a tradition that Mac Mhaighstir Alasdair had composed "The Dispraise of Morag" in the hope of regaining favour with his wife, who was hurt or incensed by his poem "*Moladh Mòraig*" ("Praise of Morag"). We need not concern ourselves with the biographical implications—if there are any—of the poems. "*Moladh Mòraig*" has been judged for long enough simply on these grounds, being denied recognition because it is not *virginibus puerisque*, because the adult public for Gaelic poetry is small. Leaving that controversy aside, what we have in "*Moladh Mòraig*" is a highly-wrought poem (in the technical, not the emotional sense), dealing exhaustively with the subject of an attractive girl's attractions—surely one of the most universal of themes. It has spice added to it in various ways. There are references to the poet's married state (and these in themselves may have started the legend of his wife's resentment), and there are parallels, sometimes involving *double entendre* drawn from piping. These latter match, as it were, the metrical structure of the poem, which is imitative, to some degree, of the structure of *ceòl mór*, or classical pipe music. We might add the spice of ecclesiastical impropriety, in the suggestion that the Pope himself might be tempted by Mòrag's charms. With these ingredients the poet makes a polished, racy, audacious, and sometimes amusing poem, deploying his great gifts of eloquence and technical brilliance. The poem runs to 336 lines, but the following extracts may suggest its mood and movement:

> O bravo, bravo,
> bravo, Mòrag!
> gay, golden-lock'd maiden
> red-cheeked and rosy;
> her cheeks are aflame,
> lit like sparkling jewels,
> her teeth white as snow,
> cleanly chiselled in order.
>
> As attractive as Venus
> for delights of the body,
> as lovely as Dido,
> surpassingly comely . . .
>
> . . . The like of the lassie,
> is not in the wide world—
> you have wounded my heart
> since I saw your gold tresses,
> locks curling and twining
> and twisted like cornets,
> with ringlets and clusters
> and loops that are glorious,
> in star-studded circlets

like jewels most graceful,
well-powdered—in fashion—
lit by sunlight, all golden.

. . . . . .

Your counsel do not hide from me,
what else to say or do now
about the girl who played these tunes
so finely on her chanter?
I cannot find the like of her
on Mainland or in Hebrides,
so absolutely beautiful,
so frisky yet so soothing.

There's one thing that I'm certain of,
I'd better not tell Jane of her,
and how I've fallen headlong,
and am going at the knees now;
there isn't enough water
in Loch Shiel, or snow on Cruachan,
to cool and heal the raging fire
that burns away within me.

When I heard the melody
played on Mòrag's chanter,
my spirit danced with merriment,
an answering most joyous:
the stately ground,[25] most elegant,
of her tune, with fingers tapping it,
a music with fine setting,
the rocks providing bass for it.
Ah! the chanter with its grace-notes,
a hard, sharp, clean-cut music,
sedate now, and now quavering,
or smooth, controlled, soft, tender;
a steady, stately march then,
full of vigour, grace and battle-zest,
a brisk and strutting *crunluath*[26]
played by sportive swift-soft fingers.[27]

This piece, in style and mood, is perhaps the closest we get to that masterpiece of Irish eighteenth-century poetry, Brian Merriman's *Midnight Court*. I think one can sense a similar potential in Mac Mhaighstir Alasdair, but it did not culminate in one large, zestful work as in the case of the Irish poet.

Mac Mhaighstir Alasdair's invention shows clearly, however, in the metrical structure of the poem. Based, at least loosely, on the succession of movements in *ceòl mór*, the poem consists of an alternation of movements called *Urlar* and *Siubhal*, or Ground and Variation, with a climactic *Crunluath* at the end. All the movements consist of one or more sixteen-line units, with fairly straightforward rhyme-schemes, but there are marked rhythmical differences from one section to another, and particularly between *ùrlar* and *siubhal*. "*Moladh Mòraig*" is the prototype of this complicated poem structure, though the most famous example is Donnchadh Bàn's "*Moladh Beinn Dòbhrain*" ("Praise of Ben Doran"). The later poet's indebtedness to the earlier model is fairly clear throughout, but is especially noticeable in the opening sections, where Donnchadh Bàn preserves the sixteen-line unit, and virtually the same rhyme scheme. The succession of *ùrlar* and *siubhal* is of course a feature of both poems, but whereas "*Moladh Mòraig*" has an extra pair of these, "*Moladh Beinn Dòbhrain*" makes all the individual sections longer, running to a total of 554 lines, as against "*Moladh Mòraig*'s*" 336. Donnchadh Bàn introduces many pleasing variations, of rhythm and rhyme. The difference in regularity is no doubt in part deliberate, and in part to be explained by the fact that Donnchadh Bàn did not *write* his verse down, but composed it in his head.

Donnchadh Bàn's work does not lack order, but it is clear that his mind did not have the hardness and intellectual grasp of Mac Mhaighstir Alasdair's. It may be, of course, that the older poet, with his readier access to the literature and thought of his time, in the neighbouring English speaking territories, was drawn somewhat to the order and temper of the Augustans, despite his tempestuous character. One sees such an Augustan temper in his "*Marbhrann do Pheata Coluim*"[28] ("Lament for a Pet Dove"), where the choice of a classical (Gaelic) precise metre may be a pointer in itself. He has no other elegies to his name, and the existence of one to a dove may suggest that he was almost thumbing his nose at the elegiac tradition he had inherited. But the intellectual qualities show through repeatedly, as in his capacity for ordered structure in the poem on Gaelic and in the invocation to the Muses; in his ability to develop a verse argument, as in *"Oran mu Bhliadhna Theàrlaich"*[29] ("A Song about 1745–6"); in his ability, and predilection, to put cause before clan, which one can deduce from his restrained handling of clan poems like *"Moladh an Leóghainn"*[30] ("Praise of the Lion"); in his method of tackling the subject in *"Cuachag an Fhàsaich"*,[31] which is a song to a milkmaid, where the milkmaid is not so much a particular girl as the representative of a genus; and most markedly in his *"Birlinn Chlann Raghnaill"* ("Clanranald's Galley"). In this latter poem, which must be regarded as his major single poem, we get vivid glimpses of the other side of his nature too, the emotional, explosive, expansive side. We must look, finally, at this poem, sampling it rather than attempting to savour it in its entirety.

The *"Birlinn"* was not included in Mac Mhaighstir Alasdair's book *Ais-eiridh*, which was published in 1751. This makes it likely that it was not written until after that date. There are traditions that it was composed in Canna, where the poet was Bailie from 1747–52, and also that it was composed in South Uist. The truth may be that parts of it were written in each of these places. It runs to some 566 lines in the first printed version, the Eigg Collection of 1776, an anthology summarily edited by the poet's son Ranald.[32] A poem of this length, falling into sections as this one does, may well have occupied the poet, intermittently, for a year or two.

The poem is concerned with a voyage made by Clanranald's galley from South Uist to Ireland, with the preparations of the galley and the choosing of the crew as well as with the actual voyage. There is no need to suppose that the poem describes an actual voyage, although it may be based in part on one. Some of the characters appear to be historical persons, probably of both Canna and Uist origin, and even those not named may have been recognizable to contemporaries. Clearly, however, parts of the poem are drawn from the imagination, and it is not particularly profitable to speculate further concerning these aspects of the poem.

It contains a great deal of technical detail, including close observation of the parts of the galley and of the functions of the various members of the crew. One of its most interesting features is the vivid description of the physical appearance of the crew members, and the connections that are established between appearance and character. There is, in fact, much human observation in the poem, although this may at times be obscured by the technical detail. This is a human drama, and this helps to give the poem its power and fascination. There are hints of humour, but humour is not one of the obvious qualities of the poem.

Despite its considerable detail, the poem is compact, with visual clarity, and a sense of tense excitement which carries it forward, reaching its climax very near the end, and subsiding rhythmically as its action subsides to a calm. The storm which the galley encounters is described in extravagant terms, but the poet is in complete control of his subject all the time: the words do not run away with him, even at the height of the storm. There is no slackness or flabbiness of thought or expression here. The verse is hard, terse and business-like, the clean rhythm of the lines like the movement of cold sea-water along the side of a boat. This poem is the ultimate demonstration of Mac Mhaighstir Alasdair's hard, exact intellectual power.

Occasionally it borrows ideas or phrases or short passages from earlier Gaelic work. The "Ship Blessing" takes a traditional form, attested for example in Carswell's translation of the liturgy in 1567. The lines referring to the hoisting of the sails borrow directly from a "run" used in traditional stories,[33] and the poet was almost certainly familiar with Iain Lom's poem "*Iorram do Bhàta Mhic Dhòmhnaill*" ("An Oar-song for MacDonald's Boat").[34] These are minor, episodic influences. The "*Birlinn*" is a new work, forged in the imagination, and plunged into the cold, sharp, setting liquid of the poet's intellect, with his technical skill ready to shape it as we see it.

The poem begins with a Blessing of the Ship, followed by a Blessing of the Arms. Then comes an Incitement to Rowing to the Sailing Point. By this time the pace is being stepped up in anticipation (for the voyage has not yet begun) with blisters appearing on rowers' hands, and washers beginning to fly off the nails in the galley's planks. The sixteen men are seated at their oars, and in Section 4 Calum Garbh, at the bow-oar, sets the boat-song going. Here are a few of the stanzas of the boat-song:

> And now that you have been chosen,
> and bid fair to be champions,
> let your rowing be strenuous, fearless.

. . . . . .

Wood dust showered on the thole-pins,
palms peeling and blistered,
oars engaging in high billows' arm-pits.

Let your cheeks flame with action,
your palms shed their whole skin,
sweat from your brow swiftly rain down.

. . . . . .

A bank of oars on each side then
mashing ocean with effort,
flashing into the face of the billows.[35]

. . . . . .

A short transitional section brings them to the sailing point, and
there follow a series of sections giving sketches of individual
crew-members and their functions. The first of these is of the
helmsman:

Let there sit at the helm a thick-set hero,
loose-limbed, powerful,
whom neither top nor base of billow
will rive from rudder;

A solid, squat, pithy fellow,
sturdy, broad-beamed,
of delicate touch, alert, careful,
very wary;

Stocky, large, calm and weighty,
lithe and lusty,
sure and patient, without flurry
when seas pour in;

When he sees the shaggy billows
coming roaring,
he keeps her bow trained trimly
on curved breakers;

Keeps her on course quite steady,
with no heaving,
sheet and tack adjusted keenly,
eye to windward;

He does not deviate an inch
from his right course
in spite of surging crests of sea
that come bounding;

He tacks to windward, if he has to,
so resolute
that every rove and peg that's in her
takes to squealing;

He must not weaken, must not panic
however fearful
the grey sea seems in its swelling
to his eyeballs:
it may not shake the strong stalwart,
no nor move him

From where he sits like a hero,
tiller in arm-pit,
awaiting the grey ancient seas,
deep-troughed, hostile.

. . . . . .

In section 12 there is a description of the man who is to give warning of particularly heavy seas, thus giving the helmsman time to
take evasive action. The helmsman speaks at this point:

Let the man who warns of high seas sit
right beside me,
and let him keep his eye sharply
straight to windward.

Choose a man who is half-frightened,
shrewd but fearful;
I don't want him to be a coward
absolutely.

Let him be on his guard when he sees
squall-before-shower,
as to whether the breeze comes astern
or on the bowsprit.

Let him give me due warning,
a quick alerting;
he must never, when danger looms,
keep his silence.

If he sees an engulfing sea
coming lowing,
he will shout to point the prow
quickly at it.

Let him be loud-voiced but prudent
as he tells the rollers,
not hiding it from the helmsman
if he sees danger.

Let there be no teller of high seas
except that one:
flurry, chatter and babble
make for confusion.

After fifteen preparatory sections, many of them quite short, we
come to the final climactic section, which contains in fact the whole
voyage. Two-thirds of the section is translated here:

Sun bursting goldenly
from its meshing;
the sky became scorched and gloomy,
awe-inspiring.

The waves grew dark, thick, dun-bellied,
angry and sallow;
the sky had every single hue
you find in tartan.

A dog's tooth* appeared in the west,
a storm threatened;
* A partial rainbow seen in stormy conditions.

swift-moving clouds by wind shredded,
squally showers too.

They hoisted the sails—speckled,
towering, close-woven;
they stretched the ropes—stiff,
tough and taut,
to the long, tall masts,
red-resined, pointed.

They were tied in trusty knots,
efficiently,
through the eyes of iron hooks
and round ring-bolts.

They adjusted every bit of gear,
smartly, neatly,
each man sat ready to watch
his own portion.

The windows of the heavens opened,
dark-grey, spotted,
to let the rough wind blow through them,
in fierce anger.

The ocean then donned completely
its black-grey cloak,
its rough, shaggy sable mantle
of horrid surging.

It swelled into glens and mountains,
rough and ragged,
the matted head of ocean spouted
up in hillocks.

The blue sea opened its jaws,
horned, capacious,
each pouring into the other
in deadly combat.

It was man's work to look in the face
of the fiery torrents,

phosphorous sparks of flame
on each mountain.

The waves in the lead, high, grey-haired,
with their harsh roaring,
the following waves in their troughs rumbling
and loud-lowing.

When we rose proudly up to
the tops of these waves,
we had to strike sail then
with quick precision.

When we fell, almost engulfed,
down in the wave-troughs,
every inch of sail that she had
came off her masts then.

. . . . . .

When we fell down from the tops
of the shaggy billows,
the heel of the ship just about gored
the shelly sea-floor.

The ocean was churned and dashed
against itself;
the seals and other great creatures
were in dire straits.

The roaring and rage of the ocean,
the ship in its movement
dashing the white of their brains
through the billows;

As they howled in horror and dread,
and bitter sorrow,
"We are the under-dogs here,
let us aboard you."

All the small fish in the sea had
their white bellies upwards,

killed by the raging storm
in their thousands.

Surfacing stones and shell-fish
from the sea bed,
were torn up by the pounding
of haughty ocean.

The whole sea turned to porridge,
foul and turbid,
with the blood and filth of splayed sea-beasts
turned red and horrid.

Creatures with horns and talons,
flippers, splay-feet,
many-headed, howling from wide jaws,
their mouths gaping.

The deep all full of goblins,
with paws weaving,
a-crawl with claws and tails
of great monsters.

. . . . . .

But when the ocean failed to win
from us surrender,
she took pity and smiled wanly,
making peace with us.

There was not a mast unbent,
a sail not tattered,
a yard-arm fast, a yard-ring whole,
an oar undamaged.

. . . . . .

The tiller was split badly,
the rudder shattered,
every plank groaned and creaked,
being cracked and split.

. . . . . .

The ocean made its peace with us
in the Sound of Islay;
the rough wind, raucous-voiced,
lay down by order.

It went away to the upper regions
of the sky,
and the sea grew smooth and white
after that barking.

We offered thanks to the High King,
shaper of Nature,
that the Clanranald were safe
from a death that was brutal.

Then we struck the thin sails
of spotted canvas,
and laid the mast, fine and smooth-red,
on the decking.

We put out oars, slim and sweet-tuned,
smooth and tinted,
of the pine MacVarish cut
in Islandfinnan.

We rowed with a smooth rocking
never missing,
and found a haven at the head
of Carrickfergus.

We cast our anchors quietly
in that roadstead;
had food and drink unstinted,
and stayed there.

Donnchadh Bàn Mac an t-Saoir (Duncan Bàn Macintyre) was
Alasdair Mac Mhaighstir Alasdair's junior by more than thirty
years, being born in 1724, but their names have been so commonly
linked that many have thought of them as almost twin-poets of the
eighteenth century. This is far from being the case. Yet there are
connections and contrasts that make it attractive to turn now to

Donnchadh Bàn's work, while that of the older poet is fresh in our minds. There was perhaps a sufficient gap in age to make a discipleship possible, but it is a discipleship that is not made explicit except by internal evidence, and there is a marked individuality also in part of Donnchadh Bàn's work which makes an interesting contrast with Mac Mhaighstir Alasdair.

The situation is complicated, and given an odd twist, by the fact that Donnchadh Bàn was not literate. We may be prepared to come to terms with the idea of non-literacy among the heroic ancients: it is more difficult to make such mental adjustments for comparatively recent times. Non-literacy is however a relative term, and I use it to avoid the pejorative overtones of "illiteracy". It is known, and it is clear from the poetry, that Donnchadh Bàn had a wide knowledge of his own poetic tradition, and a teeming, varied vocabulary which he could wield with expert ease. Nor was he the only significant Gaelic poet to be non-literate in this century of uneasy transition from one system to another. In addition, Donnchadh Bàn had literate mentors, so that his disability was to some extent mitigated. At an important period of his life he lived only a few miles away from the Manse of Killin, in which the New Testament was then being translated into Gaelic, and he belonged to the same parish as that notable minister of Lismore, the Rev. Donald MacNicol, who is said to have written down his poems for Donnchadh Bàn. We can scarcely escape the conclusion that he had become closely familiar, probably through these friends in particular, with at least that part of Mac Mhaighstir Alasdair's work which was published in 1751. When Donnchadh Bàn came to publish the first edition of his poems, in 1768, the book was seen through the press by the Killin minister's son, John Stuart, then a young man of twenty-five.

In such ways the influence of Mac Mhaighstir Alasdair's poetry on Donnchadh Bàn can be explained. It is there to see in the poetry itself. It has been stated already that Mac Mhaighstir Alasdair set the fashion in Gaelic for composing poems about the seasons. There can be no reasonable doubt that Donnchadh Bàn followed his lead, but it is instructive to observe what he did. One might deduce that he had proposed to himself to go one better: to produce a poem which would have more and fuller detail in it, and which would deploy a more impressive vocabulary. Perhaps similar ambitions made him opt for a longer line, a graver rhythm. His most recent editor thought his ambitions had been realized: ". . . the poem is a noble structure, not excelled in style by any of the Gaelic poems on Summer."[36] I cannot agree with this estimate. It is not summer one scents here, but competition. In Mac Mhaighstir Alasdair's poem the joy and freedom and brightness of summer come through to us, carried on the light, tripping rhythm, but Donnchadh Bàn's poem is for the most part "words, words, mere words, no matter from the heart". This might seem a curious way in which to contrast two poets, one of whom had a strong intellectual strain, the other a more emotional one, but the contrast applies rather to themes in which Donnchadh Bàn is too consciously trying to follow a set pattern. He has other poems in which he comes into his own as a descriptive Nature poet. But here, hoping to imitate, or excel Mac Mhaighstir Alasdair, he has a passage about birds in which these summery creatures all have leaden pellets tied to their legs; the wren laboriously tunes his chanter, but does not seem to be able to keep time. Clearly birds do not move him. But already in this poem there is a hint of his true genius, where he begins to deal with the deer. I give a translation of part of the song; it was made many years ago, and I would not now choose to make it in this style, but perhaps it gives some idea of the formality of the poem. The last line of the second stanza in particular takes some liberties with Donnchadh Bàn's text:

Summer Song

When branching summer turns the sky
from surly grey to blue,
mild airs, and warmth, and lightsomeness
draw green-ness from the dew;
the sun suffuses all the land,
bringing its power to bear
on growing things, as it begins
from its hot side to rear.

The seed, sown in its due time,
draws sap from its own soil,
the upward thrust from plain to point
fills every granary full:
the dappled crop grows lush, secure,
thick-stalked and heavy-eared,
the large grain with its brindled husk
comes surging from the braird.

Sweet scents and gleaming sprays now fill
the jewelled orchard air,
the warmth glows as rosy gems
lay their mild beauty bare:
apples and pears and figs
modestly peeping out
in the green lovely lanes
that compass them about.

. . . . . .

Each hind is lying with her calf
as Nature has decreed,
for stags and fawns must frolick
when November sows its seed;
it were a lease of life for one
who loved them and their ways
to listen to the belling stags
and closely watch their ploys.

. . . . . .

The rising sap beneath the bark
moistens the birch's veins,
till shoot and wand, and branch and bough
are clothed with leaves again;
the sultry heat sucks from the mould
the fecund birch-top's food,
no snuff's aroma can excel
this flowering of the wood.[37]

Before returning to Donnchadh Bàn's more congenial and more
mature nature poetry, which was his chief contribution to Gaelic
poetry, we may look briefly at his other work. He had assimilated
the traditional style of praise-poetry thoroughly. Although it was
as a forester or gamekeeper he was employed by members of the
Campbell aristocracy, he thought it proper that he should use his
poetic gifts to praise them in the traditional way. Seven poems of
this kind are extant, with such titles as "A Song to Lord Glenorchy", "Lament for Colin of Glenure" (the victim of the Appin
Murder), and "Lament for the Earl of Breadalbane". There are

many parts of these poems that give the impression of being very central to their tradition: they hardly needed thought, for the thoughts and phrases were ready to hand. Two of the praise-songs have a much stronger individuality: the *"Oran do Iain Caimbeul a' Bhanca"* ("Song for John Campbell, Banker"),[38] which has a fine sprightly rhythm and a most robust use of language, and *"Cumha Chailein Ghlinn Iubhair"* ("Lament for Colin of Glenure"),[39] which lies in style and mood mid-way between the formal praise-poems and the folksongs: the poet's personal involvement in his subject shows. In view of the interest which the problem of the Appin Murder has retained over the years since 1752, a short extract from this poem is given:

> Hard the message that came,
> sad what happened just now,
> if you could have avoided
> the place where death struck you first!
> Up above the wall gate-way
> you were hit by the bullet—
> my pain—no one near you
> when they came from your back;
> on your side, without talking,
> the breath of life left you,
> your fair, coursing red blood
> outpouring in spate:
> the act of a madman,
> unknowing and stupid,
> his soul sold for lucre,
> with no mercy in view.
>
> . . . . . .
>
> Your sleep is eternal
> and my spirits are mournful;
> often futile reflections
> come rushing anew;
> anguish presses upon me,
> your death sorer than fever,
> my handsome, fine foster-brother
> has been cut to the heart.
> A thousand curses on him

who by ambush surprised you,
who let go the volley
from the Spanish gun aimed.
Cheerful news that would please me
were the public announcement
of his climbing the ladder
to the gallows' worse plight.[40]

Donnchadh Bàn also composed three love-songs, one of which,
"*A Mhàiri Bhàn Og*" ("O fair young Mary") is very well known.
It was composed to his wife. The song is too long, and it is not too
clear why the verses occur in the sequence that they do occur in. It
is in a well-defined tradition of literary love-songs (for example
that of Lachlann Mac Theàrlaich Oig for Nighean Fir Gheambail)[41] being too detailed and itemizing, but it is retrieved to some
extent by the imagery of these stanzas:

I went to the wood where grew trees and saplings,
a radiant sight all around,
and my eyes' desire was a peerless branchling,
in the dense growth of twiglets above:
a bough from trunk to tip in blossom
which I tenderly bent down—
it was hard for others ever to cut it,
this shoot I was destined to win.

I set a net on fresh limpid water,
and hauled it hard to the bank,
and brought with a sweep to land the sea-trout,
lustrous as swan on the sea;
the share I won at that time has left me
contented in spirit and mind:
my dear spouse, the star of the early morning,
my partner with me in sleep.[42]

Donnchadh Bàn composed songs of drinking and conviviality,
competition songs about the bagpipes, and nostalgic recollections
of the countryside and society of his youth. He moved from the
Argyll–Perthshire borders, and settled in Edinburgh, in 1767,
becoming a member of the City Guard (a policeman in modern
parlance), and serving late in life in the Breadalbane Fencibles.

His output of verse seems to have kept up in Edinburgh, but there is reason to think that his poetry died when he left the countryside he belonged to. His greatest poetry, at any rate, had been written by the time his first collection appeared in 1768.

The poetic gift which Donnchadh Bàn was perhaps best endowed with was that of observation. His observation was not confined to one field, but there is no doubt that it was in the deer-forest, in those varied hills and mountains of the Perthshire–Argyllshire border, that it was exercised most lovingly. The highly factual nature of much of the description need not entirely obscure the emotion that underlies it, but perhaps it is when we contrast the poetry of his rural period with that of the later years that we realize most clearly that he needed this physical background of Nature to sustain his poetry. There might well be other, more prosaic explanations of the change of tone and talent, but this one is also supported by those few poems of his later period in which he returns, in person or in imagination, to the scenes of his youth. And above all his eye and his imagination open when he is within sight of the deer. There is not a hint of sentimentality in his attitude: he describes in an equally loving way the antics of the hind or the fawn, and the process of stalking or taking aim at or shooting the stag. Nor is there any attempt to philosophize. He does not question the workings of Nature, nor attempt to draw from them lessons for Man. There is no overt intellectual curiosity displayed at all. The close and detailed observation implies a strong and effective concentration, evidenced again in the transfer of that observation to verse that is tightly constructed metrically. But it may leave us with the impression of an artefact to be admired for the moment, rather than a work of art whose reverberations are unpredictable.

His two most famous Nature poems are *"Oran Coire a' Cheathaich"* ("The Song of the Misty Corrie")[43] and *"Moladh Beinn Dòbhrain"* ("Praise of Ben Dorain"). In the former he deals, in catalogue-style almost, with the natural description of the corrie, describing the kinds of grasses that grow in it, mantling the ground; the berries, flowers and herbs; and via a description of water-cress, the stream and the salmon in it; the birds, the bees; nuts and trees; and throughout the whole song, moving deer, for the deer have the power of motion, and motion is of their essence. It is very noticeable too that the birds in this poem come alive, as though they were birds he knew personally: not the birds of summer, of any summer, but the birds of the Misty Corrie. It is in such ways that we can detect the lyricism of Donnchadh Bàn's poetic nature.

We do not know when his longest and most remarkable poem, "The Praise of Ben Dorain", was composed. It has already been suggested that its metre and form were strongly influenced by Mac Mhaighstir Alasdair's *"Moladh Mòraig"*, and that this model was probably brought to Donnchadh Bàn's attention by his literary friends, after the publication of Mac Mhaighstir Alasdair's book in 1751. The internal evidence suggests that the logical sequence of composition was "The Song to Summer", followed by "The Song of the Misty Corrie", followed by "The Praise of Ben Dorain". It would be hard to imagine a poet troubling to make "The Song of Summer" after composing so successful a poem as that on the Corrie, and surely "The Praise of Ben Dorain" is the last word in this series.

The connections between the Coire Cheathaich and the Beinn Dòbhrain poems are clear. In the latter, all the individual sub-themes are taken up again and greatly expanded: the mantle of the Ben, flowers and other plants, birds, burns, fish, and the deer moving throughout the poem. The theme of the deer is developed in remarkable detail, with many sub-themes such as hunting techniques; the appearance and construction and operation of the gun; the different ages and stages of hind and stag, their way of life, food, and whimsically, their feelings. In truth, this is a song in praise of the deer, and in a sense we can say that it is the foremost praise-song in Gaelic—an ironic reflection, when we consider the generations of bards trained to praise human chiefs and patrons.

The poem moves with great rhythmic vitality and verve. The flood of words is controlled with no appearance of strain or effort, and seems as light and happy as a dance-song. There can be no doubt that this poem was Donnchadh Bàn's greatest achievement, and it must rank very high in Gaelic literature as a whole.

As a sample of this remarkable poem, one movement is quoted from Iain Crichton Smith's verse translation.[44] This is the third movement, in which we see the deer moving gracefully in their closely observed habitat:

> Pleasant to me rising
> at morning
> to see them the horizon
> adorning.

Seeing them so clear,
my simple-headed deer
modestly appear
in their joyousness.

They freely exercise
their sweet and level cries.
From bodies trim and terse,
hear their bellowing.

A badger of a hind
wallows in a pond.
Her capricious mind
has such vagaries!

How they fill the parish
with their chorus
sweeter than fine Irish
tunes glorious.

More tuneful than all art
the music of the hart
eloquent, alert,
on Ben Dorain.

The stag with his own call
struck from his breast wall—
you'll hear him mile on mile
at his scale-making.

The sweet harmonious hind—
with her calf behind—
elaborates the wind
with her music.

Palpitant bright eye
without squint in it.
Lash below the brow,
guide and regulant.

Walker, quick and grave,
so elegant to move

ahead of that great drove
when accelerant.

There's no flaw in your step,
there's all law in your leap,
there's no rust or sleep
in your motion there.

Lengthening your stride,
intent on what's ahead,
who of live or dead
could outrace you?

The hind is on the heath
where she ought to be.
Her delicate sweet mouth
feeding tenderly.

Stool-bent and sweet grass
the finest food there is
that puts fat and grease
on her flanks and sides.

Transparent springs that nurse
the modest water cress—
no foreign wines surpass
these as drink for her.

Sorrel grass and sedge
that grow on heath and ridge,
these are what you judge
as hors d'oeuvres for you.

Luxuries for does
between grasses,
St. John's wort, the primrose,
and daisies.

The spotted water-cress
with forked and spiky gloss;

water where it grows
so abundantly.

This is the good food
that animates their blood
and circulates as bread
in hard famine-time.

That would fatten their
bodies to a clear
shimmer, rich and rare,
without clumsiness.

That was the neat herd
in the twilight,
suave and trim, unblurred
in that violet!

However long the night
you would be safe and right
snug at the hill's foot
till the morning came.

The herds of the neat deer
are where they always were
on the wide kind moor
and the heathland.

When colour changed their skins
my love was most intense,
they came not by mischance
to Ben Dorain.

Donnchadh Bàn made a brief appearance at the Battle of Falkirk in 1746, fighting without enthusiasm on the Hanoverian side, but the Rising and politics play very little part in his poetry. There were a number of Jacobite poets at this time, and their work has been collected and translated by John Lorne Campbell.[45] One of the most interesting of these was John Roy Stewart, a professional soldier who had fought against Britain at Fontenoy, and came home to take part in the whole of the '45 campaign. His poems on

Culloden make some interesting comments on the battle and on the issues at stake:

> My great grief, the white bodies
> that lie on the hills over there,
> without coffin or shroud,
> or burial even in holes!
> Those that still live have scattered,
> and are now herded close on the ships.
> The Whigs got their own way,
> and "Rebels" is what we are called.[46]

Stewart himself escaped to France, dying in the early 1750s.

Other poets of the time, such as Rob Donn and Iain MacCodrum, composed poems on Jacobite or related themes, such as the Disclothing Act, which forbade the wearing of the kilt, and Uilleam Ros wrote an elegy for Prince Charlie on hearing of his death in Rome. But we do not associate these poets closely with either the '45 or with Jacobitism.

Iain MacCodrum (John MacCodrum) was born about 1700, but seems to have reached middle-age before composing much verse. Even later, he came in contact with the MacMhuirichs of South Uist, and in 1663 was appointed as bard to Sir James MacDonald of Sleat. This was an appointment of an antiquarian nature, but it seems to have stimulated MacCodrum. His output falls into two main sections: official poems flowing from his honorary office, and poems of local interest. It is all public poetry, having some sort of communal function. MacCodrum is one of the earliest of the "village" poets for whom we have a sizeable body of extant work. We have seen glimpses of such poetry in the seventeenth century, and it is hard to imagine that it was new then. Clearly by MacCodrum's time the tradition is a well-established one, and its links with present-day village poetry are clear also.

It is on this verse that MacCodrum's reputation should truly rest. It is eloquent, using a rich vocabulary and idiom, though with only occasional flashes of creative originality. There is wit and humour in generous measure, and some evidence of comic imagination, as in the Dispraise of Donald Bàn's Pipes, and in *"Oran do'n Teasaich"* ("Song to Fever"). In the former of these he describes Dòmhnall Bàn, a third-rate artist on the pipes, who has to content himself with a sooty kiln as his concert-hall, and sits

there resting against a bundle of straw, blowing his dissonant and
evil-smelling pipes:

> That mockery's-butt will
> have no joyous hall
> but a kiln that is choked
> with burnt straw and soot;
> there's no chair for Donald
> and he cannot stand straight—
> he must sit at the hearth
> with straw at his back;
> with a hell of a tune
> and a roar of bad drones,
> smell of body's decay:
> a music as loathsome
> as screeching of rooks,
> or young growing chicks
> sore for lack of their food.[47]

In "Song to Fever" we see again MacCodrum's descriptive gifts
and his wit, and (at least in a restricted sense) his comic imagination:

Song to Fever

> I came off worse in the wrestling round
> I held with the hag, for I'll be bound
> she sapped my strength, though I thought it sound,
> and laid me flat on my back on the ground.
>> My flesh and blood she drained away
>> and sent a wheeze in my chest to stay;
>> a luckless tryst we had that day;
>> God's vengeance smite her without delay.
>
> She planted confusion in my head;
> a host of men, both alive and dead,
> like those whom the Trojan Hector led,
> and Roman warriors, thronged my bed;
>> that dismal, dark and hunch-backed crone,
>> to scandal and lying tales too prone,

reduced my speech to delirious moan
and left me stripped of sense, alone.

What a wretched autumn you've given me,
the harvest's lost, as all can see;
I'm bruised and ill, as here I lie,
with tired bones, and head awry:
 My bones were weary to the core,
 lopped off they'd hardly have hurt more;
 a raging thirst had tried me sore
 I'd have drained a river from shore to shore.

The fever bed is a wretched place,
you grow lanky and grizzled apace,
shaky and weak, without a trace
of hair on your head, but too much on your face:
 The loathsome beard that you have to wear
 makes your mouth unsavoury; if you dare
 to eat or drink, the lion's share
 of the victuals comes a cropper there.

Your coat has grown too big, and throws
into relief your wrinkled hose,
your splayed, pathetic ankle shows,
long as wild-cat's the nails of your toes,
 Bandy legs that fever has made
 pithless, and strengthless thighs—I'm afraid
 they're less like the oar-shaft than the blade—
 if grass but touched them they'd bend and fade.

Your scraggy neck is long; you feel
your ribs protrude like the ribs of a creel;
your strengthless hams make it hard to kneel;
your wobbly knees begin to peel
 with rubbing together; the knee-cap's sharp
 and the skin of the knees is as black as bark;
 frightened of cold as a cat—a mark
 that it's time death folded you in its sark.

Your bonnet seems to have doubled its size,
and it sits on your wig in unsightly wise;

your sprouting ears would win a prize;
what cruel friend could thus devise
    A pate as bald as the palm of the hand
    and a body as thin as a willow wand—
there's nothing like it in this land:
death has enrolled you in its band.

You lurch and sway like a wicket gate;
the one knee hardly knows its mate;
you're starved of food but easy to sate;
though you haven't taken a drop, your fate
    is to look like a drunkard, a poor mite
    preaching peace since you can't fight,
    in action taking no delight,
    sickly and wan, a sorry sight.[48]

The County of Sutherland, in the extreme north-west of the mainland of Scotland, is sparsely populated, but still retains a small number of native Gaelic speakers. This was the county most savagely affected by the early nineteenth-century clearances, especially on the estates of the Gordon dukes of Sutherland, a family of non-Gaelic origin, employing Lowland factors. We are fortunate in having a considerable body of Gaelic verse, composed by a poet of great stature, dating from the eighteenth century, the century before that in which sheep and money talked in that unhappy region of Scotland. The work of Rob Donn unfortunately has been much neglected, although his reputation is in the ascendant again. It is sometimes suggested that the neglect is to be explained by the dialectal strangeness of his Gaelic, but it seems to me that this is not the true explanation. It might be truer to say that he was an innovator, but in a sense quite different from his contemporaries, whose innovations caught the public eye; at the same time there was a strongly localized bias in his choice of themes, and so his verse came to be regarded as remote and non-central. In fact it has strong affinities with the witty, satirical strain of local or village poetry which we have seen surfacing at various times from the late seventeenth century, and which we will find enjoying a robust health in the nineteenth and twentieth centuries. As though to add further spice to this tradition, and to the subtle, oblique intelligence of Rob Donn himself, there is reason to think that he was influenced at least marginally by the poetry of

Alexander Pope, as mediated to him by the Rev. Murdoch MacDonald, minister of Durness in Rob Donn's time.[49]

Rob Donn (Robert Mackay) was born about the time of the '15 Rising, and died in 1778. He seems to have been non-literate, but fortunate in having literary patrons. Apart from a period of service in the Sutherland Highlanders (starting in 1759) he spent his life mainly in north and north-west Sutherland, herding and droving and dealing in cattle, hunting and in the service of Lord Reay. His verse is mainly a commentary on the episodes of that life and on the people he lived among. It is a lively, amusing commentary often enough, but it is also a critical and at times satirical one, quite unsparing of rank or class, once the thin veil of ambiguity or obliquity is penetrated.

Apart from these poems of commentary, to which we shall return, he composed some love-songs, some poems of natural description, and about a score of elegies. As a curiosity it is interesting to refer to his poem on Winter.[50] This is clearly based on Mac Mhaighstir Alasdair's poem on Summer, with the appropriate inversions being made. It is cleverly done throughout, implying quite a feat of memory for a person who did not read. In "*Cead Fhir Bhioguis do'n Fhrìth*" ("Bighouse's Farewell to the Forest") he recalls nostalgically his days of hunting the deer, and the good companionship of that time.[51] Rob Donn's employers and patrons were on the Hanoverian rather than the Jacobite side, but this did not prevent him from giving views which are indistinguishable from those of the Jacobites, or perhaps more particularly the Gaelic patriots whom we have already seen speaking out. A quotation from his poem on the act proscribing Highland dress, in 1747, "*Na Casagan Dubha*" ("The Black Cassocks") illustrates this attitude clearly:

> I am saddened by Scotland!
> You've shown clearly your motives;
> your mind is divided,
> which has spoilt every venture.
> The Government read
> greed in those who had turned to them,
> and gave avarice bait
> till you tore at each other.
>
> Englishmen took the chance
> of weakening you further,

> lest you still might be counted
> among those who opposed them.
> But when you have surrendered
> your swords, and your firearms,
> you'll get a charge in your belly,
> a very swift penance.[52]

He goes on to say that he recognized the sad plight in which his countrymen are, with the finest of their hawks chained to a kite, and he shows his sympathy for Prince Charlie's cause quite plainly. It would seem that by the circumstances of his life and locality Gaelic lost in Rob Donn a political poet of some vigour and originality. But political poetry's loss was social poetry's and satire's gain, and indeed there are many sidelights on aspects of politics in his most domestic verse.

His attitude to the relationship between tacksman and tenant, with its specific praise on the one hand, and its implied criticism of people who observe another code, comes through clearly in his "Lament for Iain Mac Eachainn", who died in 1757. Rob Donn was capable of composing fairly conventional elegies. This is not surprising. Much more remarkable is his ability to compose a low-key lament for a patron and friend, in which he is constantly on his guard against surrendering his own integrity, and in which he develops, quietly and firmly, a telling indictment of those who cannot match Iain Mac Eachainn's nobility of character. I give the poem in a translation published many years ago by Iain Crichton Smith, who suggested at that time that "the influence of Pope is [noticeable] in some of its balanced statements."[53]

Lament for John MacKay

> Iain Mhic Eachainn since your dying
> where now will we find
> your equal in knowing
> how to gather and how to spend?
> The plain truth is that no one
> of your own age does know it,
> and if the gift's being grown
> few living will see it.
>
> How different your life from many
> of those who still alive hoard

every acre, every penny
for their own children to discard:
who will endure dreary days;
who'll have no friends who can be named;
whose only elegy this praise:
"Look at the acres he reclaimed."

These are legal to the letter:
to some, hard debtors, though they pay
their own friends without bitter
recrimination or delay.
But all the rest of their resources
is speedily put in store;
while both their pity and their purses
are shut equally to the poor.

In such half-honour deeply rooted
they think it neither wrong nor odd
to spend their lifetimes thus indebted
less to men than they are to God;
but when their last judgment is ready
they must listen to this arraignment:
"Why did you never help the needy
with food or drink or proper raiment?"

I would wish if I were able
to fix your deeds in clear letters,
that youth might from them learn a noble
emulation of their betters;
for your whole life's so full of use
to those who will consent to study,
as your charity was profuse
and prompt for the weak and needy.

O you who have the means and power,
if you'd pursue the purest fame,
now is your exact hour,
O do not waste this precious time;
you also are in the midst of death
which took this hero to his doom.
Let each of you emulate his worth,
assume his burdens at his tomb.

For though many scorn these rare
and generous givers, I'd rather hear
instead of mockery this pure
petition and this passionate prayer:
"May the generations as they fade
at length making us wise in tears,
teach our late wisdom not to trade
an eternity for sixty years."

Many a man did you enrich,
and many a silly lad might gather
knowledge from the experience which
you could interpret to another.
Indeed there's not a man here
(but the dolts of cowherds) who wasn't
indebted to you, either for
your wisdom or a lesser present.

You never ate your food with pleasure
if you knew of any who was without;
nor would you ever pass a beggar
without responding to his plight.
Much rather would you give a pound
than suffer an ounce of late remorse,
and what you gave so freely round
renewed itself within your purse.

Today I see the prodigal
walking in sorrow and weariness;
the inn is warm but he is chill,
dispirited and penniless.
I see the poor widow forsaken,
I see the needy full of hunger,
I see the orphan stark naked,
having helper no longer.

I see the poet neglected
with rusting skills he's not using;
I see men strayed and infected
with loss of trade and of vision.
Should I ask why this grieving,

why this sorrow and sadness,
they'll say to me weeping:
"It's because of Mac Eachainn."

I see this multitude stricken
by the death that removed you;
yet a gain may be reckoned
to the wealthy who loved you;
since this year has now shown me
unknown patrons who've risen
like stars in the gloaming
when the sun's left our vision.

In the elegies that are made here
we find an impure flattery dropping,
the corrupting gleam of a false tear
that turns the truth to worse than nothing.
But though I should be on holiest oath
to the one God who can sustain,
I have spoken only clear truth
and what I knew of this good man.

Rob Donn's elegies in general are more reflective and more concerned with spiritual values than were the elegies of tradition. A strong strain of evangelical Protestantism had taken root in the North in the seventeenth century, as evidenced for example in the hymns of Alexander Munro of Strathnaver. This tradition, reinforced by the preaching of his own day, may account for the cast of Rob Donn's thought, and his weaning from the conventional style of elegy, which was more material and heroic in tone. We see this influence even in the elegy for the Earl of Sutherland who died in 1766, although this is more conventional than others of his elegies. The break with the old conventions would have made it easier for him to develop an idiosyncratic approach to elegy. This has bequeathed to us two elegies in particular which have an amusing twist. The first is, if not a mock-elegy at least a premature one. The story is that Rob Donn, while hunting, took shelter for the night in the cottage of an old man Ewen, in a lonely place called Polla, at the head of Loch Eribol. Ewen was very ill and troubled with asthma, and appeared to be about to take leave of the world. The poet had just heard that Prime Minister Pelham had died, which dates the poem[54] to 1754, and he reflects on the way Death visits high and low, and all between, without distinction. The thought is not specially profound, but its expression is interesting, with the added piquancy that Ewen had to listen to the completed elegy, and evidently took exception to it. Rob Donn refers to Death

> with its leap from the Court
> to Ewen's poor cranny.

Addressing Death he says:

> I conclude this is true,
> your view takes in high and low:
> you snatched Pelham from greatness,
> and Ewen from Polla.

The poem ends in this way:

> Ah, my dearly loved friends,
> do these two not give fright to us!
> We're like candle in lantern
> with both the ends wasting;
> where on earth was one lowlier
> than the son of your father?
> There was none above *him*
> but the King on his throne.

The best-known of Rob Donn's reflective elegies is that on the Rispond Misers. These were two brothers who were born within a year of each other, and lived a miserly existence, looked after by an old housekeeper. All three are said to have died within a week, having turned a poor person away from their door only a few days earlier:

The Rispond Misers

> Lying in their lowly state
> are three we buried here,
> though they were strong and healthy,
> and lively at New Year;

ten days only have gone by
since then—who can be sure
that our dread Summoner is not,
unknown to us, as near?

Within one year a pair of them
had come from the one womb,
and they had been close comrades
since their childhood in one room;
their fellowship is still intact,
unsevered by the tomb—
within two days Eternity
has plucked them from Time's loom.

These brothers now departed
came from one man and wife,
their clothes were made from the one fleece,
each lived the self-same life;
their deaths came close together,
their natures were alike,
the one procession bore their dust
and laid it out of sight.

These men broke no commandments,
as far as we can trace,
nor did their deeds show anything
of what the world calls grace;
they were conceived and brought to birth,
were nursed, and grew apace,
a swatch of life passed by them
and Death put them in their place.

Surely this sounds a warning
to each one of us alive,
especially old bachelors,
unlearned in married love:
men who will not spend on food
the cash to which they cleave,
saving for a funeral feast
the gold that they must leave.

They'll never spend what they have made,
and make no heirs besides;
their treasures on the hillsides
are food for dogs and birds;
they stand condemned—though I can plead
"not guilty" in assize—
of hoarding darklier their gold
than ever did the mines.

The High King in His providence
wisely left some men short,
to test the sense and charity
of those who have a lot;
these should surely give a part
of all the wealth they've got
to poor folk who are ready
to increase their meagre stock?

In spite of this straight talking—
and I feel it's only right—
and all the words of truth I've put
directly in your sight,
I fear you will not listen,
or give the poor a bite,
any more than these did
a week ago tonight.[55]

We have spent long enough over the elegies of a poet who above
all Gaelic poets in his century clearly revelled in company, and
observed the nuances of character and behaviour as carefully as
Donnchadh Bàn observed his deer on Ben Dòrain. We must at
least sample this human observation, bearing in mind that we can
choose only a few examples from a great many, for Rob Donn left
over two hundred poems, many of them of this kind.

Refreshing critical asides occur frequently in poems dealing
with "persons of quality" in his northern world. There was ample
contact between what would in other contexts be called different
"classes" in that world, and Rob Donn seems to have moved freely
in the tacksman society of the time. This society impinged at some
points on that of the native and alien "aristocracy", for both the
Mackay chiefs and the Sutherland earls had each their own

nexus, with some points of contact. Lord Reay had married, as his second wife, a daughter of Sutherland of Proncy, who was not too popular to begin with, but she seems to have commended herself to Rob Donn in one or two ways. He makes a sarcastic reference, however, in a poem to Lady Reay,[56] to her new circle:

. . . . . .

> The fashion of that party
> in whose set you find yourself,
> is to boost their name and fame
> at expense of their own friends.

One of Lady Reay's popular actions was to rescue a local lad who had run away from his regiment and was subsequently arrested. She entertained his captors so well with liquor that the boy was smuggled out, in a fashion which Rob Donn describes with obvious enjoyment:

> There was a lady on the threshold
> who stood largely, stoutly there;
> I couldn't tell the password
> that he used, though I were killed;
> but in between a woman's legs—
> he wore no arms or hat—
> close to where he saw the light
> he was whisked away like that!

A good example of Rob Donn's serious and moral attitude, which led him to use poetry as a moral sanction in his community, is the poem in which he describes, in oblique terms, Lady Reay's stratagem in seeking to marry off a servant-girl who had been made pregnant by someone "above her station". He had ignored the request to sing dumb about the incident:

> With sharp order and counsel
> the gag was spiked in my mouth,
> regarding the mishap,
> much liker to hunting than love.
> Well, I pity the couple
> whose happiness rests on deceit;

though I wish it, I doubt whether
joy will remain in your house.

. . . . . .

Not for fear nor for favour
did I wait without making my way,
giving special obedience
to the ruler most great and most high;
but for that I would tell them
that what won for you gear, was not sense
but a hauteur degrading
you now it is lodged in your breast.

It's my view of you, hauteur,
you're contentious and dangerous too;
you proposed many shifts
to encompass your evil intent;
when persons of worth
cleanse you out of the nooks of their minds
you are sure of a welcome
in poor little brains without sense.[57]

Perhaps enough has been said and quoted to establish the point
that in Rob Donn's work a new dimension had been added to
Gaelic poetry in the eighteenth century. Probably the first person
to demonstrate in detail the deep interest of his work was Ian
Grimble, more especially in his Aberdeen University Ph.D. thesis
(1963), and in published writings. He refers to the poems about
Iain Mac Eachainn and his family as "the most graphic delineation
of a tacksman's family in the whole of Scottish Gaelic literature".[58]
Certainly there is no earlier body of Gaelic verse from which we
can get so many-sided a picture of people in a community, with the
tensions and sanctions that affect their lives. This picture has much
trivial detail as well as bolder features, and undoubtedly some of
the verse that carries this detail is trivial too. But it has the sterling
quality of being rooted in actuality. There can be little doubt that
it represents an important peak of achievement in Gaelic poetry.

A close contemporary of Rob Donn's was Dùghall Bochanan
(Dugald Buchanan) born in 1716 in Perthshire. Only a handful of

his poems survive, and these are all on religious or moral subjects, even his "Song to Winter" carrying a strong moral. It is likely that he had a body of early secular verse which was destroyed. There is evidence in his *Diary* or Confessions that he had early obsessive experiences: he says that between the ages of six and nine "the Lord began to visit me with terrible visions, dreams in the night, which greatly frightened me: I always dreamed that the day of judgement was come . . .".[59] His mother had died when he was six. And he recalls hearing, at the age of twelve (by which time he had already become a private tutor!) graphic descriptions of how the Day of Judgement would break upon the world, with thunder and lightning and hail.[60] He experienced a secular reaction, which took the form of a craving for company, and at this time he learned all the ballads and songs he could get, "which was but a bad cure for a wounded and festered conscience",[61] though perhaps a useful preparation for a poet! He tells too of his examination of a horse's skull, saying that this was one of the proofs he found of God's wisdom and power;[62] one of his own poems was to be called "The Skull". He came under the influence of the English evangelical preacher George Whitefield during his second visit to Scotland, in the year 1742.[63]

As with the other eighteenth-century poets, the influence of Mac Mhaighstir Alasdair shows in his work, marginally at least. Besides the "Song to Winter" which is much less detailed than the seasonal poems usually are, and which has a moral turn to the argument, he may well be reacting to Mac Mhaighstir Alasdair's glorification of heroic and savage qualities, in writing such a poem as *"An Gaisgeach"* ("The Hero"), where he portrays the Christian warrior. It is true, though the blessing was a mixed one, that "Buchanan and his fellow Evangelicals won the battle for the soul of the Highland people. In the generations that followed, the Christian warrior rather than the pagan hero became the accepted ideal."[64] He was influenced to some extent by northern Gaelic religious poets, such as John MacKay, and by various English writers. He was probably more widely read in English than any of his contemporary Gaelic poets, and it is clear that in subject-matter he responded to the interests and fashions of his time, with his somewhat macabre interest in the grave and in skulls.

In his poem *"Fulangas Chrìosd"* ("Christ's Suffering") he is emotionally involved in the suffering, and the poem has remarkable simplicity and clarity. *"An Claigeann"* ("The Skull") is clever and persuasive, terse in language but marred by exhaustive categorization. *"Am Bruadar"* ("The Vision") has a restrained simplicity of statement and a kind of proverbial wisdom, as in these stanzas:

> The thing most greatly you desired,
> did not its winning turn it sour?
> There's more joy to be had in hope
> than in possession of a crown.
>
> Just like the garden rose whose bloom
> soon withers after it is cut;
> you've scarcely caught it in your hand
> but it has lost its scent and hue.
>
> . . . . . .
>
> Smoke hangs above each burning peat,
> good often co-exists with pain;
> the roses grow on pointed thorns;
> honey and sting are side by side.
>
> Though one man may enjoy great wealth,
> do not suppose his joy as great;
> the cleanest spring your eye can see
> has sediment upon its floor.
>
> And if you take a sudden draught,
> swirling the water with your breath,
> the red deposit rises up
> and specks of sand befoul your teeth.[65]

Dugald Buchanan's longest poem is *"Là a' Bhreitheanais"* ("The Day of Judgement"), running to over 500 lines. It is also his most powerful and imaginative. The emphasis is undoubtedly on the pains of Hell, the aspect of the matter which had most vividly struck the poet's imagination. The kindly rewards that the righteous win seem scarcely to interest him at all; he glosses over them in a few lines, eager to come to grips with the penalties of the damned. The obsession of his immature youth had become a permanent sickness of the imagination. But if we set aside questions of humanity or Christianity, the exercise is brilliantly conducted. One sequence from it is quoted here:

A redness then glows in the sky,
like morning light arising red,
and tells us then that Christ himself
comes in its wake with a rough day.

The clouds come suddenly apart,
an opening to the High King's room,
and the great Judge is then revealed
in endless joy and glory clad.

A rainbow placed around his head,
his voice's sound like glens in flood;
like lightning, glances from his eyes
come spouting from the darkling clouds.

The sun, high lantern of the skies,
bows down before his glorious form;
his countenance's radiant sheen
smothers entirely the sun's light.

It puts the clothes of sorrow on;
the moon seems to be bathed in blood;
and heaven's powers are shaken sore,
wrenching the stars out from their roots.

They waver weakly in the skies,
like fruit on branches tossed by storm,
falling like drops of water fast,
their glory that of dead men's eyes.

On fiery chariot he sits,
with roars and thunder all around,
calling to Heaven's outmost bounds,
and ripping clouds tempestuously.

From out his chariot's wheels there comes
a stream of fire aflame with wrath,
and that flood spreads on every side,
until the world is flaming red.

The elements all melt with heat,
just as a fire can melt down wax;

> the hills and moors are all aflame,
> and all the oceans boil and seethe.
>
> . . . . . .
>
> The blue drape spread out from the sun,
> and round the universe, a cloak,
> is wrinkled up by that red flame
> like birch-tree bark in living fire.[66]

The poem turns shortly after this to deal with the cases of Biblical
characters who will now repent of their actions—Judas and Herod
and Pilate—and goes on to consider other types of person, such as
the greedy person, the blasphemer, liar, envious person and so on.
There is an interlude in which the righteous come briefly into the
picture again. Returning to Hell, he lets the suffering damned
speak:

> From nothingness, wherein I stayed,
> why did the Lord lift up my head?
> A thousand curses on the day
> my mother took me in her womb.
>
> Why was I ever given sense,
> or understanding as my guide?
> Why did you not make me a fly,
> or a mean worm in the earth?
>
> Must I be here world without end,
> and will I ever die or change?
> Am I now in Eternity,
> swimming a sea that has no shore?
>
> Though I should count all Heaven's stars,
> all leaves and grass that ever grew,
> and every drop that's in the sea,
> and grain of sand that's on the shore;
>
> Though I should spend a thousand years
> for each and every one of these,
> the march of great Eternity
> were as one started yesterday.[67]

The final part of the poem is concerned with the traditional appeal to the reader to repent and to accept the means of grace.

Dugald Buchanan's poetry is not ornate metrically, but he makes a freer, more imaginative use of imagery than most of his contemporaries do, and he has a fine feeling for language. Despite the religious obsession one can sense a keen, orderly and even a hard intellect behind some of the poetry.

He saw his own poems through the press in 1767, and in the same year helped to see through the press the Gaelic translation of the New Testament. In 1768 he died of fever.

Uilleam Ros (William Ross), the last of the group of major poets whose work falls entirely within the eighteenth century, was born in 1762, and died in 1791. Born in Skye, though he lived most of his life in Wester Ross, he was however schooled at Forres, where he learned something of the Classics. He was clearly schooled also in the tradition of Gaelic verse, composing praise-songs, both of people and of his home district, and adding his offering to the growing tally of songs in praise of whisky. There is precision and wit in the language of his whisky song; this is the gist of one of the verses:

> You would make old men merry
> and get hunchbacks, wrinkled, wretched,
> to rise to the dance, quite sprightly,
> cocking a snook at old age.[68]

He was born too late to take more than an antiquarian interest in the '45. He wrote a lament on hearing of the death of Prince Charlie in 1788, but in it one feels strongly that Rome is very far away, as is Charlie's Year and the fervour it aroused. He followed tradition also in composing a "Song to Summer". This has a light, airy mood, and he has fine touches, absolutely in tune with the mood of summer, as in his description of birds:

> their wings pointed, unresting,
> on the high twigs of great trees;[69]

We get a sense of pulsing movement, warmth and movement of sap. His Song has more people in it than the seasonal songs usually have, and is more subjective: there are girls driving cattle to pasture (with the grace of love "swimming", *à la* James Macpherson, in their faces), and we catch a glimpse of the poet himself reclining on a clump of fragrant heather. The poem is less adjectival than its earlier models, but for all that it belongs securely to its tradition.

The legend of William Ross says that he died of love, and we shall look at the poetry, some of it his best, associated with that legend. But there was a strong representation of humorous, witty and bawdy verse in his work. The two aspects are not incompatible, and there is enough evidence to show that he was fully conscious of the duality of his feeling, and conscious too of the legend which was already taking shape in his brief life-time. Perhaps there were times when he played a part, within the framework of the growing legend. But he wrote courting songs of a quite different kind, and tradition, like the *"Oran do Chailin àraidh"* ("Song to a certain Girl"):[70]

> I went to woo a lassie
> yellow, fair-haired, lovely,
> but I turned me home again
> like a bald old man.
>
> A dun-dark night, a Sunday—
> Paul wouldn't have prescribed it—
> I sallied over moorland
> for kisses and for love.
>
> Seeking love and kisses
> from the lovely lassie,
> comliest in Europe
> though she lives up here.
>
> It had to be a duke at least
> to win her with approval;
> we made nothing of it,
> the venture went awry.
>
> I set out feeling sprightly,
> in the early twilight,
> striding long and lithely
> not hunched like a carle.
>
> I fell in many a bog,
> had my fill of mud,

with my cassock flapping
against heath and rocks.

But I had a guide there,
mountain-bred MacDonald,
of swan and geese the hunter,
of the bailiff's merry kin.

When I heard her statement
I threw the halter at her,
Roger started barking
but, the bissom, she kept mum.

There was nothing for it
but go home, a poltroon,
like one who lacked the gear
to give a girl a ride.

When I go and lie down
I can't sleep a wink now,
with my merry member
rising by my side.[71]

The song is reminiscent in tone of some of the songs of the great
fourteenth-century Welsh poet Dafydd ap Gwilym, both poets no
doubt drawing ultimately on a medieval European tradition which
had been carried far and wide by the troubadours, the *clerici
vagantes*, and in Gaelic lands by the Cliar Sheanchain, or strolling
bards and entertainers.

Ross, however, has one poem in particular in which it appears
clearly that he had reflected on the duality of his nature and his
poetry. This is the *"Oran eadar am Bàrd agus Cailleach-mhilleadh-
nan-dàn"* ("Song between the Poet and the Hag-who-spoils-
songs").[72] This takes the form of a debate which the Hag wins
hands down. He seems to be making fun of himself—in a remark-
ably healthy way—and of that love-poetry which shows too little
understanding of life and its complexity, which does not recognize
the co-existence of ugliness and beauty, asperity and sweetness,
meanness and maidenliness. Perhaps the poem is coloured by
Ross's personal experience in the matter of his love for Marion
Ross. It seems, at any rate, to fall late in the series of his poems
about women.

Three poems of his surviving output[73] are concerned with the short unhappy affair with Mòr Ros (Marion Ross), a young lady from Stornoway, in Lewis, which William Ross had visited, probably along with his father, who went there as a travelling pack-man. We know that she married in 1782, and went to live in Liverpool with her husband, who was the captain of a sailing-ship. The affair was therefore over by the time Ross was twenty, though it may be that the obsession lasted for some time.

John Mackenzie, Ross's fellow-countryman and first editor, is responsible for the story that *"Feasgar Luain"* ("Monday Evening") was composed by Ross on seeing Marion Ross at a ball in Stornoway. Mackenzie's first draft of this legend is cautious, but by 1841, when he published his famous anthology of Gaelic poetry, *Sàr Obair nam Bard Gaelach*, its outlines had become quite firm. He says of the song, "Its history like that of its author, is one of love and brevity—it was composed in a few hours to a young lady, whom he accidentally met at a convivial party—and sung, with all its richness of ideality and mellowness of expression, before they broke up."[74] The internal evidence of the song, however, in specific detail as well as in tone, shows that this was not the case, but that it was composed on the mainland and very probably after Mòr Ros's marriage. It was the sound of dance music that "ferried his thoughts over" [to Lewis] and he proceeds to reconstruct the detail of his first meeting with Mòr Ros. He sees her sedately turning in time to the music, on the dance-floor, and describes her, comparing her to Diana and Venus, and then hinting at her noble and heroic ancestry, and that of her clan, which was his own clan also. The poem ends:

> Sad my sighing, hard my fortune
> no means of rest, no hearty joy,
> as I think of my beloved
> who took my love without return.
> The Powers imposed a double penance
> to humble me without delay.
> I was enticed to drowse by Cupid
> but I wakened bruised and weak.
>
> Take farewell greetings to the maiden,
> of great clan and noble ways,
> bring to her my warm good wishes—

I love her fair and yellow hair.
It was no dream that moved my spirit—
would that it would give me peace—
whether on near or distant voyage
I will for ever think of you.[75]

The poem does not in fact give the impression of uncontrollable emotion. It is carefully ordered, rather formal in its images and its progression, and has time and inclination to nod courteously in the direction of these formal literary traditions, both Classical and native, which Ross knew. It is a controlled reconstruction of a situation, and only the reference to the "double penance" strikes really deep in emotional soil. Indeed, somewhat contrary to the legend, Ross's poetry is generally tightly controlled. His experience with Mòr Ros seems, however, to break surface in poems which are not ostensibly concerned with her, as in this verse:

That was no sign of wisdom
in me that I fell then in love
with a girl who has left me
and airily sets me at naught.
If I thought of it coolly
that flame would burn low in my breast,
I would drown it completely,
not letting it gnaw me again.[76]

The emotional drive behind the lines finds its expression in a simplicity of words and thoughts but the urgency shows in the rhythm.

Another love-song attributed to Uilleam Ros, the *"Oran Cumhaidh"* ("Song of Lament"), has verses that may belong to an earlier love-song, but whether they were composed by Ross or merely retouched by him, they seem characteristic of one side of his poetic personality:

I find your converse sweeter
than the mavis in the trees,
than cuckoo in May morning,
or than harp with its strings,
than the Bishop on a Sunday

when he preaches to the crowd,
I'd have it before Hanover
with all its riches strewn.

Why was I not born sightless,
dumb, without power to see,
before I saw your modest face
that dimmed a hundred's light;
since first I ever saw you
your virtues were renowned,
and death to me were easier
than to live now you are gone.[77]

The barest, most desolate of his love-songs, the one most firmly pruned of extraneous ornament, is the *"Oran Eile"* ("Another Song" [on the same theme]). This has no elaborate analogy, such as mars the "Song of Lament", nor classical and fashionable adornment such as we find in *"Feasgar Luain"*. It is a song without bravado either. It is short, and tightly reined, so that the emotion which sets it in motion is kept compact and compressed. The emotion declares itself in the use that is made of language, which is disturbed and pressed into unusual shapes, as happens when the imagination's temperature rises. There is a telling example of this in the third line of the first verse, where he refers to a maggot or grub hatching its eggs within him: these eggs from which disease comes. In one sense the word he uses for hatching, *gur*, is a homely, everyday word which would be used of a hen hatching its eggs, but it is used here in a dark threatening, macabre sense, as of bacteria multiplying in a diseased body. Ross died of TB, and perhaps knew he was dying. The image, however, is one which has the power to expand, to fill and jolt the imagination. He plays elsewhere in the poem with the double meanings of words, in a more obvious but still a very effective way, as where he refers to Mòr Ros's journey over sea *fo bhréid*, which means (1) under sail and (2) under kerch, the headgear that was the badge of the married woman. Again, he plays with the senses of *dàn*, (1) poem and (2) destiny. People say of him that he is a mere poet, and that no poem/destiny that is worth while will come his way. And throughout he is drawn to images and thoughts that suggest to us that things which were alive and in motion are now proceeding to dumbness, immobility and death. I give the poem in Iain Smith's verse translation:

Another Song on the Same Theme

I am lonely here and depressed.
No more can I drink and be gay.
The worm that feeds on my breast
is giving my secret away.
Nor do I see, walking past,
the girl of the tenderest gaze.
It is this which has brought me to waste
like the leaf in the autumn days.

O girl of the ringletted hair,
how much I deplore you, and miss.
In spite of the riches you wear
I shall never curse you, but bless.
What can I do but despair
like the wounded soldier whose pain
cries out from the field of the war
he'll never join battle again?

I'm a stray who is far from the herd
or a man to whom love is dead.
The voyage you took as a bride
wrung the hot tears from my head.
Better not to have stored
your beauty and fame in my mind
or the affable grace of your word,
a language to music refined.

Ill-wishers who hear of my plight
call me a coward and worse.
They say that I'm only a poet
whose fate is as dead as my verse.
(His father's a packman. You know it.
His father, in turn, couldn't boast.)
They'd take a good field and plough it.
I cut better poems than most.

My spirit is dulled by your loss,
the song of my mouth is dumb.
I moan with the sea's distress

when the mist lies over the foam.
It's the lack of your talk and your grace
which has clouded the sun from my eyes
and has sunk it deep in the place
from which light will never arise.

I shall never praise beauty again.
I shall never design a song.
I shall never take pleasure in tune,
nor hear the clear laugh of the young.
I shall never climb hill with the vain
youthful arrogant joy that I had.
But I'll sleep in a hall of stone
with the great bards who are dead.[78]

William Ross died in 1791, a long time indeed after Mòr Ros's marriage in 1782, too long no doubt to give credence to the legend that he died for love of her. Yet the legend has its own truth, or so it seems when we consider the ways in which his poetry differs from that of his fellow Gaelic poets of the eighteenth century. His personality seems the most vulnerable, and he either wears his heart on his sleeve or pretends he hasn't got one: two reflexes of the same emotional disturbance. This subjective element, and more especially the conscious manipulation of it, was new in the poetry of the century, though perhaps not entirely original.[79]

We have seen, momentarily, that James Macpherson's writing of the years around 1760 had left a slight mark on Ross's sensibility.[80] No doubt they both responded to the atmosphere of their time, though Macpherson did something to create that atmosphere too. There are some superficial resemblances between Ross and Burns also, although these cannot be pressed hard. James Macpherson had some influence on subsequent Gaelic writing, almost always a pernicious or trivial influence. This produced poems like *"Miann a' Bhàird Aosda"* ("The Aged Poet's Wish"), John Smith's *Sean Dàna* (*Ancient Lays*) and archaized poems such as *"Mordubh"* and *"Collath"*. These have some place in a history of Gaelic poetry, but need not detain us here.

As the century drew to a close, the last of the eighteenth-century poets, Ewen MacLachlan, had just begun to publish. He was the most learned of the group, and served as Headmaster of Aberdeen Grammar School and as Librarian to King's College. He is the only one of these poets who has to his name a poem on each of the four seasons. He also wrote a short pibroch-type poem, after the manner of Donnchadh Bàn. His verse lacks the strong individuality which marks that of all the others, in their various ways, and he is chiefly remembered nowadays as the translator of seven books and a fragment of the eighth, of the *Iliad*.[81] The *Odyssey* had to await its translator for another 150 years, being translated by the late John Maclean, Headmaster of Oban High School, in the 1960s.[82]

The century had opened with the old age of Niall MacMhuirich, one of the last of the literate bards of the old school. By 1800 the representative of the MacMhuirichs, Lachlann, was not able to read or write, but the poets had nevertheless got their second wind, and were in command again in their own house. Much of the old society lay in tatters around them, but the pen is at the end of the day mightier than the sword, and a nation's spirit can be stronger than either.

6

Gaelic Poets in Lowlands and Highlands

THE NINETEENTH CENTURY is above all others the century of the Gaelic diaspora. It was chiefly in this period that people of Gaelic descent and language became distributed throughout the Scottish population, but especially the population of the Lowland industrial belt, and also went further afield, in particular to the Americas, where in company with Lowland Scots they proved to be hardy and capable settlers. The language and music and life-style they took with them survived for varying periods and with varying intensity where they went, or influenced the texture of the life around them, and that influence can still be traced from Milngavie to Milwaukee. There is room for a serious historical study of this diaspora.

This dispersal of the Gaelic people had begun, in a significant way, in the second half of the eighteenth century. The magnets were those that were to work so effectively in the nineteenth century—the industrial Lowlands and the undeveloped spaces of the New World—but these magnets were to grow enormously in strength and attraction. The movement had indeed begun earlier. We may note, for example, the settlement of a group of 350 people from Argyllshire in North Carolina in 1739, and subsequent grants of land to persons with Highland names in 1740 and spasmodically for several years thereafter.¹* A large number of pardoned Jacobite "rebels", to use the official description, had been transported to America as "indentured servants", which is sometimes a polite circumlocution for "slaves", and this movement had begun before the '45 Rising. We have seen already that Donnchadh Bàn, the poet, had moved to Edinburgh in the 1760s, becoming one of a growing Highland community in the city. Around the year 1770 there were considerable migrations to America, led by tacksmen, the middlemen of the land-leasing system in the Highlands. These

tacksmen had lost their military function with the collapse of the
'45, and the subsequent repression, and as their rents were steeply
increased a number of them made arrangements to go abroad, with
their tenants, to areas where land was plentiful and cheap. The
famous Flora MacDonald and her husband Allan MacDonald of
Kingsburgh, settled in North Carolina, having sailed from Camp-
beltown in 1774. She, however, returned to Skye after five years in
America.[2] Some 2,055 Highlanders are listed as arriving off emi-
grant ships in North Carolina alone, between 1739 and 1775, most
of these coming from Argyllshire and Skye.[3] There was migration
abroad to other places also, for example Jamaica, where two of the
poet Ewen MacLachlan's brothers were settled, the elder having
gone there about 1793.[4]

In addition to the social and political changes which had produced the revolt of the tacksmen, there were powerful economic
changes beginning to make themselves felt, notably the development of sheep-rearing in the Highlands, with consequent enclosures
and evictions, and in some areas a population explosion which
current land-use and employment patterns could not accommodate.
These pressures begin to become noticeable in the southern Highlands first of all. Already by 1760 Lowland sheep-farmers were
leasing hill grass-lands, and by the end of the century sheep-rearing
on a large scale had penetrated the Northern Highlands, eventually
leading to large-scale evictions: the infamous Highland Clearances
which blotch the face of Highland history in the nineteenth
century.

Also, the demand for labour, in the rapidly growing industrial
economy of the Central Belt of Scotland, was a powerful positive
attraction for Highlanders in the nineteenth century, and led to
the growth of very large Gaelic-speaking populations in that
region, and to the growth of a literature which reflected the circumstances and sentiments of this body of Gaelic immigrants to
the Lowlands. The lines of connection and tension between the
various old and new Gaelic communities, and between these and
the new host-communities, help to make new patterns in the Gaelic
poetry of this period. Much of the poetry of the century is connected, in one way or another, with these matters that have been
briefly summarized.

Though there had been earlier poets, such as Iain MacMhur-
chaidh of Kintail and North Carolina, it was mainly in the nineteenth century that the tradition of New World Gaelic verse was

established. The Rev. James MacGregor is the earliest Gaelic poet to have left any considerable body of verse composed in Nova Scotia. He held a charge in Pictou County, and his verse consisted mainly of hymns. Iain MacGhillEathain (John Maclean) is usually regarded as the main patriarch of Nova Scotia Gaelic verse. He had acted as bard to Maclean of Coll before leaving Scotland in 1819, and had published a collection of poetry in the previous year. His Scottish verse is very much in the panegyrist style of the eighteenth century. More interest attaches to what he wrote in Canada, and particularly to his poem *"Am Bàrd an Canada"* ("The Poet in Canada"), in which he gives his early reactions to his new country (contrasting it with his windswept native Tiree) and castigates the emigration agents whose picture of life in Canada was evidently too rosy. A few stanzas of this will be sufficient to give its flavour:

> It's little wonder that I am gloomy,
> where I live now behind the hills,
> in a wilderness by Barney's River,
> bare potatoes my only food.
> Before I fell all these lowering trees,
> and till the soil, and produce a crop,
> my arms' strength will have tired and failed
> before my children have come of age.
>
> This is a country where hardship's common,
> although the immigrants don't know of that;
> we were hard done by those enticers
> who brought us here with their glowing tales.
> If they prosper, their wealth won't last long,
> they'll reap no comfort—I'm not surprised—
> pursued by wretched people's curses
> as they are driven from place to place.
>
> They make their promises strong and steadfast,
> praising the new land to the skies;
> they will say that your relations
> are happy, wealthy, and do not lack.
> They tell you all these enticing stories
> to make you desperately keen to go;
> if you come safely, when you see them
> the "states" are no better off than you.[5]

He goes on with his anti-immigration propaganda, referring to the emigration agents in Scotland as cattle drovers, and saying that one sees little of the famous green dollars, and that barter is still prevalent. It is an interesting enough testimony of disillusionment, and must have been composed very early in MacGhillEathain's sojourn in Canada. He survived there until 1848, composing some other songs in a similar vein, but in the main reverting to what must have been his natural bent in verse: a miscellany of panegyric (for persons in Scotland and in Canada) and of occasional village-verse.

It was a grandson of his, the Rev. Alexander Maclean Sinclair, who edited a large number of anthologies of Gaelic verse, including Nova Scotian verse, in the latter years of the nineteenth century. The family MSS., some of which Iain MacGhillEathain had brought over from Scotland, include some important items, especially Dr Hector Maclean's MS. collection of verse, partly compiled before the '45.

Nova Scotia continued to produce Gaelic poets throughout the century, and well into the twentieth century also. Representatives of the MacMhuirich bardic family had emigrated there early in the nineteenth century, and continued to produce versifiers. Donnchadh Blàr (the Rev. Duncan Blair) composed a poem in praise of the Niagara Falls,[6] Malcolm Gillis of Cape Breton composed many "homeland" songs which were very popular, Vincent MacLellan published a collection of songs in 1891, and much verse appeared in Nova Scotian publications, especially in the weekly (later fortnightly) Gaelic paper *Mac-Talla*, which was published in Sydney from 1892 to 1904.[7] The links with the Scottish tradition were closely kept; there were occasional new themes suggested by the new environment, but no new voice or style.

At home in Scotland there were some more adventurous developments, together with much verse of an unambitious nature. A great deal of religious verse was composed in a century which saw many collections of sermons published, and many translations made of religious and pious prose. The work of Pàdraig Grannd (Peter Grant) and Iain Gobha na Hearadh (John Morrison) is the most famous in this field. Pàdraig Grannd (1783–1867) was strongly influenced by the English hymn-writer Isaac Watts. His rhythms are flowing and evangelical, his thought is not very demanding, and his clear exposition and relatively lively turn of phrase make his verse easy and pleasant to read. It became very popular, appearing in many editions throughout the century.

Iain Gobha na Hearadh (1790–1852) is, however, a much more original and forceful poet. He handles his themes at times with great freshness, robustness of language, and on occasion with dramatic power, as in this extract from his long poem *"An Nuadh Bhreith, no Gleachd an t-Seann Duine agus an Duin' Oig"* ("The New Birth, or the Struggle of the 'old' and the 'new' Man"), which is a dialogue between the converted Christian and his unregenerate self:

> I am drowned in the "old" man's sea,
> in sharp cold dew and winter's coldness,
> the glorious "new" man comes to his temple
> and he sets my feet a-dancing.
> > It is the "old" man who made me gloomy,
> > the "new" man is my blazing lantern.

> . . . . . .

> The "old" man set me in the miry clay,
> and made me wallow in eternal mud,
> the "new" has raised me up to safety,
> and rescued me from that mud's choking:
> > the "old" man is licking the dust,
> > the "new" man is pleading his case. [8]

Some of his verse is highly evangelical, but his thought and expression remain robust and agile, unweakened by sentimentality:

> But O! how great our need is
> now of believing,
> that we find ourselves
> with that sun bedizened:
> the righteousness of Christ
> a garb to give us beauty,
> making us clean, pure-white—
> no spot or wrinkle:
> if that were our garment,
> though the world should mock us,
> we would be like heroes,
> above the world and steadfast. [9]

The third-last line shows the resilience of the poet's mind.

The commonest theme of Gaelic verse in the nineteenth century is that of "homeland". This was no doubt to be expected in a period of upheaval and uprooting, much of it of an involuntary nature, whether people were forced to migrate by physical action or by economic circumstances. The homeland is seen primarily in a nostalgic light: a place of youthful associations, family and community warmth, a Paradise lost. But this in itself is not sufficient to explain the simple and unambitious nature of so much of the verse of this period on such themes. It should be recalled that the condition of the Highlands was very unsettled, with periodic pounces being made by landlords and factors, villages uprooted, and new communities set up to take the displaced persons. Schooling must have suffered severely. The introduction of English, first of all to the southerly and eastern communities, introduced Gaels, not to the glories of English literature but to the simpler ephemera of the elementary schoolroom, to the chapbook and to the models of semi-literate taste. All this is reflected in the "new" Gaelic verse of the nineteenth century, which largely turns its back on its own relatively learned, aristocratic tradition, and grovels contentedly in its novel surroundings.

As always, there were survivals from the older order, individuals who made an effort to cling to the tradition. Thus we find, for example, Gilleasbuig Grannda (Archibald Grant) of Glenmoriston, a poet who was born in 1785 but whose verse was not published until 1863, producing praise-poetry and local verse written against a strong background of knowledge of language, clan and legendary history, and traditional versification, using robust rhythms, and handling with assurance and skill the strophic verse paragraph which was so popular in the late seventeenth and early eighteenth centuries. In one of his poems in particular, *"Beannachadh Bàird do Luing ùir"* ("Poet's Blessing for a new Ship"),[10] there is an interesting seam of fantasy based on the old Fenian and other legendary lore which is slightly reminiscent of Iain MacAilein's work.

But the staple verse of the nineteenth century is that of poets such as Iain MacLachlainn (John Maclachlan, of Rahoy), Eóghan MacColla (Evan MacColl, of Lochfyneside), Iain Caimbeul (John Campbell, of Ledaig in Benderloch), Dòmhnall MacEacharn (Donald MacKechnie, of Jura), Calum MacPhàrlain (Malcolm MacFarlane, of Lochaweside and Paisley), Niall MacLeòid (Neil

MacLeod, of Skye), and Iain MacPhaidein (John MacFadyen, of Mull). With the exception of Niall MacLeòid, all these were Argyllshire poets. The earlier nineteenth-century pattern of migration to the Lowland cities (where virtually all the Gaelic publishing took place) has a strong bearing on this distribution.

We may attempt to describe the overall flavour of this verse, without going into great detail. Homeland verse was perhaps the most prominent variety, but the theme of homeland is frequently combined with that of love, and especially lovers' partings. These frequently take place on the shore. Iain MacLachlainn writes:

> O, do tell me, western wind,
> when you come across the sea,
> what state is my sweetheart in,
> is she thinking now of me?
>
> When I stretched my hand to you,
> leaving land, on the shore,
> I could scarcely speak the words
> "Fare you well, my adored."
>
> When I turned my back to you
> I saw your tears begin to swell;
> though I took the tiller then
> it was on you my eyes fell.[11]

Such romantic, idyllic settings are characteristic of the homeland/ love verse of the period. We find a closely similar situation in Niall MacLeòid's song *"Duanag an t-Seòladair"* ("The Sailor's Ditty"):

> She gave her picture on the shore,
> a smooth lock of her fair hair,
> these bring always to my mind
> the love my sweetheart gave to me.

Earlier in the song this verse occurs:

> The wind is rising, driving spray,
> and I am lashed against the wheel;
> it put new strength into my hands
> to think of my girl's love for me.[12]

The invented detail and the spurious emotion are plain to see. This has little or nothing to do with the fact that Niall MacLeòid was a tea-traveller rather than a sailor, but it does throw serious doubts on his artistic integrity. Another highly popular song of his, "*Màiri Bhaile Chrò*" ("Mary of Baile Chrò") uses an idyllic setting on a shieling. The travelling poet is offered a night's hospitality by the lovely and charming Mary. There is no mention of a chaperon, and it would be improper to question the propriety of Mary's hospitality. Again, his "*Cumha an t-seana Ghaidheil*" ("Lament of the Aged Gael")[13] appears to suffer from the same defect of simulated emotion issuing in sentimentality. The aged Gael has lost his wife and three of his children by death, but has time and inclination to reflect on the vanished cowherd and especially the milkmaid, whose ditties he loved to hear; he recalls her with her hair down over her shoulders in braids of gold. This passage seems to show that the emotional experience was not deeply imagined, and a similar perfunctoriness of identification is common in the popular verse of the period. Eóghan MacColla has a long series of "love-songs" addressed to a large number of ladies from different locations.[14] I must confess that I have not checked on whether he was a peripatetic lady's man, but I suspect, from internal evidence, that many of these love-songs are simulated and stylized. Iain Caimbeul of Ledaig has a series of poems on human "tragedies", e.g. "A Mother bewailing the Loss of her Daughter, who perished in the Wreck of the 'Royal Charter' ", or "Written on the death of a sister and her two children, as if by her Husband".[15] Again the emotion is simulated, and produces sentimentality, as does Niall MacLeòid's "*Bàs Leinibh na Bantraich*" ("The Death of the Widow's Child").[16]

There are other kinds of "set subjects" also, in which the poet retains a totally external relationship with his theme. Niall Mac-Leòid's "*An t-Uan*" ("The Lamb"),[17] "*Rainn do Neòinean*" ("Verses to a Daisy"), and "*Tobar Thalamh-Toll*" ("The Well of Talamh-Toll") are cases in point. The latter in particular is a verse sermon rather than poetry, and in the poem on the Daisy the moral obtrudes. Dòmhnall MacEacharna's "*An Sruthan*" ("The Burn") might be regarded as veering towards the set subject, but it is saved from total failure by the vitality of its rhythm and some clarity of observation. Poems and songs on Gaelic, on the state and future of the language, are often set pieces also. Expressions of love for land and language tend to be repeated until they can only

H

rank as clichés, for example in Iain Caimbeul's work, even in his "*Is toigh leam a' Ghaidhealtachd*" ("I love the Highlands"),[18] Niall MacLeòid's "*Brosnachadh na Gàidhlig*" ("Incitement to Gaelic"),[19] with its fashionable praise of Professor Blackie, and Calum MacPhàrlain's "*Na Gaidheil an guaillibh a chéile*" ("The Gaels shoulder to shoulder").[20] Too many of these poems, and the last referred to is a good example of this, are plain transcriptions of arguments and sentiments, having the minimum metrical adornments of verse but virtually no heightening of language.

Niall MacLeòid's "*An Gleann san robh mi òg*" ("The Glen where I spent my youth") is often taken as a symbol of the poet's work. Perhaps this is not entirely just, but it may serve as a fair sample of "homeland" verse, and it would be appropriate to quote from it for that reason. It was translated by Henry Whyte who wrote under the pseudonym of Fionn, and was very active in Highland circles in Glasgow. The translation's pawky smattering of Scots words offends against linguistic good taste, but despite Niall MacLeòid's original having more dignity in this sense, the translation is not too unfair a representation of it:

> When the simmer bricht returnin',
> decks each grove and buddin' tree;
> when the birds amang the branches
> are a' pipin' loud and free;
> an' the bairnies fu' o' glee
> pu' the roses in the den
> O! 'twere dear delight tae wander
> in my bonnie native glen.

> In my bonnie native glen,
> in my bonnie native glen,
> O! 'twere dear delight tae wander
> in my bonnie native glen.

> . . . . . .

> When the lasses gae'd a-fauldin',
> aft I joined the merry thrang;
> in their hands their milkin' coggies
> an' frae ilka voice a sang;
> while the echoes sweet and clear

wad gi'e answer frae the ben—
but we hear nae mair their liltin'
in my bonnie native glen.

. . . . . .

There was routh o' sport an' pleasure
tae keep a' the young in glee;
for the loch, the moss, the muirlan'
then tae a' alike were free;
now the bailiff's keepin' ward
on each streamlet, creek, an' fen;
an' ye daurna fish a burnie
in my bonnie native glen.

Now the dwellin's are in ruins,
where ance lived a gallant clan;
theirs was aye the frien'ly welcome,
an' theirs aye the open han';
aft the needy an' the puir
found a place at their fire-en';
now, alas! there's nane tae greet them
in my bonnie native glen.[21]

The note of protest appears, though in a muted form, in the second-last stanza quoted, and this is heard, with varying degrees of urgency, throughout the "homeland" poetry. Iain MacLachlainn voices it rather more effectively, in his *"Och, och mar tha mi"* ("Alas, my state"). This belongs to an important sub-variety of the homeland verse: verse about the evictions and clearances, symbolized by the new sheep and shepherds and their new language:

Not sweet the sound that waked me from slumber,
coming down to me from the mountain tops:
the Lowland shepherd whose tongue displeases,
shouting there at his lazy dog.

In May, on rising at early morning
there's no birds' music nor moorland lowing,
only creatures screeching in English,
calling dogs, setting deer a-scamper.[22]

Niall MacLeòid, in his poem *"Na Croitearan Sgitheanach"* ("The Skye Crofters") does come to grips with the situation of eviction, and the question of human rights, as actuality, but only in some stanzas, while others slide into the grooves of jingoism or braggadocio:

> I find sad the account
> tonight from my country,
> my friends are being scourged
> by Lowland poltroons;
> with sticks at the ready
> being beaten like cattle,
> like slaves quite uncared for
> being shut in a fank.
>
> The folk who were friendly,
> and kindly, warm-hearted,
> have now been pressed sore
> by landlords' conceit;
> their freedom has left them,
> their fields are deserted,
> sheep have taken the place
> of free men in the glen.
>
> Unremembered the heroes
> who saved us our country,
> with bared blades of battle
> defeating the foe;
> not bending to slavery,
> no justice refusing,
> leaving that reputation
> unsmirched with their seed.
>
> . . . . . .
>
> An end will come to oppression;
> food and possessions,
> peace and joy also
> will abound in the land;
> the youth will sing sweetly
> their tunes and their ditties,

and lovely young maidens
tend the calves at the fold.

The heir and the bailiff
will with tenants deal kindly,
with no pride or deceit
as they did in the past;
and Gaels without number
will live in the Highlands,
enhancing the country,
enjoying good name.[23]

This poem might be regarded as a key-poem in a deeper study of
Niall MacLeòid and poets similar to him at this time.

In different poets throughout the century one can detect
nationalist feeling. It is often of the "land and language" variety,
although it is noticeable that this strain of protest did not flourish
nearly so strongly in Gaelic Scotland as it did in Wales. There is
not much of this nationalist feeling in Niall MacLeòid's work. In
"Na Gaidheil" ("The Gaels")[24] there are indeed nationalist sentiments, but one senses a lack of real commitment, and perhaps the
final stanza quoted above illustrates his lack of political acumen.
Nationalist feeling shows more clearly in the work of Eóghan
MacColla, who spent some thirty years of his life in Canada. His
"Fóghnan na h-Alba" ("Thistle of Scotland")[25] has been revived
in a nationalist context in recent years. Calum MacPhàrlain, it may
be worth noting in this context, makes the point that he is not
singing of one region or district, but of the Highlands as a whole.[26]
There can be little doubt that there are connections to be seen
between these occasional demonstrations of nationalist feeling and
the rise of what Professor H. J. Hanham calls "the first effective
nationalist movement [of modern times], the National Association
for the Vindication of Scottish Rights",[27] in the 1850s, and successive movements and devolutionary developments in the second
half of the century.

Eóghan MacColla has one poem in particular in which he shows
himself master of a style and technique which is characteristically
Gaelic. This is the poem *"Moladh Abhainn Ruaile"* ("Praise of the
river Ruail"), which has some clear observation, communicated
with precision and economy, and without sentimentality. Similarly,
Niall MacLeòid's *"Fàilte do'n Eilean Sgitheanach"* ("Salute to

Skye") has a dignity and weight that is unusual in his work. There is a strong sense of local patriotism here too. The language is clean and hard, and some interesting variety is introduced by the use of staccato rhymes in some of the stanzas. This is how the poem begins:

> A salute to your peaks
> and your lowering corries,
> your grass-covered mountains
> where roe-deer run fast.
> The winter with darkness
> round the hill-tops is closing;
> the wind-sounding groves
> are stripped to the base.
>
> And I see the Coolins
> like a lion all fearless,
> with their beard of white snow
> encircling their head;
> down the cheeks there are pouring
> waterfalls with their fine spray,
> falling and looping
> to the floor of the glen.[28]

The other salient positive virtue that some of this poetry has is that of humour. This is a characteristic it shares with the village poetry, and of course this is essentially what it is in many instances. The village has changed, perhaps from Skye or Lewis or Mull to Overnewton or Pollokshaws or some other locality in Glasgow or Clydeside, but the essential conditions for the verse have not changed beyond recognition. Probably the outstanding example of a village bard who found his village and his public in Glasgow was Iain MacPhaidein (John MacFadyen), of Mull. The first edition of his poems and readings, under the title *An t-Eileanach* (*The Islander*) was published in 1890, at a time when the communal life of Highlanders in Glasgow was well organized in societies of various kinds, when communities were tight-knit, churches well-established, shinty played in "the Shaws" and elsewhere, and the printing-presses still turning out cheap Gaelic books. MacPhaidein tends to use tripping though regular metres, and his humour is more often quiet than boisterous, as in the "*Oran*

dh'Oidhche-Shamhna" ("Song for Hallowe'en") which gives a
light, humorous description of a Hallowe'en party in a hall south
of the "Shaws" district in Glasgow. A non-Gaelic policeman appears intent on keeping the peace, and gets a ducking in a pond for
his pains.[29] In another song, about a Hogmanay spree, the statues
in George Square begin to dance,[30] while in *"Oran Margaidh-an-
t-Salainn"* ("Song of the Saltmarket")[31] we meet the uninhibited
Irishry of Glasgow, dancing and fighting in the street. Many of the
songs are peppered with references to streets, shops and characters
in Glasgow.

MacPhaidein has another type of composition which has not
worn well: longish dialogue-poems, e.g. between the Author and
an Owl, or the Author and a Wood-pigeon, or the Author and a
Mermaid.[32] These tend to be more serious, with desultory argument, moral advice (e.g. not to drink too much), though the second
of those referred to above has passages on the plight of the Highlanders at the time. Dòmhnall MacEacharn shows a liking for the
dialogue-poem also. His *"Còmhradh eadar am Bàrd 's an Cìobair"*
("Conversation between the Bard and the Shepherd")[33] contains
some three hundred lines of rather inert argument (the verse
equivalent, perhaps, of the somewhat prosy and long-winded
dialogues of the time). His *"Impireachd Bhreatuinn"* ("The British
Empire")[34] is a conversation between the Bard and the Sun, presumably in its never-setting capacity; the Sun comes up with the
assurance that the British Empire is still strong and fine. Mac-
Eacharn's verse as a whole is dull and pedestrian, in distinction
to his prose, which has humour, gaiety and a sense of style. Perhaps
several of his poems suffer from being competition-pieces. The
jingoist strain appears in his verse also.

Many of the poets whose work has been referred to composed
pop songs which have enjoyed a long popularity. This is partly to
be explained by the elaborate system of *céilidhs* and concerts staged
in Glasgow and Clydeside generally, and the early links between
the organisers of these, and the song-writers themselves, and the
National Mod, which began in 1893. There was a strong contingent
of Argyllshire singers in the earlier decades of the Mod, and indeed
afterwards also, and this body of modern pop-song was well maintained until recent times. One thinks of Mac Colla's *"O till, a
leannain, o till, o till"* ("Return my love, return, return"),[35] Iain
Caimbeul's *"O théid mi gad amharc"* ("I shall go to see you"),[36]
Dòmhnall MacEacharn's *"Bean a' Chòtain Ruaidh"* ("The Lady

in the brown Coat"),[37] Calum MacPhàrlain's *"Mo Dhachaidh"* ("My Home"),[38] a pretty picture postcard of a song, Iain Mac-Lachlainn's *"Seinn an duan so"* ("Sing this Song")[39] and Niall MacLeòid's *"Sìne Chaluim Bhàin"* ("Jean"),[40] *"Doire na Smeòraich"* ("Grove of the Mavis"),[41] *"Far an robh mi'n raoir"* ("Where I was yestreen")[42] and many others. Niall MacLeòid would seem to be the example *par excellence* of the popular poet in Gaelic, and he more than any other became part of the pop culture of his time. It would be useful to analyse his work carefully, as it, and his popularity, throw valuable light on the dynamics of Gaelic society in his time.

It was suggested earlier that some of the hymns of this century showed metrical influence from English hymns, and that elementary English school texts and popular literature in the Lowland context may have influenced the "new" Gaelic poets in the Lowlands. At any rate, it is particularly noticeable that the pop songs of the period show a strong tendency to be written in quatrains, or in eight-line stanzas with simple rhyme-patterns which may be regarded as juxtaposed quatrains or couplets. The quatrain rhyming a b a b, and the eight-line stanza rhyming a b a b a b a b are common, with variant patterns such as a a a b and a b c b. The assonantal character of Gaelic rhyme make these patterns quite unexacting. Niall MacLeòid chooses the quatrain in close on two-fifths of his poems, and an eight-line stanza in a slightly larger number of instances. He also shows a subdued liking for the rhyming couplet, a form that had been a favourite of the Islay poet Uilleam Mac Dhunléibhe, whose work we have still to consider. MacDhunléibhe probably took the form over from Sir Walter Scott's work in particular. In the present century we find this chain of metrical influence reaching the work of Somhairle MacGhillEathain (Sorley Maclean), in his case perhaps as a devotee of MacDhunléibhe.

Niall MacLeòid and Iain MacLachlainn in particular, but these poets we have been discussing in general, make a strong feature of vowel melody in their work, and this poetry is also characterized by rhythmic regularity. This may be in conformity with its character as a poetry basically lacking in surprise, shock, tension.

Besides the poetry we have been considering, much of it published in individual collections, there is a good deal of similar verse published in anthologies, particularly district or island anthologies. The anthology *Na Bàird Thirisdeach* (*The Tiree Bards*), for example, includes work by some fifty bards, many of them nineteenth-century ones such as Iain MacGhillEathain (John Maclean of Baile

Mhàrtainn), the author of highly popular songs such as *"A Chaluim Bhig"* ("Little Calum")[43] and *"Hi ho ró's na hóro éile"*.[44] The latter is a direct and simple love-song, which gains enormously in effect from being set to a fine traditional melody. Another such anthology is *Bàrdachd Leódhais* (*Poetry of Lewis*), and we shall meet one poet in particular whose work was published there. And beyond the individual collections and the anthologies there is much verse that has never achieved systematic publication at all, although some of it has been written and recorded. A case in point is Iain Dubh MacLeòid ("Black" John MacLeod), a brother of Niall MacLeòid's, whose work is sometimes said to be of a distinctly higher quality than that of his famous brother. Their father, Dòmhnall nan Oran (Donald MacLeod), it is of interest to note, had published an anthology of verse, including some of his own, in 1811.

There are three poets whose work seems to have a special individuality, strength and *gravitas* in this age of flux and resignation and triviality. Gaelic poetry, and Gaelic self-respect, would have suffered had they not produced their work. All three were concerned, in different ways, times and places, with their countrymen's struggle for freedom. The notable bid for freedom in religious and ecclesiastical matters, which had led to the Disruption and the birth of the Free Church in 1843, showed the desire for freedom issuing in action, and strangely enough little or no memorable poetry issued from this campaign. The other great campaign of the nineteenth century was the long-drawn-out one for land rights, starting with the smouldering resentment against landlords, chiefs and factors at the time of the Clearances and Evictions (and it must be remembered that these went on for close on a hundred years, erupting in different places at different times), and finding a solution at last in an organized struggle, using both constitutional means and violence. In the events leading to the final dénouement an important part was played by Lowland Gaels, attuned to current political tactics, and in touch with Irish developments also, but one of the trio of poets we are to consider took an active part, as poet, in the campaign which won security of tenure for the crofters in the mid-1880s. This was Màiri Mhór nan Oran or Mary MacPherson of Skye. The other two poets were dead by this time.

The eldest of the trio was Uilleam MacDhunléibhe (William Livingstone, of Islay) who lived from 1808 to 1870. MacDhunléibhe, who was a tailor by trade, was a keen self-taught student.

He acquired a diffuse knowledge of several classical and modern languages: Latin, a little Greek and Hebrew, French and Welsh. His editor, Robert Blair, says that he remembers "calling upon him in his little garret at 68 Dale Street, Tradeston, Glasgow, and finding himself and his wife busily engaged in translating a French history of the Druids".[45] He also read widely in Scottish history, and published several parts of a projected History of Scotland. His intense Scottish patriotism often took the form of a deep hatred of the English, and his work is much coloured by these opinions.

Many of Livingstone's poems are concerned with dramatic reconstructions of incidents in the earlier history of Scotland, or imaginary battles between the racial groups whose struggles for supremacy looms so large in earlier Scottish history. *"Na Loch-lannaich an Ile"* ("The Norsemen in Islay") and *"Blàr Shunadail"* ("The Battle of Sunadale"),[46] each running to over 1,000 lines, are set in Norse times, and purport to deal with the struggle between the Gaels and the Norsemen. These poems are full of anachronisms, many of them deliberate, and it cannot be said that they carry much conviction. The characters are not sufficiently developed, and the poems have a vagueness of plot which is reminiscent of James Macpherson's "translations" of Ossian, and they were no doubt influenced by these, or perhaps more likely, by the Gaelic version of these. It is difficult to keep the thread of the action in mind, though there is some vivid writing, especially in the descriptions of battle scenes. He has other battle-poems also, e.g. on the Wars of Independence, and on the battle of Tràigh Ghruineaird,[47] in Islay, fought in 1598 between the Macleans of Mull and the MacDonalds of Islay. This latter poem has an imaginative and visual quality which many of the historical poems lack, and the poet's lyricism comes to the surface here too.

But the poles between which his emotions sway are a *saeva indignatio* and a brooding melancholy, and these are the qualities which give his poetry its distinctive stamp. It is the former one we see in this passage from the poem *"Cuimhneachan Bhraid-Alba"* ("Memorial of Breadalbane") where his themes are depopulation, dispersal of the Gael, and the intrusion of the hated English. He surpasses the invective of Mac Mhaighstir Alasdair himself in this context:

> Scotland, bless now my cry,
> waken, Mother beloved,

before cursèd enslavement binds you;
the old valiant clans
have been scattered abroad,
heroes' offspring inured to hardship;
their halls overgrown, nettles sprouting through stones,
deserted and damp and wailing;
owls of sadness are seen,
bats emerge from the holes,
unafraid in the gloomy dwellings
where heroes were reared,
a free Christian stock,
now driven the whole world over,
by glum envious toads,
seed of gluttons most gross
and shameless sows with their lips drooping,
a dirty treacherous brood
whom our fathers called *Goill*,*
sad the grief of the remnant left by them.[48]

But the most effective of his poems, partly because they are the most sustained, are "*Eirinn a' gul*" ("Ireland weeping") and "*Fios thun a' Bhàird*" ("A Message to the Poet"). In the former he recalls how he was used to seeing Ireland from Islay in his youth, and to hearing stories of Ireland, so that it was for him a magic land, although now he sees it as a beaten land. There was still more than half a century to run before Ireland won a measure of freedom:

· · · · · ·

In the innocent morning of youth
I heard the tales of ages past
at Islay's Clan Donald hearths
before the Gaels were driven out.

· · · · · ·

Today as before I discern
your coastline over the sea,
from South Islay's wave-lapped shore,
and sad to tell is your state.

* *Goill* is used of strangers, especially Lowlanders.

Tale of sadness, oppression, exile,
starvation, injustice and grief,
no means of relieving your pain
since you yourself shattered your strength.

Where's the valour of the three Hughs,
heroic O'Donnell, O'Neill,
Maguire with no fear of the foe,
no yielders—they stood till they died.[49]

"*Fios thun a' Bhàird*" begins on a deceptively mild note, describing a sunny morning in Islay, and going on to several stanzas of evenly-flowing Nature poetry, with brief descriptions of herds of cattle, flocks of sheep, flowers, and the peaceful yet teeming life of the countryside. But half way through the poem—literally and exactly half way through it—there is a sudden reversal of mood, which we must conclude was anticipated and planned. Islay, teeming with sheep, has lost its human population, and this is the central theme of the poem, the first half being a disarming introduction which serves in the end to underline the human desolation of the scene. The poem has fourteen stanzas; three are quoted in translation from each half of it:

The morning's bright and sunny,
and the west wind softly blows,
the loch is smooth and peaceful
with the strife of sky at rest.
Under its lovely canvas
the ship's lively—does not tire,
as it carries this clear message,
as I see it, to the Bard.

. . . . . .

There are cattle in their thousands,
on the plains, white sheep on slopes,
and the deer in the wild mountains
undisturbed by foreign scent,
their offspring, wild and powerful,
wet with dew from mildest breeze;
will you carry this clear message,
as I see it, to the Bard.

The great sea-bay lies murmuring
in its everlasting power,
majestic in its beauty,
head-high to waves that roll,
with its seven-mile white halo
of sand swept from edge of tide;
will you carry this clear message,   3
as I see it, to the Bard.

. . . . . .

Though the rays of sun may ration
heaven's warmth to meadow's bloom,
though the shielings have their cattle,
with folds full of lowing calves,
Islay has lost her people,
the sheep have emptied homes;
will you carry this clear message,
as I see it, to the Bard.

Though a stranger, in his wanderings,
comes to harbour in the mist,
the hearth has no light shining
any more upon this coast;
for Lowland spite has scattered
those who will not come again;
will you carry this clear message,
as I see it, to the Bard.

. . . . . .

The poor will find no shelter,
nor the traveller his rest,
nor will preacher find an audience;
strangers, wrong and tax have won.
The spotted adder's coiling
on the floors whereon there grew
the great men that I saw here:
take this message to the Bard.[50]

A similarly deep and bitter anger, finely controlled, shows perhaps in only one other Gaelic poet of the century, Iain Mac a'

Ghobhainn (John Smith, of Iarsiadar), who died in 1881, aged thirty-three. He had been a medical student at the University of Edinburgh, but was forced by ill-health to abandon his course. It is thought that the main body of his surviving work—some 1,400 lines or so—was composed after he returned to Uig, in Lewis, from Edinburgh. Some of this work had survived only in oral sources, as so often happened with Gaelic verse.

He composed village verse of a high standard, fluent, controlled and humorous, including burlesque which is reminiscent of Uilleam Ros in his *"Gaisgeach mór na Féinne"* ("Great Fenian Hero"),[51] songs about night-visiting or courting expeditions, and occasional songs about local episodes. His *"Oran an t-Seana Ghille"* ("Bachelor's Song")[52] is a fine example of humour with a clean, hard bite. There is evidence of nationalist views in several of his poems, though little evidence of that strong anti-English feeling we saw in MacDhunléibhe. Even this following reference is restrained compared to the Islay poet's:

> The violent Saxon
> most stupidly thinks
> we'll yield to his power—
> that we ought to be tame.
> That the Gael should stay quiet
> in a corner alone
> were like a dog putting
> the lions in pen.[53]

Earlier in this poem, *"Am Brosnachadh"* ("The Incitement"), after praising the Gaels and the Scots for their warlike qualities, and their fighting for the country, there comes this withering comment, with its reference to the encroachments of deer forests and foreign hunters:

> It was not for fawns
> with their bottom's bald patch
> that this mantling blood flowed,
> filling up all the pools.[54]

Though relatively few poems by Mac a' Ghobhainn survive, a good range of style and interest appears in them. His *"Coinneach*

Odhar", a poem about the legend of the Brahan Seer, is a modern heroic ballad. It is influenced distantly, mainly in matters of nomenclature, by James Macpherson's work, but weaves legend and imagination to make a new blend. It shows narrative strength, and has a startling clarity, and a power with words, here in the main simple, terse vocabulary.

The poetry which forms the core of his work, however, is quite different from those types so far mentioned, though we have seen a hint of it in his "Brosnachadh". That core consists of a poetry of social, political and moral criticism. It resembles Rob Donn's poetry in some respects, showing a similar realism and barbed wit. Its thought processes are less oblique and subtle than Rob Donn's, but the poetry has a greater *gravitas*. In the whole of nineteenth-century Gaelic verse this is probably the most considered and the most damning and scathing indictment we have of those policies which decimated the Gaelic people. The fearless quality of Mac a' Ghobhainn's mind shows through repeatedly.

Besides *"Am Brosnachadh"*, which we have glanced at, the main poems in this core are *"Oran Luchd an Spòrs"* ("Song for Sportsmen"), and the two longer poems *"Spiorad an Uamhair"* ("The Spirit of Pride") and *"Spiorad a' Charthannais"* ("The Spirit of Kindliness"). In *"Oran Luchd an Spòrs"* he examines the policy of turning large tracts of the Highlands into deer-forests, for the benefit of landlords and visiting sportsmen. The problem which exercised Mac a' Ghobhainn a century ago is still with us, a grisly if often discreet reminder of the colonizing temper of the palmier days of Empire. The problem has attracted its soap-box orators and its pamphleteers,[55] parties have hinted at tackling it, and it still remains. Mac a' Ghobhainn seemed to see it, perhaps not entirely correctly, as a Scottish problem. At any rate he addresses his complaint to Scotland, which has rejected her own sons, and taken instead sportsmen whose pockets are filled with money. He reflects on the practical consequences of this in the event of war, born as he was in the year of revolutions (1848), and living as he did in the shadow of the Crimean War, and the longer shadow of Waterloo. Addressing Scotland, then, he says:

> Now that you've sent them abroad
> you're no longer "the land of the brave":
> you're the land of the gadabout Saxons,
> land of the setters and grouse.

> When battle and slaughter begin,
> and the deerhound folk go to war,
> I'm afraid, facing that, they'll crack up,
> though they're smart at maiming the hare.[56]

Later in the poem he refers to the power whisky distillers have gained over the Highlands, both by broadcasting their product and as landlords and dictators of policy. Speaking of other kinds of proprietors, he says:

> Some of them trafficked in opium,
> they gathered a great deal of riches,
> their vice made the Chinamen suffer,
> their people destroyed by the poison;
> men without kindness or mercy,
> who were hard to prick in the conscience;
> in payment for all of their plunder
> they deserved to be stabbed with a whinger.[57]

He had in mind the Matheson proprietor of Lewis, a member of the firm of Jardine and Matheson, which had an extensive business in the East. The poem is written from a thoroughly radical standpoint. It shows a strong control of verse argument, and an ability to use robust expression, realist detail, and original turns of thought.

These characteristics mark "*Spiorad an Uamhair*" also. He expresses his radical views on the nobility, and on the wealthy, with a realism that cuts through cant and cliché, as in these lines:

> Though your wealth were of the order
> that the world were yours entirely,
> a simple twist of your intestines
> would make it worthless as potatoes.[58]

And when he turns from the rich and the high-born to the poor, who yet suffer from spiritual pride, he is as it were on his home ground, and the poetry gains in immediacy. His description of the Pharisee (and it can scarcely be doubted that he is describing the Lewis variety) seems to come straight out of his own experience:

I'm certain I'm a child of grace,
numbered for ever with the elect;
my belief is firm and strong,
and I loathe the name of pride.
I am conscious of that love;
my new nature's Spirit-given,
I praise the One who quenched my hauteur;
I'll find favour, being a lamb.

Better the pride of a Caesar
than that false pride coming near us.
It makes us think that we are Gods
to chasten everyone around us.
That pride comes in like sneaking serpent,
but coils about their hearts and preens it;
it thrives mid poverty and patches
more lustily than in a palace.[59]

Yet this poem is not so successful overall as his *"Spiorad a'*
Charthannais". The latter begins with a well-ordered discussion of
the action of the spirit of kindliness in society. He uses a succession
of balanced statements to build up a case and generate some
emotion. In the first part of the poem he addresses the world,
which he thinks has too often renounced kindliness. Here his
argument is a general, abstract one. But as the poem proceeds he
moves from the general to the particular, and we find the emotional
temperature rising, and the language becoming more figurative
and compelling. There is an interesting intermediate passage in
which he attacks the loquacious and dogmatic, or alternatively the
broody minister or Christian, making the point sharply that creeds
and religious organizations are not what matter most, and in the
context of Lewis society he here shows a clear independence of
thought and judgement, and the courage of his convictions. The
latter section, in which he deals with the particular case of evictions,
is very vivid in its detail. Here he had in mind the land-troubles
which came to a head in Lewis in the 1870s, and in particular
the infamous case of Donald Munro, Sir James Matheson's
Chamberlain, whose oppression of tenants and general double-
dealing were notorious. The translation which follows selects
stanzas from these various sections of the poem:

. . . . . .

I fear that you have left us now,
departed up to heaven;
men favour now injustice,
your nature quite remote from them.
The surly hide of selfishness
engarbs them all around;
nothing I know will tear through it
but the shaft of the Lord of Hosts.

. . . . . .

(Addressing the world:)

The gracious man is grieved by you,
the evil man wins through;
you stroke the man in luxury
and strike the one who's hurt;
you're generous to the wealthy,
you scorch the man who's poor;
you warm the man who's well-clad
and freeze the man who's bare.

. . . . . .

The preaching sermonizer
shouts with his lusty cry;
we're cursed if we don't listen
to his creed—no other's right—
instead of ever urging us
to answer duty's call,
and making us use reason
before Almighty God.

. . . . . .

The gentle man who rises up
to heaven on love's wings

does not backbite, nor yet debate
too keenly about creeds:
Episcopal or Orthodox,
of Presbytery or Rome;
he's one whose heart has human warmth
and finds a place for love.

O kindliness, most lovely,
O grace of highest worth!
but many never give you room
in hearts that are too hard.
And if the Muses granted me
some eloquence a while
I'd tell you something of the deeds
of the beasts who bore you hate.

. . . . . .

They handed over to the snipe
the land of happy folk,
they dealt without humanity
with people who were kind.
Because they might not drown them
they dispersed them overseas;
a thralldom worse than Babylon's
was the plight that they were in.

They reckoned as but brittle threads
the tight and loving cords
that bound these freemen's noble hearts
to the high land of the hills.
The grief they suffered brought them death
although they suffered long,
tormented by the cold world
which had no warmth for them.

Does anyone remember
in this age the bitter day
of that horrific battle,
Waterloo with its red plains?
The Gaels won doughty victory

when they marshalled under arms;
when faced with strong men's ardour
our fierce foes had to yield.

What solace had the fathers
of the heroes who won fame?
Their houses, warm with kindliness,
were in ruins round their ears;
their sons were on the battlefield
saving a rueless land,
their mothers' state was piteous
with their houses burnt like coal.

While Britain was rejoicing
they spent their time in grief.
In the country that had reared them,
no shelter from the wind;
the grey strands of their hair were tossed
by the cold breeze of the glen,
there were tears upon their cheeks
and cold dew on their heads.

. . . . . .

O tremble midst your pleasures,
oppressor strong and hard!
What death or pain will fall on you
for the hurt you did to men?
The grievous sighs of widows
blow up your bloated wealth,
and every cup of wine you drink
is full of paupers' tears.

Though your estate were spacious,
and though people bowed the knee,
Death's laws are also stringent,
you must bow before his power.
That landlord makes arrangements,
giving equal rights to all,
for your estate he'll give a shirt
and six feet of green turf.

That will be your abject ending,
O man of mounting pride,
with your summonses and warnings,
that cast over all a cloud.
In that serene inheritance
your hauteur won't be high;
the bailiff's scolding can't be heard
nor the ground-officer's rage.

The wriggling worm will praise you then
for your flesh's enticing taste,
when it finds you placed before it
on its table, silent now,
saying "This one's juicy flesh
is good for earthy worms,
since he made many hundreds thin
to feed himself for me."[60]

It was the most savage and final indictment of the men and the
policies that cast their cloud of shame over the century, and a real
measure of reform was only a few years away when Iain Mac a'
Ghobhainn died in 1881. His greatest poem has the heartbeats of
his countrymen in it, but also the pulses of their intellect, and an
observer a century later may confess to a sense of relief that heart
and mind combined to produce a great poem before the century
was out.

The remaining poet of note in the nineteenth century was Màiri
Nic a' Phearsain (Mary Macpherson), of Skye. She was known as
Màiri Mhór nan Oran (Big Mary of the Songs): she was, by her
own testimony,[61] seventeen stones in weight, and she sang and
composed many songs. The Rev. Kenneth MacLeod of Gigha, Mrs
Kennedy-Fraser's collaborator, recalled at the 1951 Mod having
heard Màiri Mhór singing songs at the first Gaelic Mod,[62] and she
has become something of a figure of legend. This is partly because
of several of her songs which have remained popular and partly
because she had become a legend even in her life-time, especially
in her championship of land-reform. It has been said that her songs
contributed significantly to the victory of the popular land-law
reform candidates in the Highlands in 1885 and 1886, and she was
indeed the bard of that movement. Her song "*Brosnachadh nan
Gaidheal*" ("Incitement of the Gaels")[63] was composed for the

1885 elections. Her *"Oran Beinn-Lì"* ("Song of Ben Lee")[64] recalls the Skye land-reform fighters in glowing terms, and it is clear that she took an independent and fearless stand on this issue. She shows independence of mind also in her poem *"Clò na Cùbaid"* ("The Cloth of the Pulpit"),[65] where she voices criticism of churchmen, and even of Free Churchmen. Her language here is vigorous and picturesque, combining homely metaphor with plain speaking. It is with a sense of surprise, then, that one reads her *"Oran an Diùc Chataich"* ("Song for the Duke of Sutherland"),[66] with its string of compliments. Another theme which touched her closely was a personal one. She had been imprisoned in Inverness on a charge of shop-lifting, and claimed that she had been "framed". She returns to the bitterness of this theme frequently, claiming at one point that this was the incident that had made her turn to verse, and in *"Na dh'fhuiling mi de dh'fhòirneart"* ("The Oppression I suffered")[67] producing a fine series of Biblical parallels.

Her political verse is of course of great interest in an historical context, and other parts of her work are of interest to the social historian. They do not seem to me to carry much weight as poetry, though her work has indeed a great deal of pithy, down-to-earth realism which jolts it out of the nostalgic rut of the period. She has a large number of celebratory songs on various topics, addressed to Shinty Associations and friends and dignitaries in Skye, Inverness and Clydeside. Yet, despite the very real legend of her life, what will perhaps survive longest are her evocations of Skye and the community she knew there in her youth. She belonged to the people there, and had a voice that could reach them, and that is the voice that survives. She touches, skilfully, on one of the great themes of the century in *"Soraidh leis an Nollaig ùir"* ("Farewell to the new Christmas"):[68]

> But change has come upon the clouds,
> on the hills and on the fields,
> where once kindly people lived
> now there are "big sheep" and lambs.
>
> When I came into the place
> where my people once had stayed,
> dogs were barking at my heels,
> O their welcome sounded cold.

And, when I reached the Mounds,
my grandfather's house in dust,
a clump of bracken in the room
where my heart was joyous once.

She has several songs in praise of Skye which are effective in their
blend of emotion and vowel music, and fortunate in their melodies.
The one which has the greatest density of texture is "*Nuair bha mi
òg*" ("When I was young"),[69] and part of this is translated:

I wakened early, with little sadness,
on a morning in May in Òs;
with cattle lowing as they gathered,
with the sun rising on Leac an Stòir;
Its rays were shining on the mountains,
covering over in haste night's gloom;
the lively lark sang her song above me,
reminding me of when I was young.

. . . . . .

It brought to mind many things I did then,
though some eluded me for all my days,
going in winter to waulkings, weddings,
no light from lantern but a burning peat;
there were lively youngsters, and song and dancing,
but that is gone and the glen is sad;
Andrew's ruins overgrown with nettles
reminded me of when I was young.

When I walked by each glen and hillock
where I once was carefree, herding cows,
with happy youths who have now been banished,
the native stock without pride or guile,
the fields and plains were under heath and rushes
where I often cut wisps and sheaves of corn;
could I but see folk and houses there now
my heart were light as when I was young.

It is perhaps fitting enough to end this chapter, not on the note
of the period's greatest poetry, but on the highly characteristic one

of the exile's nostalgia, tinged with anger. Our period spilled over into the twentieth century. Màiri Mhór had died in 1898, but several of the poets we have looked at were active in the early years of the twentieth century. The effective watershed is the 1914–18 War. The literary stage was being set anew some time before then, for example by the publishing activities of Ruaraidh of Erskine and Mar, the promoter of the periodicals *Am Bàrd* and *Guth na Bliadhna*, and we shall see that some of the earliest new voices came from the battlefields of France.

7

Renaissance

VIEWED FROM WITHIN the tradition, one of the most striking characteristics of Gaelic poetry in the twentieth century is that it is a poetry of innovation. We have seen before that there were phases of innovation in earlier centuries, whether these affected style or subject-matter, or both, and that there were clear instances of individuals, whose innovatory skills can be seen to be at the "cutting-edge" of the tradition: those poets who belong to the tradition in one or many ways, but who are prepared or compelled to drive new shafts into the darkness ahead. It is doubtful, however, if innovation has ever featured so largely and persistently in the Gaelic verse tradition of a period as in the present century. It has been a matter of controversy affecting readers as well as writers, and it can be said without exaggeration that virtually whole generations of writers have thrown in their lot with the innovatory styles. The older styles have survived to a muted extent, especially among older writers, but one would feel a sense of great surprise if a new writer were to appear on the scene now, using older styles. So drastic a change calls for some comment.

A difficulty which exists in discussing these matters objectively has to be admitted, particularly by one who has been deeply involved in these movements for the last thirty to thirty-five years. It is not likely that anyone can attain perspective on the matter for some time yet. And there are difficulties in discussing, from within, the work of a small group of writers who mostly belong to different circles or cliques. There is evidence, for instance, that political affiliations enter into such groupings, and that attitudes which at first might appear to be literary have political undertones. It may be that some future historian of the literature will wish to investigate these ramifications. The purpose of this work is different. For all that, personal considerations and questions of perspective dictate an approach different from that taken in some earlier chapters. The work of contemporary poets will not in the main be considered in compartmented sections, but an attempt will be made to discuss and illustrate the new styles and techniques and subjects, with a muted relation to the personalities of poets involved.

Before coming to that, which may be regarded as the core of the matter, it is desirable to sketch the conditions which are the setting, or the background, to the verse of the twentieth century. In previous centuries we have seen particular instances of poets whose personal contacts with English literature have been reflected in their work. But always behind that border contact, as it were, there were the depths of Gaelic country. There is a sense in which we can see these contacts taking place at borders which have retreated perceptibly to the west and the north over the centuries, and in such a series we would place the twentieth-century contacts in the far west of the country, in the Western Isles. This is much the same as saying that English influence has penetrated to all parts of the Gaelic area. There is now no linguistic hinterland to which the Gaelic writer can retire, except for that hinterland of the imagination which can be summoned up at times, though it too needs its defences. It might be thought that this situation needs to be pushed only a little further to reach crisis level: that the language of poetry has only a limited life-expectancy where that language is shrinking in terms of daily use, and developing use at that. This may well be so, and in that case the use of the reservoirs of the imagination and of conscious learning could only add a modest period to that life-expectancy. But we have still to discover whether a prolonged and healthy bilingualism is possible in the Scottish situation, and whether such a bilingualism can sustain a Gaelic poetic tradition of value. In addition we have now the novel development of Lowland learners of Gaelic contributing to the literature.

The pace of bilingualization is speeded up enormously for those whose careers lie in the professions, though it is possible for them also to regain lost ground through greater opportunities for reading. The 1872 Education (Scotland) Act led blatantly to the suppression of Gaelic Schools, and to the enshrining of English as the vehicle of education and advancement in Gaelic Scotland. In this context, which has been challenged only very spasmodically, the dice are heavily loaded against the survival of a secure Gaelic personality, whether in the arts or in other contexts.

It was against this background, almost predictably, that revival burgeoned. The situation of repression (whether overt or otherwise) has produced the necessary tension, as it did in Mac Mhaighstir Alasdair's time. It is of course no accident that similar tensions have operated in the wider Scottish context. The steady growth of Home Rule sentiment, and the gradual extension of devolutionary instruments, characterize the period from the mid-nineteenth century onwards, although the contrary centralizing tendencies may in many sectors of life have more than cancelled out these. There was a parallel movement in the arts, and especially in poetry, and a clear involvement among poets with political movements which aimed at Scottish independence. This can be seen clearly in the movement spear-headed by Hugh MacDiarmid, especially in the twenties and thirties, and in the work of his successors in the forties and since. Beneath the ideological attitudes, whether Communist or Socialist or otherwise, there is usually a hard core of Scottish separateness. It would, perhaps, be impossible to imagine a Scottish poetic renaissance without it.

In the Gaelic context there was indeed a strong element of Gaelic nationalism again, as in the eighteenth century and in the latter half of the nineteenth. Some at least of the poets became Scottish nationalists because they were Gaelic nationalists. It might at any rate be said, without offence to anyone's political sensibilities, that it was the desire, or the compulsion, of a Gaelic identity that kept them writing in Gaelic.

The bilingual situation, and the prominence of English in the educational system, naturally shows strongly in the poetry of the time, as it had shown in the latter part of the nineteenth century. Probably, however, English literary influence shows in a much more assimilated and pervasive way in twentieth-century verse. Some of it, indeed, makes the silent assumption that it proceeds out of a bilingual, bicultural context, and is addressed to such a public. There are other alternatives: to cultivate the Gaelic garden assiduously, and to quell English weeds with whatever will serve as pesticide in this situation, or to tend Anglicized blooms lovingly, and trample on Gaelic dockens. The former of these has sometimes been attempted. This may be one way of assessing Aonghas MacDhonnchaidh's (Angus Robertson's) Gaelic writing,[1]* and parts at least of the work of a number of other poets. But more generally, and with greater assurance as the century wore on, the Gaelic poets have frankly written out of a bilingual background, and without much self-consciousness about impinging on two literary traditions. Probably such an attitude could not have existed within a generation of the new school system introduced in 1872,

* For Notes, see pp. 318–19.

and it was rare to find it in writers who had gone to school at all in that first generation. Right on this border-line are writers such as Murchadh Moireach (Murdo Murray) and Iain Rothach (John Munro), two Lewismen who were born within a year of each other (1890 and 1889), and who had recently graduated from King's College, Aberdeen, when they joined the army in the 1914–18 War. Their writings which have survived from the battle-fields of France show the bilingual and bicultural influence strongly, sometimes in obvious ways, as where Murray's war-diary fluctuates continually between Gaelic and English,[2] sometimes in style, choice of theme or metre. Murray uses the sonnet form and the Burns stanza, and in 1916 was moved to translate Charles Murray's "Auld Scotland counts for something still".[3] Yet it was Munro, who was killed in action in 1918, who most clearly showed his sensitivity to change, and probably his war-poem *"Ar Tìr 's ar Gaisgich a thuit sna Blàir"* ("Our Land, and our Heroes who fell in Battle") is the finest early burgeoning of the "new" poetry of the century. Its novelty lies in metre and rhythm and construction, and it is clear that it was in some ways influenced by the work of his contemporaries in English poetry.

Our Land, and our Heroes who fell in Battle

(i)

Snow mantle on the mountain peaks,
like white hair lie the mist streaks,
the runnel and the moor-burn
leap and pour
tumbling and rumbling down the rough glens
that skirt and buttress the high bens;
antlered stags and red deer
roam the long slopes, heather-dun—
this is the Land of Brave Men,
a hero's land of hill and glen,
this is the Land of Brave Men.

(ii)

Many a handsome man, young, agile, quick of hand,
with gay mien matching warm heart,
who had often climbed, with strong step, light, foot-sure,
  bright

to the high upland of the great hill,
went to his meeting with death—
often fore-knowing its skaith—
went out to the war:
the green grass grows over
the shreds his enemies' arms
left, when holocaust had had its fill.

With some of them, when they were alive,
we had our differences, did not see eye to eye.
Ah! they have fallen on the battle-field:
We found them lying, wounded to death—
their unsightly dust was all that was left—
five of them lying, like fingers outstretched,
summoning, guiding,
urging fresh effort upon us,
asking us to press on, together,
as when they fell, advancing,
over the plain of the battle-field.

Stay with me for a little while,
close your eyelids over your eyes,
and in the treasure-house of your mind,
(with the soft light of early morning, calm June morning
    filling it, dawn at the back window),
in the repository of loved things,
in your soul's shrine,
there, take, cherish a picture of them
lying, as they fell, in the field;
        feel, hear
        their summons, their speech in our ear—
the ideal for which they gave their breath
        lying there
        on the slaughter-floor,
their image kept alive for us
as though a cunning craftsman had carved
a priceless memorial in stone:
        "Be ready to leap up,
        with firm step, bold, fearless,
        crossing the plain of strife,
        do not weaken, be strong,

> attack them, requite,
> destroy their trust in themselves;
> forward, forward,
> this is the road,
> set up the standard,
> firm and high,
> that the glory of Peace may come again."[4]

The translation attempts to recapture the rhythms and to suggest many of the rhymes and half-rhymes of the original. I know no work in Gaelic from the earlier part of the century which has the rhythmic strength and assurance of this poem. Unfortunately only a handful of Munro's poems survived.

Dòmhnall Mac na Ceàrdaich (Donald Sinclair) had begun to publish Gaelic poetry, at an early age, a few years earlier, and his long sea-poem, *"Là nan seachd Sìon"* ("A Day of Tempest") had appeared in the periodical *Guth na Bliadhna* in 1915 and 1916. It was a longer poem than Mac Mhaighstir Alasdair's *"Birlinn"*, and while clearly inspired by that work, has its own virtues. Sinclair's imagination and his linguistic virtuosity show in it. Yet it strikes one as another attempt to cultivate the Gaelic garden assiduously, and therein may lie the seeds of its failure. Sinclair seems slightly more in tune with the incipient innovation of his time in such a poem as *"Slighe nan seann Seun"* ("The Path of the old Spells"), where the language is indeed densely-packed but where the lines, regular as they are, show rhythmical strength and sinuousness. The poem, which laments the passing of the old Gaelic world, ends:

> No wonder my folk's churchyards beside the sea are dumb,
> no wonder tops of graves swell with the worth that's gone,
> O world, my grief no withered hour returns,
> nor can my constant wish from dead men's sleep wring words.[5]

Sinclair died young, in 1933, and his poetry, which survives in manuscript, has never been collected and published. Its importance remains to be assessed in detail.

A number of poets modified their style in a marked way, in tune with the strong reaction to the older tradition, but without cutting themselves off from that tradition significantly. Seumas Mac-Thómais (James Thomson) is a case in point. A contributor to

Guth na Bliadhna in the second decade of the century, and first crowned bard of the National Mod in 1923, his collection *Fasgnadh* (*Winnowing*), published in 1953, contains a large number of later poems which show a marked freedom of movement and structure although they do not abandon rhyme. Many of the poems are on religious themes, and both these and others have as a salient characteristic a quiet epigrammatic grace. The break-up of the native Lewis community of his youth is one of the poet's recurring themes: the early part of the century had seen heavy emigration from Lewis to the New World. A poem such as *"Tha 'm fraoch fo bhlàth"* ("The Heather is in Bloom")[6] captures this mood succinctly and with restraint, while poems such as *"Mo Ghrian-éirigh"* ("My Day-spring")[7] are effective evocations of Lewis, particularly of its coast and seascape. Love and religion are fused in an effective lyricism in the short poem *"Companaich Slighe"* (Companions on the Way"):

> On my way I have a trinity
> and two of them I love—
> the one who gave her heart to me,
> whose words I most approve,
> and He who promised me a place
> in His own heart for ever.
> In company of these two
> it's natural to seek then
> cheerfulness and kindliness,
> comeliness and tenderness;
> but how then should I view my claims
> to be the third one of the three,
> and when will these two with a heart
> in their image fashion me?[8]

Donnchadh MacDhunléibhe (Duncan Livingstone) was born in Mull in 1877, being eleven years older than Seumas MacThómais. After serving his time as an ornamental mason in Glasgow he settled in South Africa at the beginning of the century. He was still writing prose and verse in Gaelic in the 1950s and 1960s, usually on contemporary issues. He contributed a poem on the "Wind of Change" theme to the periodical *Gairm* some appreciable time before Harold Macmillan made his famous speech on that topic,[9] and he celebrated the appearance in the Southern

Hemisphere of the Russian sputnik. His poetry, like his private correspondence (which was conducted in Gaelic whenever possible) shows a strong radicalism and compassion for the underdog. In terms of Scottish politics he would have been a Jacobite rather than a Nationalist, but his championship of the black peoples, at least in his verse, was of a strongly humanitarian rather than a political kind. Here is part of his indictment of the white man in his imperialist phase:

> . . . fickle, restless like the winds that blow over Europe's north,
> the white men moved in swarming hosts; their strength like
>   yeast in dough.
> Ingenious as the Devil's son; pitiless to poor or weak;
> intolerant of rule or guide; loving sword's edge more than right.
> Courageous, without fear or fright; ready for tempest or for
>   calm;
> sure, and trusty, lacking doubt; wealth and power their two
>   gods.[10]

He links his two countries beautifully in an elegy for his wife:

Anguish

> I ought to be happy in this sun-drenched land
> with its skies of light-blue, and its plains of the greenest,
>   and the warmth of its breezes;
> a land full of blessings, of ease and of leisure,
> a land without poverty, rich in its earnings,
>   a land made for pleasure.
>
> . . . . . .
>
> But far in the northlands a vision disturbs me:
> Mull of the cold hills, where I found my darling,
>   fine rose of the garden.
> I am drawn back to Mull by her lovely remembrance;
> I would fain have lived there, with my sweetheart and treasure,
>   but fate has withheld it.
>
> And in spite of the pull of each fragrant remembrance
> I don't wish to leave the land of the blossoms,
>   the home of my love now.

In this soil there is laid my fresh rose for safe keeping;
O, love, your white hands on your bosom are folded
    in the silence that seared me.

My love, who was noble, now shrouded in windings,
in the shade of bright trees, with blossom above you,
    in your grave like a garden.
My dearest, my kind one, when the time came to call you,
and you lay all alone, you made this land holy,
    and made holy its beauty.[11]

. . . . . .

Dòmhnall Ruadh Mac an t-Saoir (Donald Macintyre) wrote
some ten thousand lines of verse in his life-time, though much of it
was not published until after his death.[12] His affiliations are much
more clearly with the village-verse tradition. He was a South Uist
man, and had inherited in that environment a rich vocabulary and
store of verse and song and story. Without abandoning that store,
he had made part of his being the radical tradition of Clydeside,
and a thorough acquaintance with the poetry of Robert Burns.
He translated some of Burns' works with brilliance, notably *"Tam
O Shanter"*[13] and *"The Twa Dugs"*,[14] and deals in a lively, sometimes ribald, but certainly disrespectful style with topics such as
Mussolini,[15] the British Establishment of the 1930s[16] or the coming
of the Unemployment "Buroo" to the Highlands.[17] In his middle
and later years his views were strongly Nationalist and Leftist (this
was a time when it was possible to hold strong Nationalist views
within the Scottish Labour Party). There are many poems of
homeland, and poems on humorous topics, in his large corpus of
verse, which constitutes a quite remarkable linguistic and socio-
logical document for this period. We may sense his flavour from
this translation of some stanzas from his song about the taking of
the Stone of Destiny:

The Stone of Destiny

    The Stone of which my grandma
    and grandpa told me stories,
    has come back as it left us—
    hurrah for the Stone!

It can be in Kerrera,
in Callander or Calvie,
so long as it's in Scotland
its own rugged home.

. . . . . .

Let us indite our verses,
and polish them for those
who took the Stone from Spain once;
if it goes back to Scone now
our nation's reputation
will stand higher than it did;
for they took it from the rabble
who sat on it with their buttocks,
and the rogues have other articles
they ought to hand back.

. . . . . .

The Dean was tired and weary
that morning when he wakened,
his eyes were red and bleary
as he rose from his bed;
he walked and walked the floor then,
now sighing and now praying,
and looking in the corner
where the Stone had been.

What a clatter and a stamping,
and a running there was there then,
and all his conversation was
"Where is the Stone?"
and "Mary, Mary Mother
what will I do tomorrow
for I know that the Queen
will go clean off her head."

He spoke, with deathly pallor,
"I could never have believed that

anyone could move it
an inch off the floor.
What Destiny's in store for me?
May Providence be kind to me—
the man who moved that Stone
was as strong as a horse."

. . . . . .

Highlanders and Lowlanders
are both now chirping proudly
elated with vainglory
since we got the Stone.
When first it came from Ireland
it then was said about it
that we would stay united
so long as it stayed.[18]

Dòmhnall Ruadh Chorùna (Donald MacDonald), of North Uist, was a composer of very popular songs, one of which *"An Eala Bhàn"* ("The White Swan") is widely known and sung. The earliest group of his poems dates from the 1914–18 War, with titles such as *"Oran Arras"* ("Song of Arras") and *"Air an Somme"* ("On the Somme"), but they are in marked contrast to John Munro's poem:[19] the horror of the Somme becomes almost trite, and the lack of clean-cut detail produces a muzziness of emotional response in the reader.[20] The main part of his verse output was on themes of local interest, with a group of poems concerning old age and approaching death. They do not have the verbal felicity of Donald Macintyre's work, nor his range of interests and sensibility, but they make very pleasant reading.

Many of the true village-poets do not achieve book publication, for reasons of a practical and financial nature, though it is likely that with their numbers growing smaller, and the demand for Gaelic books increasing, a higher proportion will be published in future years. The work of Murchadh MacPhàrlain (Murdo MacFarlane) of Melbost, Lewis, has a keen local public, and several successful songs have made him known more widely in recent years. His collection, *An Toinneamh Dìomhair*, has newly appeared (1973). Similarly, a collection by Donald J. MacDonald of South Uist is projected. It would not be difficult to name a dozen more poets of marked talent, from each of the Outer Isles, from Skye, and from other areas, whose work awaits collection and publication. Many of them are now in their sixties and seventies, and the signs are that they are not being replaced by a younger generation. There are, however, isolated instances of younger poets, like Donald R. Morrison of Scalpay (Harris), who uses both traditional and non-traditional styles. A number of these poets have contributed spasmodically to *Gairm*, and a series of poems by Lewis bards has been published in book form.[21] This continued a well-established earlier tradition of area or island anthologies, and this tradition has probably not come to an end yet.

One of the most remarkable of the poets represented in the recent anthology of Lewis rural bards was Aonghas Caimbeul (Angus Campbell), better known by his nickname Am Puilean. A collection of his poems, *Moll is Cruithneachd* (*Chaff and Wheat*) appeared in 1972, and makes an interesting study in the context of innovation and conservation. Some of the poetry belongs securely to the tradition of village-verse, some seems to be ambitiously reworking the linguistic riches of monoglot Gaelic days, while some is frankly of its own time, and of much more than local relevance. The choice of subject-matter helps in this, for some of these poems were reflections in a Polish prison-camp during the 1939–45 War. From this period also comes the hilarious "*Deargadan Phóland 1944*" ("Polish Fleas 1944"), which must have boosted the morale of the Gaelic group in Aonghas Caimbeul's Stalag. Addressing the fleas and one of his more emaciated companions together at one point, he says:

> If you followed Gaelic instead of just Polish,
> you might use a talented strategem slyly;
> you need not expire on grass-thin unfed body
> when the full lap of plenty is right by your side.
>
> See Rory More, fifteen stones to his credit,
> a plumpness derived from a lush youth in Shader,
> food with its spice that would keep you and feed you
> a twelvemonth or more if your rationed it out.[22]

There is much humour, satire and social criticism in Aonghas Caimbeul's work—qualities which appear in good measure also in his recent autobiography.[23] These qualities may be illustrated by a

quotation from his poem to the Devil, "*Am Fear nach ainmich mi*"
("The One I shall not name"):

The One I shall not name

Black Donald of the tricks,
Wily Planner, thieving Rascal,
most to-be-avoided here,
nails on you like a hay-fork;
peace you never leave behind
where you happen to visit,
strategist who's cunning, sly,
hooved and taloned destroyer.

. . . . . .

With your cloven feet of deer
from a colt's thighs protruding,
antlers of horn, you beast,
jaws and chin of a seal;
fiery vapour from your mouth,
and teeth like a sea-lion's,
devil's-light from your hide,
phosphor-gleam from your nose.

. . . . . .

How attached you are, my lad,
to this place beyond others;
it may be that Gaelic
is the language you know,
all these foreigners there
with their purposeless stammer,
hardly know about peats,
ceilidhs, tatties and herring.

. . . . . .

But you dearly love your own,
black accursed evil-doers;
giving alms from the poor,

with interest, to well-to-do;
what you do is to clart him
with soft-soap of applause,
conscience sealed in holy blubber
though the deeds he does stink.

No one else is as respected
when the coins chink in your purse;
no one gives a thought to honour—
"what the eye doesn't see . . .";
yet they like a goodly name,
searchers after excess wealth;
you're the greaser of their palms
though their faces may grimace.

. . . . . .

Here's a health to you, Donald,
I'd be better not to quarrel;
you can listen to a leg-pull
and forgive me after all;
if my luck and fortune hold,
when I reach my home again
I'll drink my glass off to the dregs
in the *Caley* to your health.[24]

A close friend and collaborator of Aonghas Caimbeul was Tormod MacLeòid (Norman Macleod), who was widely known by his sardonic pseudonym Am Bàrd Bochd (The Poor Poet). His work still awaits collection, but enough appeared in periodical form to establish his persona and his reputation. He was a poet of some range and sophistication. His work leaned towards the humorous and local, and he believed that this was the best way, perhaps the most democratic and humane way, to use his talent. A teacher of various subjects in Lewis, and latterly a teacher mainly of Gaelic, he had a hand in the production of a most lively Junior Secondary School Magazine which had a large Gaelic content—the magazine *Tàintean*—was an indefatigable collector of songs, words and traditions, an active Labour Party stalwart, and a great lover of drams and company. His humorous poems about local incidents have touches of comic genius as well as passages of very broad

humour. In a scathing satire of the proposals for crofters to earn
their living from tourism, he advises the crofter to learn his new
trade carefully:

> Buy a mutch-like chef's tall hat,
> white jacket and striped trousers;
> learn by practice how to point
> your bottom smartly upwards;
> wax and "spittle" your moustache
> until it sticks out finely;
> so no one twigs that you were born
> in these Western islands.
>
> . . . . . .
>
> But I must sound a warning
> though the words will take some finding:
> somewhere behind the cornyards
> is no toilet for the strangers;
> there's a danger there of pimples
> where the skin is somewhat tender,
> and most of all when they don't know
> a docken from a nettle.[25]

He finishes this poem on the sardonic note that the notorious
mess of pottage, and the sold birthright are going to be more tangible
rewards than a pride in independence and a good reputation.

Am Bàrd Bochd's verse reflects a lively interest in current affairs,
and he uses a mélange of prose and verse to describe a fantasticated,
but shrewdly conceived version of the Summit Meeting between
Khrushchev, Kennedy, Macmillan and de Gaulle. He could write
in a quieter, lyrical vein also, and we may leave him, a little uncharacteristically, on that note:

Glen Ramadale

> Glen Ramadale;
> my love in the dew of twilight;
> a morning glory in her hair,
> setting it alight;
> the hidden cuckoo's call
> encircling her.

I heard the cuckoo yesterday;
a shadow fell across the evening;
beauty tearing apart memory's harp
in Glen Ramadale:
Darling! where did you go?[26]

It may be worth remarking here that the concept of a short lyric of this kind had become foreign to the Gaelic tradition. I use the phrase "had become" advisedly, for although it is true to say that the longer, more exhaustive poem has always predominated in the tradition, the shorter lyrical vein was once practised. But in the modern period one of the rough rule-of-thumb tests that can be applied to a poet, to discover his attitude to the tradition is this: does he essay the short lyrical form? I forbear from suggesting the use of more complicated statistical measurements.

There were in fact some attempts also in our period to construct poems of more epic proportions, ranging from T. D. Mac-Dhòmhnuill's "*An Déidh a' Chogaidh*" ("After the War") (1921) and the epic veteran Land League champion, the Rev. Donald MacCallum's *Domhnullan* (1925), to Aonghas MacDhonnchaidh's (Angus Robertson's) *Cnoc an Fhradhairc* (1940) and Niall Ros's (Neil Ross's) *Armageddon* (1950). Of these, *Cnoc an Fhradhairc* approaches most nearly the conditions of poetry. It is grossly over-burdened with exotic (and sometimes invented) vocabulary, and carries too great a load of detail as it muses, in the words of the Foreword, "on the ethos of his race, their society—their love of home and kindred—", but it has passages of well-judged description and some lyrical inserts which raise its general temperature.

In the case of the poetry we have been considering up to this point in the chapter, where any considerable quantity of a poet's work survived or was accessible it could be seen that the older tradition was still exerting a strong influence on it. The effectiveness of that influence depended to some extent on personality, but it was also influenced by questions of age and date. Proximity to the first generation of the post-1872 regime seemed to inhibit a surrender of the traditional values, perhaps because the new external influences were less fully assimilated at that stage. Educational opportunity, and the poets' environment—both physical and job environment—influenced directions also, sometimes with interesting cross-currents being brought to bear, as in the case of Am Bàrd Bochd for example. In the main, however, a steady process of polarization can be observed, as the century advances. This polarization is no longer one simply of poetic styles but one which involves life-styles as well. The non-traditional poets belong quite clearly to a society far advanced in bilingualism and biculturalism, and are usually involved in professional or academic activities. The influence of their work, and perhaps of propaganda associated with it, has been so strong and pervasive as to win over partial converts from the ranks of the traditional poets. Both types of poetry gain prestige from publication, but the non-traditional type probably has the edge on the other in this respect. The intermediate style, which is traditional but not village-poetry, is gradually being squeezed out by this polarization. This represents a remarkable shift of style over the last half-century, and more particularly over the last thirty years. The rest of this chapter will be mainly concerned with this new poetry, which will be examined in relation to its themes and styles. There are those who feel that this verse, which is almost by definition more cosmopolitan than the other type we have characterized, is less characteristic of the Gaelic temperament, and therefore less worthy of study by students of Gaelic matters. It may be freely admitted that it offers less to the advances of antiquarians, but it may be that future generations will find in it evidences of a Gaelic genius as salient as those to be found in the poetry of earlier centuries. It would be presumptuous to attempt to give an answer one way or the other at this stage.

The poetry of the last thirty years has been dominated by a relatively small group of poets, consisting of an older generation and a younger one, with a still younger group in process of forming now. The eldest of these groups is that consisting of Somhairle MacGhilleEathain (Sorley Maclean) (b. 1911), Deòrsa Caimbeul Hay (George Campbell Hay) (b. 1915), and Ruaraidh Mac-Thómais (Derick Thomson) (b. 1921). The second wave consists of Iain Mac a' Ghobhainn (Iain Crichton Smith) (b. 1928) and Dòmhnall MacAmhlaigh (Donald MacAulay) (b. 1930). The third and youngest group has as its most prominent members at the present time the two sisters Catrìona and Mòrag NicGumaraid (Catriona and Morag Montgomery), still in their early twenties, and Aonghas MacNeacail (Angus Nicolson), who is slightly older, but a number of other poets who publish more spasmodically might seem to have affinities with this group, for example Dòmhnall Iain MacLeòid (Donald John MacLeod). Again there are poets, mainly publishing spasmodically, whose affinities with these various groups are less clearly defined, for example Uilleam Niall (William Neill), Iain Moireach (John Murray), Calum Greum (Calum Graham), Iain MacDhòmhnaill (Iain MacDonald) and Eóghan Gilios (Ewen Gillies). The poetry we are about to examine has mainly been composed within the last thirty-five years, and is still flowing fairly strongly. It seems likely, therefore, that this wave of poetry will last until the end of the century.

The chief markers of the non-traditional Gaelic verse of this century are perhaps of a technical nature, although this depends on the range of matters we class as technical. Clearly the choice and handling of rhyme, stanza form, and the usual metrical ornaments, are matters of a technical nature, and there has been a clear tendency to use these in a freer way, or to dispense at times with some of them. Rhythm, on the other hand, has come to form a more important part of the poet's technical armoury. And, especially in the case of those poets who use *vers libre*, and whose concept of writing is generally affected by views that tolerate *vers libre*, all these devices tend to be used in an organic way: that is to say, not as an adjunct to the matter of the poetry but as a vital part of the communication. But furthermore, the shaping of a poem, the progression of ideas, the symbolic devices used, the patterns that are made, may all be said to be matters predominantly of technique. A fuller and freer appreciation of what constitute the poet's technical resources would seem to be implicit in the work of the non-traditional poets, although at first sight it might seem that by departing from the rule-book of the bardic poets and their successors they were throwing technique to the winds or the wolves. If we interpret technique as widely as that, and there seems no good reason why we should not, its pervasive importance can be easily seen, and by comparison the other marker of innovation, the thematic one, dwindles to some extent in importance.

Yet in such a new departure in a poetic tradition, the choice of themes has its own obvious importance, and this may be considered first. Linked to this topic, inevitably, is the availability of the language for a wide, or new, range of topics. It is no doubt true to say that prose is the normal vehicle for the discussion of novel topics. But even if this were so, or were inevitable, poetry has need of a reservoir of words and images and concepts that belong to the world it seeks to understand or describe. And if poetry consciously excludes a significant part of the world from its purview it would seem to have relinquished a part of its own significance. A poetry, or indeed more generally a literature, that exists on a partial range of experience, and whose words are a partial vocabulary, is not operating to the top of its bent. This is one practical reason for the policy, in the case of Gaelic, of introducing new vocabulary for new concepts—a policy that is often misunderstood or derided by those who do not pause to consider the philosophy that underlies it. We shall see that there are various instances of such new vocabulary affecting thematic choices in Gaelic verse, but we can hardly anticipate what the end result will be, for poetry, of such a policy. If our theory is right there will indeed be results. The chief initiator of this policy in Gaelic, in our period, has been the periodical *Gairm*, but it has been endorsed also by the Gaelic service of the B.B.C. and by other bodies. The policy is capable of infinite extension and must only be guided by practical considerations.

Again, if we are to make a fair contrast between the new and the old poetry in the matter of themes, we must distinguish between (1) themes which *happen* to be first treated by the new poets, (2) those which are new because they concern events or subject-matter which did not exist earlier, and (3) those which were available before but for some dogmatic reason were not regarded as suitable for poetry. It is not proposed to examine this topic exhaustively, but these distinctions should be borne in mind. There could have been no post-Hiroshima poems until after 1945: no poems on the Budapest rising until after 1956; no poems about Bolsheviks until the second decade of the century. It is of some interest that such topics have become topics of poetry, although that cannot be the chief interest of poems if they are living poems. Iain Mac a' Ghobhainn brings Hiroshima into a number of his poems, and seldom as effectively as in this instance, where he parodies the air and rhythm of a popular nineteenth-century pastoral-romantic song:

> Will you go with me, my youthful maid,
> across to Japan where all our sense
> is wasting in the mighty bomb
> that fell on towns and moors and hills?
>
> Not to Uist among the trees
> or to Lewis, green among the heather,
> not a last farewell to Fiunary
> burning quietly on the kyles,

> not a hall in Glasgow or Edinburgh,
> where Duncan Bàn moves elegantly
> with a bright gun in the untruths
> that mushroom clouds about our time.[27]

Somhairle MacGhillEathain uses juxtaposition and paradox to make a point wittily about the strength of his love for Eimhir:

> As a Bolshevik who gave no heed
> to queen ever or to king,
> if we but had Scotland free,
> Scotland equal to our love,
> a white, lively, open Scotland,
> a lovely, happy heroic Scotland,
> without petty, paltry, vapid bourgeoisie,
> without the loathsomeness of capitalists,
> without sly and hateful graft,
> a mettlesome Scotland of the free,
> Scotland of our blood, of our love,
> I would break the strict law of the kings,
> I would break the sure law of the wise,
> I would proclaim you queen of Scotland
> whatever the new Republic said.[28]

Irony tinges both these poems, as also Ruaraidh MacThómais's poem "Budapest";

> A heap of corpses at the roadway's edge,
> rumble of tanks, the volley of huge guns,
> carving of bullets on a smooth wall
> writing history plain as on a plaque
> or tablet sculptured by a mason—
> now the carved face of the mason lies under the chisel.
>
> The walls of Budapest—this image will be seared
> on freedom's retina for many an age,
> though short the body's memory of pain,
> though smoke extends a pall over the wounds,
> though leaves will cover them in course of time,
> though white snow, smoothly gliding down, will freeze
> the human stench on the deserted road.[29]

We have seen the upsurge of radical feeling colouring Gaelic
poetry in the nineteenth century. There is strong evidence of this
again in the new poetry of the twentieth century. We find it at
many points in Somhairle MacGhillEathain's poetry, sometimes
taking the form of anti-landlordism and of anti-clericalism. In the
short poem *"Calbharaigh"* ("Calvary") the context is a Lowland
city one:

> My eyes are not on Calvary
> or on Bethlehem the blessed,
> but a rotting room in Glasgow
> where there's festering decay,
> and another room in Edinburgh,
> of poverty and pain,
> where a sick and scabby infant
> writhes and turns before its death.[30]

And in Dòmhnall MacAmhlaigh's *"NATO 1960"* political feeling
breaks the surface more unambiguously than is usual for this poet
(the translation is the poet's own):

NATO 1960

> The sabbath
> descending upon the town
> with silence,
> mist-fine rain drizzling
> and the wind still;
> men as if half-dead
> crawling;
>
> the question
> rising out of the image, sudden,
> frantic,
> that the hail and shout and spindrift,
> the sidetracking of a mode of life
> stored up
> in the back of the mind's safe keeping
> (livelihood and weapons of destruction)
> exploding articulation, convention,
> symbol:

"is this
what the end of the world will be like
—a sabbath crawling without question or frenzy?"

(carrying its interest)
"is this the symbol
that commands respect—
the vapid quiet before the bang?"[31]

The theme of Scottish Nationalism features prominently in the new verse. This is of course not so much a new theme as the modification of a very old one, which we have seen recurring in Gaelic verse from early times. Nationalism as distinct from a romantic patriotism does not loom large in the Gaelic verse of the twentieth century until the 1930s. There are signs of it earlier, in Dòmhnall Mac na Ceàrdaich's poetry, but the first strong wave of it comes in the poetry of the older group of non-traditional poets. We have seen it appear in MacGhillEathain's poem above. It forms the groundwork of a number of poems by Deòrsa Caimbeul Hay and Ruaraidh MacThómais. There was a notable surge of national feeling in Scotland in the early years of the War, and this finds expression in MacThómais's poem *"Faoisgneadh"*, which first appeared[32] in 1943. A longish poem, it was written in 1942–3, in RAF camps in Bradford and Cranwell. A short quotation may serve to give its flavour:

. . . . . .

O hot heart of Scotland,
break the shell of the ice you're encased in,
let the warm sun of hope come inside
to bring growth to the plants of the summer,
new summer of greatness.
Wake, wake from your slumber, array yourself then
with beauty of morning:
your history's cloak is unsmudged;
draw your mettle around you, O plaid of the blood.

Far away, on the hill-tops, I heard the blast of the bagpipes
like news of the spring of the world,
like the clean wind of March,

like the laughter of waves as they strike
on the pebbles on beaches,
like an infant's sore cry,
hunter's cry of elation—
the hope-blast of Scotland.
And I saw the kilt and the plaid,
red-coloured, bare-kneed and strong-calved,
smothering Scotland's thick bracken
with the braird of new hope.

. . . . . .

At the gate of your prison the pipes are being blown,
the chanter is tuned,
the north wind plays with the tartan.
O cut through your bonds, my country's spirit,
hold up your proud head, and stand on your rights,
blow up embers of anger, set light to your honour,
seize the chance while you have it—it has marrow and music.

Deòrsa Caimbeul Hay's nationalist verse was, much of it, composed in more distant barracks, or has its origins in these, although one poem which is no doubt a nationalistic one, even if not explicitly so, is dated "Catterick, 1942".[33] One of these poems carries an Arabic title, "*Meftah babkum Es-sabar*" ("Patience is the key to your door"),[34] and the juxtaposition of the Arab and Scottish situations adds piquancy to the poem. A different kind of perspective (of time rather than of space) is achieved in the poem "*Feachd a' Phrionnsa*" ("The Prince's Army"):

When the army forded the river,
and stood on the first fields of England,
they turned, without cry or speaking,
they looked with steadfast devotion
at Scotland; each unsheathed his sword.
They gazed silently for a while,
and promised her their strength and courage.

The sheaths screeched as the steel returned,
the pipes cried out and the march went on.

The rest of it we remember.
The promise they made then was kept
with weary steps and bloody wounds.
They set great Goliath rocking,
and, one to three, at last they fell.

They closed their spell on earth with honour—
one spell, one spell we have on earth
to show the temper of our metal,
to test the edge of our courage,
to win fame for our land or shame it.

What we ought to do is stop and turn round,
look at our land with deep affection,
with warm promise, no boast or threatenings,
and bare the blade of our hot spirit,
the old white-flaming sword of our country—
so many years of rust and slumber
have blunted it in its sheath unopened.

It was a black sleep—this is the waking.[35]

The theme of Nationalism, in various forms, continued to be an important one appearing much later also in Ruaraidh Mac-Thómais's work, e.g.:

Sheep

In the still morning the surface of the land was flat,
the wind had died down, its rumbling and thrusting
drowned under the whiteness, each snowflake at rest,
set in its soft fabric like a white blanket.
We had lost the sheep that were out on the moor
when that storm unloaded its burden,
and we spent the morning desperately seeking them.

A storm came over my country,
of fine, deadly, smothering snow:
though it is white, do not believe in its whiteness,
do not set your trust in a shroud;
my heart would rejoice

were I to see, on that white plain a yellow spot,
and understand that the breath of the Gael was coming to the
surface.[36]

Nationalistic themes are also very characteristic of Deòrsa Caimbeul Hay's more recent, and uncollected verse, but they tend
latterly to be handled in a more patently propagandist form which
does some injury to the poetry. Uilleam Niall writes on nationalist
themes also, but they loom larger in his Scots than in his Gaelic work.

Dòmhnall MacAmhlaigh finds new themes in distant places—a
perennial source of innovation in literature. A short stay in Turkey
in the middle 1950s produced a very interesting short sequence of
poems. His *"Latha Féille"* ("Holiday"), with its sense of history
and its compassion, is a very effective poem, and its free, lightly
adorned style adds to this powerful effect: simple and profound
things go well together:

Holiday

They come down from the hills
Tuesdays and Fridays
a farmer on an ass
and three daughters
bent
under creel and yashmak:

The townspeople
whom they supply with fuel and fruit
always mock their fashion—
they walk on their bare
feet.

And people come down from Ankara
to spend their holidays
who say the townspeople
are old-fashioned, prone to sloth
and dirt.

I am there
numbered among foreigners
who deride

indiscriminately
the people of that land . . .

and me as well—
since I see
with my uncouth eyes
a tradition
that overrides the world of my companions

that orders in its folds
England's queen
and Ankara
and the town, a stronghold
that has stood almost as long as the hills;

since I see
on the streets in the heat of the day
footprints in the dust:
a neat-stepping dance
of bare feet;

under black shawls
stirred by the wind of history
a living eye waiting
though burdened and disparaged;
teeth white as lime about
a tuneful tongue, and cheeks
like the pomegranate.[37]

The poem is of course given an extra piquancy by the very fact that it bears a relationship to the Gaelic community that Mac-Amhlaigh often writes about, and to the Gaelic verse tradition to which he belongs. He places neatly, with a flick of the pen, the categories of people and ideas that the poem is concerned with: not only the Turkish ones, with their grades of sophistication, but also those who think of Elizabeth as "England's queen", while the bare feet and black shawls straddle two traditions in the poet's mind.

Deòrsa Caimbeul Hay also finds some of his innovatory themes abroad. One of the finest examples of this is the poem "Atman". This poem also shows deep compassion. An ethical judgement is expressed, but in poetry's terms:

Atman

You thieved when you had need to,
you tried to lie to get off,
condemned, reviled and whipped by them,
put under lock and key.

The honourable mouth that judged you,
had small blubber lips in a grey face;
Justice was blear-eyed from studying
its account-books that were full and fat.

But the mouth they proved to be lying
was mannerly, cheerful and sweet;
I got repartee and tales there
though it often had nothing to eat.

You would lift your eye from your work
to draw pleasure from the world's shape;
you praised Jebel Yussuf* to me
its colour and its form.

I know you well, Atman,
your five youngsters and wife,
your few goats and your ass,
your plot of rye and your cow.

. . . . . .

You have tried hatred, grief and laughter,
experienced both tempest and sun,
you have tried life's texture
and never once have shrunk.

Were you wealthy, your intestines
thick with your tired ploughmen's dearth,
you would not be the lice's fellow
in the black prison of Mondovi.

When the fine judge of the court
gets an eyeful of my back,

> * An Algerian mountain.

I'll cross the street to bid you welcome
if ever I see you again.

Sidna Aissa* was crucified
with robbers on a hill's top;
it were blasphemy to deny, Atman,
that you are a brother of mine.[38]

New themes, or old themes with a difference, appear in such poems as Deòrsa Caimbeul Hay's *"Bisearta"*[39] a moving account of the conflagration at Bizerta, Somhairle MacGhillEathain's poem in which he muses on a symphony by Beethoven and the classical music of the pipes,[40] the same poet's series of poems on the conflict between love and reason,[41] Iain Mac a' Ghobhainn's poems on psychological themes, and on Freud in particular,[42] Mac-Thómais's "exile's farewell" to Lewis[43] or his poems on the Highlands seen in terms of India or Tibet,[44] or MacAmhlaigh's *"Iain a-measg na reultan"*[45] with its philosophical, amused reflections on a child's summary dealings with the laws of dynamics and gravity. There are senses in which many of these represent new approaches to old themes. Any poet who writes introspectively, or who analyses other people's minds and motives may exercise a skill in psychological understanding, but we feel that this is somewhat different to what Iain Mac a' Ghobhainn is doing in his poem *"Tha thu air aigeann m'inntinn"* ("You are at the Bottom of my Mind"):

Without my knowing it you are at the bottom of my mind
like one who visits the sea's floor
with his helmet and goggling eyes
and I don't rightly know your looks or your ways
now that five years of time's tempests
have poured between me and you:

nameless mountains of water pouring
between me, as I haul you aboard,
and your looks and your ways in my weak hands.
You went astray
in the sea-floor's mysterious foliage

        * Our Lord Jesus.

in the green half-light without love,
and you'll never come to the top of the sea,
though my hands are ever hauling without cease,
and I do not know your road at all,
you in the half-light of your sleep
haunting the bottom of the sea without rest,
and I hauling and hauling on the sea's surface.[46]

Probably such a poem needs for its groundwork an acquaintance with pycho-analytical theory, though it makes no use of technical language. Mac a' Ghobhainn's interest in such theory appears in many of the poems.

Another novel theme, which played an important part in the poetry of Somhairle MacGhillEathain, was that of the Spanish Civil War. It was the over-riding political and humanist obsession of the 1930s, and coloured English verse of that period deeply. Some of that colouring is transferred to MacGhillEathain's verse, sometimes quite deliberately, as in the echoes of John Cornford's verse, e.g. "To Margot Heinemann" and "A Letter from Aragon" in MacGhillEathain's poem *"Urnuigh"* ("Prayer"). But what is chiefly interesting about the use made of this Spanish theme is that the political passion of the time rages against the emotional or erotic passion which is the other mainspring of this poet's work in the later 1930s, and his attitude to Spain is often used as one of the touchstones of that other passion, as in this poem, which is given in Iain Crichton Smith's translation:

> I walked with my intelligence
> beside the muted sea:
> we were together, but it kept
> a little distance from me.

> And then it turned and spoke these words:
> "Is it the truth that I have heard
> that your white lovely darling
> on Monday will be wed?"

> I checked the bitter heart that rose
> in my swift torn side
> and answered: "It is certain.
> Why should I have lied?"

How could I think that I could catch
that jewelled golden star
and place it in a prudent purse
where my wise treasures are?

I who avoided the sore cross
and agony of Spain,
what should I expect or hope,
what splendid prize to win?

I who took the coward's way,
the mean road of the slave,
how should I expect to meet
the thunderbolt of love?

Yet, if I had a second chance,
still standing, proud and tall,
I'd jump with undivided heart
from heaven or from hell.[47]

The younger poets, of the late fifties and sixties, despite political
leanings to the left, have not brought Vietnam into Gaelic verse in
a comparable way, but political viewpoints have added interest and
colour to recent work, as in this poem by Catrìona NicGumaraid
(Catriona Montgomery):

I see you supervising the tables,
your fine-checked, pleated kilt to the knee.
You talk loudly, shouting—
the badge of the education you got
in a college whose reputation is a mystery to most.
And you came to dig your livelihood in this village,
to fill your belly like a worm
with the earnings of poor creatures
who spend their health scraping
a livelihood from the lazy-beds
that climb from the shore Park to Healabhal—
perhaps that will bring peace to your shallow mind—
the sprightly little tit-larks still find the large silly cuckoo.
And I think when I see you with your feathers proudly cocked
that Catherine the Great of Russia has come from the grave to
    visit us.[48]

We can see that there is undoubtedly novelty in choice of themes in the new poetry, and this includes a whole class of private and personal poems which would not easily have been committed to print in earlier periods, and probably this reticence extended further, so that few would have been composed either. The "public" character of Gaelic verse had become a deeply ingrained one. We must exclude the passionate "folk" love-songs of an earlier period from this generalization, as also the laments, which could be personal enough. But there was a feeling abroad that it was improper for a poet to stand up, as it were, while in his right mind, and deal with his private affairs in public. It was an attitude understandable in a small society, and especially in a strongly oral tradition.

Changes in society have led inevitably to this literary change. We see it demonstrated in many ways: in love-poems by most of the poets discussed, in poems by Iain Mac a' Ghobhainn about his mother, in poetry describing the author's thoughts and feelings about his native community. This latter theme falls into a broad class very familiar in the previous period: the songs of homeland. Perhaps nowhere is the change of direction in the poetic tradition so starkly shown as here, with the new poetry leaning no longer on simple nostalgia or on melodic sweetness, but bringing to bear a complex set of emotions, analyses and rationalizations to describe the poet's relationship to his theme. The modern fashion of introspective analysis, with various degrees of conscious sophistication, adds a new dimension to poetry of this kind, and the relative freeing of personal inhibition makes this poetry on an old theme very different to the old poetry. We shall have occasion to quote examples of work on these themes of love and homeland later in this chapter.

Yet what makes this poetry different from its predecessor is not wholly, and not mainly differences in theme, in interpretation of theme, or in the poet's standpoint *vis-à-vis* society, though this last point is close to the heart of the matter. The main difference lies in the structure of the poetry.

The traditional structure was basically linear. A poem had a rational progression, based largely on concepts of description, and it attempted to fit facets of the theme into a composite picture, which could be assessed as a photograph is assessed. This structure was not, of course, confined to poems of a descriptive or naturalistic nature. With modifications, it can be seen to fit, for example, the poems of political argument, or the religious verse of Dùghall Bochanan, or even the philosophical elegies of Rob Donn.

As an alternative to this type of structure many of the new poems use one which is not linear, and which has a freer time progression. These fundamental differences allow the poem a closer relationship to the creative sequence or process: they allow it to record or simulate the creative process. It is likely that the widespread interest in psychological processes has put something of a premium on poetry which is constructed in this way. This is not, of course, to suggest that such a way of making poetry is new. But in the Gaelic context—and the same is true to some degree of the English one also—the non-linear poem structure belongs to this century as a generalized phenomenon.

There can be many different kinds of realization of non-linear structure. At times the subject is scarcely capable of linear development, as in this instance, a poem by Dòmhnall MacAmhlaigh. The poem is entitled *"Do Fhear-sgrìobhaidh ainmeil"* ("To a famous Writer"). The point to be made, obliquely and in poetic terms, is that the writer in question no longer takes pains over his writing, and is contented with some sort of posturing. There is little artistic interest in making a statement in these terms, and perhaps it is offensive to paraphrase a poem thus crudely, even to illustrate a theme. MacAmhlaigh, at any rate, sets up the situation in one context (a concrete one), that of the fisherman gathering bait, doing this meticulously and with exact references and then finally and suddenly applies the whole image (which is virtually the whole poem):

> The black slabs were slippery;
> who could keep his feet
> but one who knew how to read
> the suction of the tide?
> —and he was without doubt skilled
> in finding his point of balance
> on the tips of rocks:
>
> his practice was to go down each spring-tide
> to poke among the tangle,
> to catch the shrimps
> and pull out the brown crabs;
>
> but the shellfish
> he used for bait

had a rest from his hook and tooth:
he was content
with the contortions of his dance
on the slippery surface.[49]

Ruaraidh MacThómais's poem "*Air Mòinteach Shuardail*" ("On Swordale Moor") is another example of the technique of making a statement in terms of another system. Here the character in question is a Lewisman who has re-settled in Lewis after long years in South America. This is another slant—an ironic one—on the theme of nostalgia for the homeland.

At daybreak you set out
for Swordale moor.
It was hardly reminiscent of the pampas,
but you had your dog at heel
and spoke to him in Spanish.
Passing Keose Loch
you saw a rowan growing on an island,
with no other tree in sight,
and you remembered the forests of Chile,
Punta Arenas and Santiago,
women wearing the mantilla,
and wine, and fruits,
and a ship leaving the quay in Valparaiso.[50]

Non-linear structure can be seen not only in single poems but also in extended sequences. The last poem quoted comes from such a sequence, *An Rathad Cian* (*The Far Road*), which attempts to analyse a community, and the poet's complex and changing relationship to it, in poetic terms. The structure of Somhairle Mac-GhillEathain's sequence *Dàin do Eimhir* (*Poems to Eimhir*) is non-linear also. Here the links are made, e.g. by recurring references to Spain and the complex relationship in which the poet finds himself in relation to Spain and to Eimhir, or by the recurring use of images of light and jewels, or by reference to the continuing though changing conflict between love and reason. These are the two main unified sequences of poems in our period, but both Dòmhnall MacAmhlaigh and Iain Mac a' Ghobhainn have sequences, e.g. MacAmhlaigh's "homeland" series and his love series, and Mac a' Ghobhainn's "*Ochd Orain airson Céilidh Ùir*"

("Eight Songs for a new Ceilidh"),[51] and *"An t-Oban"* ("Oban"), which is here quoted entire. In this poem Mac a' Ghobhainn brings the twin themes of his Gaelic collection, Bibles and Advertisements, together brilliantly, in the final section:

Oban

(1)

The rain is steadily drenching Oban,
and the circus has gone home:
the lions and the wild-cats
and the other beasts (we have no Gaelic
for them). They went home
through the papers, advertisements.
The seats are emptying
at the sea-front, in front of the houses,
in front of the hotel—rain falls
into the midst of the heavy brine of the sea.

(2)

Shall I build a town of paper,
with coloured lions on the wall,
with huge savage tigers,
the big wheel with its music turning?

Shall I build a paper sky,
paper clouds, white lights?
Shall I build myself of paper,
with my verses being cut on paper?

(3)

The sea tonight is like an advertisement,
book after book shining.
My shadow runs down to the sea.
My skin is red and green.

Who wrote me, who makes a poetry
of advertisements from my bones?
I will brandish my blue fist at them:
"A strong Highlander with his language".

(4)

The circus has gone home.
They've swept away the sawdust.
The pictures of the animals are gone.
Rain is falling on the bay.

The big wheel has taken itself off.
The season is over now.
The lion is running through sunlight.
He has given a clean pair of heels to the rain.

(5)

The great bell began to chime.
The church is opened.
I sat down in it, in my imagination,
and I saw on the window
instead of Nazareth and Christ
beaten earth and sawdust,
a lion moving in the explosive circle
of Palestine without cease.[52]

The new poetry is also characterized by its use of images and symbols, and perhaps conversely by its hyper-sensitive avoidance of clichéd images of the past. MacAmhlaigh, in one of his series of poems on his own relationship to his native island (which he insists is Bernera rather than Lewis), uses powerfully the image of the iceberg:

Landmark

There goes the island out of sight
as the boat sails on,
as seen by many a bard
through sorrow and beer
and by others, tongue under tooth,
and tears blinding—
an ill-defined shadow and windows fading.

But the matter is not so simple
to the one who's a yearly pilgrim
out of returning sorrow rises
from a region the world has derided.

And, that is not my island;
it submerged long ago
the greater part of it
in neglect and tyranny—
and the part that submerged in me of it,
sun-bower and iceberg,
sails the ocean I travel,
a primary landmark
dangerous, essential, demanding.[53]

The imagery of Somhairle MacGhillEathain's "*Rinn sgian m'eanchainn gearradh*" is developed in detail throughout the poem:

The knife of my intellect made a cut
in my love's stubborn stone.
The blade tested every part.
Its scrutiny was keen.

I turned each section of the stone
to the inspecting glass
of the intellect sparkling in its own
chill and searching space.

But after glass and knife and fire
the blade's piercing ray,
after the cutting, burning stare,
there was no change in the stone's hue.

The enchanted stone cut by the ardour
of my keen intelligence
(though pounded lightly into powder)
remained entire and hard and dense.

And the more it was broken to a myriad
scattered pieces in my sight
the more it became a monad,
compact, adamant and white.

It expanded to a thousand oceans,
each part a drop within a wave.

but all the water in its motion
contracted to my massive love.

The stone my intellect had cut
in its cold hard inspecting course
gathered to the arrogant light
and majesty of a universe.

Struck from my breast, its greatness
was measureless to my eye.
It crouched in its giant brightness
like Betelgeuse in the sky.

The love-stone springing from my head
by paradox of active passion
became the genesis of the red
skies of the mind's imagination.

The love begotten by the heart
is a love that dances in its chains
when it embraces intellect—
love of the scrutinizing brain.

And the stone that's always broken
by the assiduous mind
becomes a bright entire stone
made harder by each new wound.

Dearest, if my heart's love
were not as strong as the jewelled stone
surely the intellectual knife
would have cut it from my flesh and bone.[54]

More lyrical, and less elaborated, is the imagery of MacThómais's
"*Achadh-bhuana*" ("Harvest Field"):

One deceptive evening, among the sheaves,
with some of the corn uncut, you came by,
and I put my scythe then in hiding
for fear that the edge of the blade would cut you.

Our world was rounded like the harvest field,
though a part was ripe and a part green,
the day to work and the night to dream,
and the moon rose in the midst of content.

I left a little to cut on the morrow,
and we walked together between the swathes;
you fell on a scythe that another had left,
and your skin was cut, and refused healing.[55]

The image of the wedge is very effective in Aonghas MacNeacail's short poem:

This is the new Road

This is the new road:
we'll go together
down to a river
   bold and certain.

Flaunting plumage on our cloak
and a warm breeze in our soul:
   we will not be wedged between
      death and eternity.

O comrade, we will not think of
   yesterday, that's history:
      we will not listen to the ploughman's warning.

Now we will be,
tomorrow, sleep will come.[56]

On the other hand, a simple unadorned style can be most effective, especially in the creation of atmosphere, as in Iain MacDhòmhnaill's "*Turas*" ("Journey"):

We went back in the evening
to where we had been cutting.
We reached the bay in the boat.

High-tide near
and the seaweed beginning to float.
We began to collect it.

The sea was lukewarm.
We pulled the rope hard,
made it fast at the edge.

It was not too large a raft of seaweed
but it was thick, well-packed.
It would grow enough potatoes for us.

We set off with it,
tied to the thwart.
The gathering held, did not give way.

It had grown cold
before we got home, a red splash
in the west growing larger.

A pale moon
rising, a petticoat
of clouds below it, a high-tide calm.

That was another night, another year.[58]

MacGhillEathain has several poems of great lyrical purity and
intensity, as this one:

My boat was under sail, the Clàrach
with laughter at its bows,
my left hand on the tiller
and the other holding the sheet.

On the second thwart, to windward,
you sat, love, by my side,
with your flaming rope of hair
gold-entwined about my heart.

O God, if but our voyage
were to the goal I desire,

the distant Butt of Lewis
were too near for my sail.[57]

It was suggested already that there was a close correlation between the use of non-traditional poem structure and non-traditional
metres, but this is far from being a one-for-one correlation. The
subject can only be touched on here, as it is particularly difficult to
discuss matters of metre, rhythm and those elements of style which
depend heavily on language, except by direct reference to the
original language. But a general summary can be attempted.

The range of metrical and rhythmical pattern and experiment
over the period is considerable. None of the poets restricts himself
entirely to one type of metrical technique, but naturally clear
predilections can be discerned where there is a sufficient volume of
work. Sometimes a clear movement can be seen over the period.
Deòrsa Caimbeul Hay's work, particularly the earlier part of it,
shows the strongest interest in traditional metrical technique, and
carries this interest so far as to reproduce many of the effects of the
strict metres, although not being bound by these. The metrical
effects of the Irish *trì rainn is amhrán*, a sixteen-line poem which is a
near-equivalent of the sonnet, are several times reproduced by him,
following the pattern of Irish *dánta grádha* or love-songs. It is of
interest that Hay translated a number of Petrarchan sonnets[59]
successfully, and has always showed a keen interest in metrical
translation. Apart from these instances, Hay favours on the whole
the rhyming quatrain. Yet already in his first collection (the Foreword is dated late 1947) he was showing a freedom of movement,
albeit with fairly regular rhymes within sections, in such a poem
as *"Tilleadh Uiliseis"* ("The Return of Ulysses"). This poem is
quoted in full (in a translation which conveys only some of its
rhythmical variety, and not its rhyming patterns) since it is a good
example of a successful organic matching of metre and rhythm to
content, and since this fine dramatic reconstruction of Hay's is so
well worth quoting for its own sake generally.

The Return of Ulysses

I

The son of Laertes reached,
a little before day broke,
Ithaca and the shores of his youth.

In the melancholy moments
before the sun rises suddenly, the high ship
was close in the lee of the old coast.

The aged world was stirring,
sighing under the growing burden of centuries;
a sigh of longing for the sun
in every creature's mouth before daybreak;
and the highest peak newly golden.
> He was asleep, and the boat,
> with lively movement, was kicking foam from her heel,
> weathering the well-known bays and headlands.

In the dark of the dewy woods
and the close-set thickets, birds busied with their broods,
cheeped their intermittent complaints;
a sandpiper on the tide-mark
was calling out its hurt in the half-light.
And still Ulysses slept a sleep of peace,
tired after exile.
> After action and wandering,
> like a child, he slept
> wrapped in his cloak.

II

Ulysses slept;
and they left him stretched on the shore,
along with all his riches.

He slept. And when he wakened
he did not recognize the land he loved,
for the goddess had covered it with mist.

The tick-infested blind old dog
was the first living creature to recognize him
when he came back alive from hundreds of torments.

Unwelcomed and unknown,
a butt for others' mockery,
he found a corner in his lordly dwelling.

III

Chewing his anger, disguised as a beggar
in his own fortress, stormy
was his sidelong glance under his brows at
    the banquet of the chiefs.

Then, his bow-string sang loud,
cool the waft of his arrows
through the hall on the cheeks of the throng.

Many a haughty drunkard was pierced,
left off his mockery and laughter,
and slumped in his own blood, his red
    hands at his throat.

And many a soft suitor was knocked down,
falling face-first, spewing a puddle of blood
amongst the wine, meat, bread, goblets and chessmen.[60]

Hay's second collection (1952) still shows a strong interest in rhymed and regular metres, and includes a large number of rhymed translations, but it also includes more poems in irregular and especially in irregularly rhymed metres than did his first. He seldom lets go of rhyme, although he does this successfully for a moment here and there in such a poem as *"Bisearta"*.[61] The use of irregular rhyme, however, is highly effective here and in other poems such as *"Ar Blàr Catha"*.[62]

Somhairle MacGhillEathain is less attracted to the bardic metres, but uses regular rhyming metres to an even greater extent than Hay. The poems in *Dàin do Eimhir* use in an overwhelming majority of cases such regular rhymed metres, the quatrain being by far the commonest, with the rhymed couplet also very popular. He uses also various varieties of five-, six-, seven-, and eight-line stanzas. In a handful of instances rhymes occur at irregular intervals, and there are two unrhymed poems in the collection. A strong predilection for monorhyme shows, whether in the couplet or in more extended sequences. To compensate, as it were, for this regularity, his rhythms are strong and varied, and this often disguises the relative monotony of the rhyming patterns. MacGhill-Eathain has not published much since *Dàin do Eimhir* appeared in 1943. His *"Coille Hallaig"*, a longish poem which appeared in

1954, is in rhymed quatrains, and his *"Cumha Chaluim Iain MhicGill-Eain"* ("Lament for Calum Maclean"), which appeared in 1970, uses regular and irregular rhymed stanzas. Of three poems published in *Contemporary Scottish Verse 1959–1969* (1970) two use irregular rhyme patterns, and in one of these the rhymes are tending to become minimal. There would seem, on that evidence, to be a movement away from regular rhyme. On the other hand, in various public poems, especially those composed in his capacity as Bard to the Gaelic Society of Inverness, we can see a strong tendency to use the traditional eight-line rhyming metre. Overall, however, the couplet and the quatrain are the stanzas most closely characteristic of the metrical side of his work, as in the fine poem *"Ban-Ghaidheal"*. The translation suggests the rhythm to some extent; in addition, the rhyme-pattern of the original quatrains is a b c b, with, normally, internal rhyme in the second couplet:

Highland Woman

Have You seen her, mighty Jew
who's called the Only Son of God?
Seen her like upon Your way,
at distant vineyard's toil?

A load of grapes upon her back,
bitter sweat on brow and cheek;
vessel of heavy clay upon
her bent, poor, wretched head.

You have not seen her, Joiner's Son
whom they call the Glory King,
among the rugged western coasts
sweating beneath the creel.

This spring and that spring that is gone,
and every score of springs there were,
she carried the cold seaweed for
her children's food and her lord's fee.

Each twenty autumns that have gone
she lost the summer's yellow bloom;
black drudgery has ploughed a rut
across her white and smooth-soft brow.

And Your kindly Church declaimed
of the lost state of her wretched soul;
and relentless drudgery laid
her body in the grave's black peace.

Her time has gone like sooty ooze
drenching the thatch of a poor home;
hard black drudgery was hers;
grey the sleep she sleeps tonight.[63]

The metrical pattern of Iain Mac a' Ghobhainn's main Gaelic collection, *Bìobuill is Sanasan-reice* (1965) is an interesting one. He shows a fairly strong predilection for regular rhymed stanzas, especially quatrains, but uses three-, five-, six- and eight-line stanzas also. His three- and eight-line stanzas are normally rhymed, but the other varieties are usually unrhymed. There is a strong representation of unrhymed poems, and in fact some two-fifths of the poems in this collection use irregular rhyme, minimal rhyme or no rhyme at all. This pattern confirms and accentuates the metrical pattern which appears in the verse section of his earlier book *Bùrn is Aran* (1960). Throughout his work, his rhymes tend to be subdued, often half-rhymes even in the laxer terms of modern Gaelic rhyme. The poem "Oban", quoted above (p. 282) may be regarded as fairly typical of Mac a' Ghobhainn's metrical style, moving as it does from the minimal irregular rhyme of the first paragraph, to the rhymed quatrains of the second, the unrhymed and rhymed quatrain (one of each) in the third section, to the similar pattern of the fourth, and to the final eight-line section with only one closing rhyme.

The two remaining poets—Ruaraidh MacThòmais and Dòmhnall MacAmhlaigh—of the five poets we have been chiefly discussing in this section, are the main exponents of *vers libre* in Gaelic. MacThòmais's first collection, *An Dealbh Briste* (1951) has a considerable number of poems using regular rhymed stanzas, especially quatrains, but including other types, even a ten-line stanza with rhyme a b b a b c a b b b.[64] Yet already approximately one-third of the poems are in some form of irregularly rhymed or unrhymed verse. Considerable use is made of internal rhyme, though in a form different from the traditional use made of this. These tendencies already appear in the poem published in 1943.[65] In *Eadar Samhradh is Foghar* (1967) the same tendencies are confirmed, with poems of a non-traditional kind forming more than half the total. *An Rathad Cian* (1970) goes over, virtually entirely, to *vers libre*. There are many novel developments in the use of rhythm in this body of verse, including a simulation of speech-rhythms used to gain a range of effects. Some of these may be suggested in this translation of "*Cisteachan-laighe*", from MacThómais's middle period:

Coffins

A tall thin man
with a short beard,
and a plane in his hand:
whenever I pass
a joiner's shop in the city,
and the scent of sawdust comes to my mind,
memories return of that place,
with the coffins,
the hammers and nails,
saws and chisels,
and my grandfather, bent,
planing shavings
from a thin, bare plank.

Before I knew what death was;
or had any notion, a glimmering
of the darkness, a whisper of the stillness.
And when I stood at his grave,
on a cold spring day, not a thought
came to me of the coffins
he made for others:
I merely wanted home
where there would be talk, and tea, and warmth.

And in the other school also,
where the joiners of the mind were planing,
I never noticed the coffins,
though they were sitting all round me;
I did not recognize the English braid,
the Lowland varnish being applied to the wood,
I did not read the words on the brass,

I did not understand that my race was dying.
Until the cold wind of this Spring came
to plane the heart;
until I felt the nails piercing me,
and neither tea nor talk will heal the pain.[66]

MacAmhlaigh's work, collected in *Seòbhrach ás a' Chlaich* (1967) shows a distinct preference for *vers libre*. A high proportion of his poems use irregular or minimal rhyme, or no rhyme at all. A small minority of the poems (approximately one-eighth of them) use regular rhyme, usually in quatrains, but his characteristic form is the minimally or irregularly rhymed variable verse paragraph, also using internal rhyme in non-traditional ways. His rhythms are very subtle, and vary widely, being an organic part of his verse technique. Some of this is suggested in his own translation of "*An t-sean-bhean*":

Old Woman

You walked feeble,
with your stick,
down by the wall;
you stopped and raised
the weight of your bent head,
you put your hand
between your eyes and the sun.

From that shade
you stared out at the spring,
at the furrow the plough turned;
at the boundaries of the croft
and the mountain
(and you looked to see the cow was not trapped).

And you turned, then,
your feet—
no space between them and the ground—
and walked them stiffly
in
(with your stick
and a hand on the wall)

to the house
where the threshold had grown
into an obstacle.

And you sat there in your seat.[67]

In the original especially, the rhythms, line-lengths and the weight of particular words, form a perfect expression of the poet's thought.

We are not concerned with prophecy in this account of Gaelic poetry over the centuries, but looking back over the history of that poetry we can scarcely fail to notice how tenacious tradition has been, and yet how innovation is eventually acclimatized within tradition. In the poetry of the last half-century or less we have seen such a process largely accomplished once again, and the possibilities of exploitation of new and new-old styles seem considerable still. The reservoir of talent still seems formidable, for a relatively small population, and we may await the next half-century with lively interest.

BIBLIOGRAPHY

Bibliography

Adv. MS. 72.1.48 (Old Gaelic MS., Nat. Lib. of Scot., XLVIII)
Ais-Eiridh na Sean-Chanoin Albannaich (Mac Mhaighstir Alasdair's Poems), Edinburgh, 1751
Am Bàrd, Edinburgh, 1901–2
An Gaidheal, An Comunn Gaidhealach, Glasgow, 1923–66
Bàrdachd Leódhais. See MacLeòid, Iain N.
Book of the Dean of Lismore. See Watson, W. J., Ross, Neil, and Quiggin, E. C.
Brant, S., *The Ship of Fools* (trans. William Gillis), The Folio Society, 1971
Bromwich, Rachel S., "The Continuity of the Gaelic Tradition in Eighteenth-Century Ireland," in *Yorkshire Celtic Studies*. IV
Brøndsted, J., *The Vikings*, Pelican, Harmondsworth, 1960
Butler, W. F. T., *Gleanings from Irish History*, Longmans, London, 1925
Caimbeul, Aonghas, *Moll is Cruithneachd*, Gairm Publications, Glasgow, 1972
Caimbeul, Aonghas, *Suathadh ri Iomadh Rubha*, Gairm Publications, Glasgow, 1973
Calder, George (ed.), *Gaelic Songs by William Ross*, Oliver and Boyd, Edinburgh, 1937
Cameron, Alexander, *Reliquiae Celticae*, 2 vols., Inverness, 1892, 1894
Cameron, Hector (ed.), *Na Bàird Thirisdeach*, The Tiree Association, Glasgow, 1932
Campbell, John, *Poems*, Edinburgh, 1884
Campbell, J. F. (ed.), *Leabhar na Féinne*, Irish Universities Press, 1972
Campbell, J. L. (ed.), *Gaelic Folksongs from the Isle of Barra*, The Linguaphone Institute, for the Folklore Institute of Scotland, n.d.
Campbell, J. L. and Collinson, F. (ed.), *Hebridean Folksongs*, Clarendon Press, Oxford, 1969
Campbell, J. L. (ed.), *Highland Songs of the Forty-Five*, John Grant, Edinburgh, 1933
Campbell, J. L., "The Royal Irish Academy Text of 'Birlinn Chlann Raghnaill'," in S.G.S., IX, 39–79
Carmichael, A. (ed. A. Matheson), *Carmina Gadelica*, Vol. v, Oliver and Boyd, Edinburgh, 1958
Carney, J. and Greene, D. (edd.), *Celtic Studies: Essays in memory of Angus Matheson 1912–1962*, Routledge, London, 1968
Carswell. See Thomson, R. L. (ed.)
Celtica (Edd. T. F. O'Rahilly; M. Dillon). Dublin Institute for Advanced Studies, 1946–
Child, F. J., *English and Scottish Popular Ballads* (ed. H. C. Sargent and G. L. Kittredge), London, 1904
Co-chruinneachadh Nuadh do dh'Orannibh Gaidhealach, Inverness, 1806

Craig, K. C. (ed.), *Orain Luaidh*, Glasgow, 1949
Cúirt Fhilíochta, *Eire-Alba 1972*, Comhdháil Náisiúnta na Gaeilge.
Dublin, 1972
de Saussure, Necker, *Voyage en Écosse et aux Îles Hébrides*, Geneva, 1821
Dòmhnallach, Dòmhnall, *Dòmhnall Ruadh Chorùna*, Gairm Publications,
Glasgow, 1969
Dunn, Charles W., *Highland Settler: A Portrait of the Scottish Gael in
Nova Scotia*, University of Toronto Press (reprint), 1968
Eigg Collection. See MacDomhnuill, Raonuill, *Comh-chruinneachidh
Orannaigh Gaidhealach*
Éigse (ed. G. Murphy; B. O Cuív), Dublin, 1939–
Ériu, Royal Irish Academy, Dublin, 1904–
Fernaig MS. See MacPhàrlain, Calum.
Gaelic and Scots Folk Tales . . . Folk Songs . . . University of Edinburgh,
1960
Gairm (ed. Ruaraidh MacThómais), Glasgow, 1952–
Gillies, Eòin, *Sean Dain . . .* (The Gillies Collection), Perth, 1786
Grannda, Gilleasbuig, *Dàin agus Orain*, Inverness, 1863
Grimble, Ian, "John Mackay of Strathan Melness, Patron of Rob Donn",
in S.G.S., X
Guth na Bliadhna (ed. Ruaraidh of Erksine and Mar), Edinburgh . . .
Glasgow, 1904–25
Hanham, H. J., *Scottish Nationalism*, Faber and Faber, London, 1969
Hay, Deòrsa Caimbeul, *Fuaran Sléibh*, William Maclellan, Glasgow, 1947
Hay, Deòrsa Caimbeul, *O na Ceithir Airdean*, Oliver and Boyd, Edinburgh,
1952
Hector Maclean's MS.
Henderson, George (ed.), *Dàin Iain Ghobha*, Glasgow and Edinburgh,
1896
Inverness Collection. See *Co-chruinneachadh Nuadh do dh'Orannibh
Gaidhealach*
Jackson, K. H., "The Poem *A Eolcha Alban uile*", in *Celtica*, III
Journal of the Folk-song Society (J.F.S.) (No. 16. Collection by Frances
Tolmie), London, 1911
Kennedy-Fraser, M., *Songs of the Hebrides*, Boosey and Co., London,
c. 1909–21
Lamont, Donald, *Strath: In (the) Isle of Skye*
Lindsay, Maurice (ed.), *Modern Scottish Poetry*, Faber and Faber,
London, 1946
Lines Review (ed. Alan Riddell . . . Robin Fulton), M. Macdonald, Edin-
burgh, 1952–
L. na F. See Campbell, J. F.
Mac a' Ghobhainn, Iain, *Bìobuill is Sanasan-reice*, Gairm Publications,
Glasgow, 1965
Mac a' Ghobhainn, Iain, *Bùrn is Aran*, Gairm Publications, Glasgow,
1960
MacAirt, Seán, "Filidecht and Coimgne", in *Ériu* XVIII (1958)
MacAmhlaigh, Dòmhnall, *Seòbhrach ás a' Chlaich*, Gairm Publications,
Glasgow, 1967

Mac an t-Saoir, Dòmhnall Ruadh (ed. Somerled Macmillan), *Sporan Dhòmhnaill*, Scottish Gaelic Texts Society, Edinburgh, 1968

Mac-an-Tuairneir, Paruig, *Comhchruinneacha do dh'Orain taghta, Ghaidhealach*, Edinburgh, 1813

MacBean, Lachlan, *Buchanan the Sacred Bard of the Scottish Highlands*, Simpkin, Marshall, Hamilton Kent and Co., London, 1919

MacCaig, Norman and Scott, Alexander (edd.), *Contemporary Scottish Verse, 1959–1969*, Calder and Boyars, London, 1970

MacCaluim, Dòmhnall, *Domhnullan*, Alexander MacLaren and Sons, Glasgow, 1925

MacCoinnich, Iain (ed.), *Orain Ghàelach le Uilleam Ros*, Glasgow, etc., 1834

MacColla, Eóghan, *Clàrsach nam Beann*, Archibald Sinclair, Glasgow, 1937

MacDhonnchaidh, Aonghas, *An t-Ogha Mór*, Alexander MacLaren and Sons, Glasgow, 1913

MacDhonnchaidh, Aonghas, *Cnoc an Fhradhairc*, Alexander MacLaren and Sons, Glasgow, 1940

MacDhunléibhe, Uilleam, *Duain agus Orain*, Glasgow, 1882

MacDiarmid Collection (1770). In MS.; as yet unpublished.

MacDiarmid, J. M., *The Deer Forests and how they are bleeding Scotland White*, The Scottish Home Rule Association, Glasgow, 2nd ed., 1926

MacDomhnuill, Raonuill, *Comh-chruinneachidh Orannaigh Gaidhealach* [Eigg Collection], Edinburgh, 1776

MacDonald, A. and A. (edd.), *The MacDonald Collection of Gaelic Poetry*, Inverness, 1911

MacDonald, A. and A. (edd.), *The Poems of Alexander MacDonald*, Inverness, 1924

MacDonald, A. R. (ed. Mackinnon, D.), "The Truth about Flora MacDonald", *The Northern Chronicle*, Inverness, 1938

Macdonald, John (ed.), *Ewen MacLachlan's Gaelic Verse*, University of Aberdeen, 1937

MacDonald, K. N. (ed.), *The Gesto Collection of Highland Music*, 1895

MacEacharn, Dòmhnall, *Am Fear-ciùil*, An Comunn Gaidhealach, Glasgow, 1940

MacFarlane, M. See MacPhàrlain, Calum

MacGhillEathain, Somhairle, *Dàin do Eimhir agus Dàin Eile*, William McLellan, Glasgow, 1943

Macinnes, John, *The Evangelical Movement in the Highlands of Scotland*, Aberdeen, 1951

Mackechnie, E. E. (ed.), *The Poems of John Roy Stewart*, Sgoil Eòlais na h-Alba, Glasgow, 1947

Mackechnie, John (ed.), *The Dewar Manuscripts*, W. McLellan, Glasgow, 1964

Mackenzie, Annie M. (ed.), *Orain Iain Luim: Songs of John MacDonald Bard of Keppoch*, Scottish Gaelic Texts Society, Edinburgh, 1964

Mackenzie, John (ed.), *Sar-obair nam Bard Gaelach*, Edinburgh, 1877

Mackenzie, W. Mackay, *The Poems of William Dunbar*, The Porpoise Press, Edinburgh, 1932

MacLagan MSS. *c*. 1755–1803. In Glasgow University Library

Maclean, Donald (ed.), *The Spiritual Songs of Dugald Buchanan*, John Grant, Edinburgh, 1913

Maclean, Sam, "Mairearad Nighean Lachainn", in T.G.S.I., XLII

MacLeod, D. J., "The Poetry of Rob Donn Mackay", in S.G.S., XII, 3 ff

MacLeod, A. (ed.), *Sàr Orain*, An Comunn Gaidhealach, Glasgow, 1933

MacLeod, A. (ed.), *The Songs of Duncan Ban Macintyre*, Scottish Gaelic Texts Society, Edinburgh, 1952

MacLeod, M. C. (ed.), *Modern Gaelic Bards*, Eneas Mackay, Stirling, 1908

MacLeòid, Iain N. (ed.), *Bàrdachd Leódhais*, A. MacLaren and Sons, Glasgow, 1916

MacLeòid, Niall, *Clàrsach an Doire* (5th ed.), Alexander MacLaren and Sons, Glasgow, 1924

MacLeòid, Tormod (ed.), *Bàrdachd á Leódhas*, Gairm Publications, Glasgow, 1969

Mac-na-Ceàrdadh, G. (ed.), *An t-Oranaiche*, Celtic Press, Glasgow [*c*. 1876]

MacPhaidein, Iain, *An t-Eileanach*, A. MacLaren and Sons, Glasgow, 1921

MacPhail, J. R. N. (ed.), *Highland Papers*, Vol. i, Scottish History Society, Edinburgh, 1914

MacPhàrlain, Calum (ed.), *Dorlach Laoidhean* . . . Dundee, n.d.

MacPhàrlain, Murchadh (ed. Alasdair I. MacAsgaill), *An Toinneamh Dìomhair*, *Stornoway Gazette*, Stornoway, 1973

MacTalla (ed. J. G. Mackinnon), Sydney, Nova Scotia, 1892–1904

MacThómais, Ruaraidh, *An Dealbh Briste*, Serif Books, Edinburgh, 1951

MacThómais, Ruaraidh, *An Rathad Cian*, Gairm Publications, Glasgow, 1970

MacThómais, Ruaraidh, *Eadar Samhradh is Foghar*, Gairm Publications, Glasgow, 1967

MacThómais, Seumas, *Fasgnadh*, Stirling, 1953

Martin, Martin (ed. D. J. MacLeod), *A Description of the Western Islands of Scotland*, Eneas Mackay, Stirling, 1934

Matheson, W. (ed.), *An Clàrsair Dall*, Scottish Gaelic Texts Society, Edinburgh, 1970

Matheson, W. (ed.), *The Songs of John MacCodrum*, Scottish Gaelic Texts Society, Edinburgh, 1938

Memoirs of . . . the Marquis of Clanricarde, Dublin, 1744

Meyer, Duane, *The Highland Scots of North Carolina*, 1732–1776, The University of North Carolina Press, 1961

Moireach, Murchadh (ed. A. I. MacAsgaill), *Luach na Saorsa*, Gairm Publications, Glasgow, 1970

Morrison, Hew (ed.), *Songs and Poems in the Gaelic Language by Rob Donn*, Edinburgh, 1899

Murphy, Gerard, "Bards and Filidh", in *Éigse* II.

Murphy, Gerard (ed.), *Duanaire Finn*, Vol. iii, Irish Texts Society, Dublin, 1953

Nic-a-Phearsain, Màiri, *Dàin agus Orain Ghàidhlig*, Inverness, 1891

Ó Baoill, Colm (ed.), *Bàrdachd Shìlis na Ceapaich*, Scottish Gaelic Texts Society, Edinburgh, 1972

Ó Cuív, B. (ed.), *Seven Centuries of Irish Learning 1000–1700*, Stationery Office, Dublin, 1961

Ó Duibhginn, Seosamh, *Dónall Óg: Taighde ar an amhrán*, An Clóchomhar Tta., Dublin, 1960

Ó Tuama, Seán, *Caoineadh Airt Uí Laoghaire*, An Clóchomhar Tta., Dublin, 1961

Proceedings of the Third International Congress of Celtic Studies (ed. W. F. H. Nicolaisen), University of Edinburgh, 1968

Quiggin, E. C. (ed. J. Fraser), *Poems from the Book of the Dean of Lismore* (P.B.D.), Cambridge University Press, 1937

R.C. See Cameron, Alexander.

Red Book of Clanranald (MS.)

Ramsay, Allan, *The Tea-Table Miscellany*, Edinburgh, 1724–37

Rankin, R. A., "Oran na Comhachaig", in *Transactions of the Gaelic Society of Glasgow*, Vol. v

Ros, Niall, *Armageddon*, Edinburgh, 1950

Ross, Neil (ed.), *Heroic Poetry from the Book of the Dean of Lismore*, Scottish Gaelic Texts, Edinburgh, 1939

Scottish Gaelic Studies (S.G.S.), (edd. J. MacDonald, D. S. Thomson), Oxford, 1926–58; Aberdeen, 1961–

Shaw, Margaret Fay, *Folksongs and Folklore of South Uist*, Routledge, London, 1955

Shaw, William, *An Analysis of the Gaelic Language*, Edinburgh, 1778

Shetelig, Haakon (ed.), *Viking Antiquities in Great Britain and Ireland*, Oslo, 1940–54

Sinclair, A. Maclean (ed.), *Clàrsach na Coille*, Glasgow, 1881

Sinclair, A. Maclean (ed.), *Maclean Bards*, 2 vols, Charlottetown, 1898

Smith, Iain C., *Ben Dorain*, Akros Publications, Preston, 1969

Smith, Iain C., *Poems to Eimhir*, Victor Gollancz, London, 1971

Smith, John, *Sean Dana le Oisian, Orran, Ulann, etc.*, Edinburgh, 1787

Stewart, A. and D., *Cochruinneacha Taoghta de Shaothair nam Bard Gaeleach*, Edinburgh, 1804

S.V.B.D. See Watson, W. J.

Tàintean, Lionel Jun. Sec. School, Lewis, 1959–

The Irish Monthly

The Shorter Poems of William Wordsworth, Dent, London, n.d.

Transactions of the Gaelic Society of Glasgow, Vol. v, Glasgow, 1958

T.G.S.I., *Transactions of the Gaelic Society of Inverness*, Inverness, 1872–

Turner Collection. See Mac-an-Tuairneir, Paruig, *Comhchruinneacha* . . .

Thomson, James (ed.), *An Dìleab*, An Comunn Gaidhealach, Glasgow, n.d. [*c.* 1932]

Thomson, James (ed. J. Logie Robertson), *The Complete Poetical Works of James Thomson*, Oxford University Press, 1951

Thomson, Derick S., "Bogus Gaelic Literature. *c.* 1750–*c.* 1820" in *Transactions of the Gaelic Society of Glasgow*, Vol. V

Thomson, D. S., "Gaelic Learned Orders and Literati in Medieval Scotland", in *Proceedings of the Third International Congress of Celtic Studies* (ed. W. F. H. Nicolaisen), University of Edinburgh, 1968

Thomson, D. S., "The MacMhuirich Bardic Family", in T.G.S.I., XLIII (1966)

Thomson, D. S. "Unpublished Letters by the Poet Ewen MacLachan", in S.G.S., XI, 203

Thomson, R. L. (ed.), *Foirm na n-Urrnuidheadh*, Scottish Gaelic Texts Society, Edinburgh, 1970

Tolmie, Frances. See *Journal of the Folk-song Society*

Watson, J. C. (ed.), *Gaelic Songs of Mary MacLeod*, Scottish Gaelic Texts Society, Edinburgh, 1965

Watson, W. J. (ed.), *Bàrdachd Ghàidhlig* (3rd ed.), Glasgow, 1959

Watson, W. J., *Classic Gaelic Poetry of Panegyric in Scotland* (reprinted from T.G.S.I., XXIX, with the addition of two bardic poems)

Watson, W. J. (ed.), *Rosg Gàidhlig*, An Comunn Gaidhealach, Glasgow, 1915

Watson, W. J. (ed.), *Scottish Verse from the Book of the Dean of Lismore*, Scottish Gaelic Texts Society, Edinburgh, 1937

Yorkshire Celtic Studies, No. IV, The Yorkshire Society for Celtic Studies, Leeds, n.d.

NOTES AND REFERENCES

Notes and References

An Introductory Note

1 For some detailed discussion of these matters see MacAirt, Seán, "Filidecht and Coimgne", in *Ériu*, XVIII (1958); Gerard Murphy, "Bards and Filidh", in *Éigse*, II; B. Ó. Cuív (ed.), *Seven Centuries of Irish Learning*; and D. S. Thomson, "Gaelic Learned Orders and Literati in Medieval Scotland", in *Scottish Studies* XII, Part 1 (1968)
2 See, for example, *Carmina Gadelica* V, 306 ff
3 See, for example, W. F. T. Butler, *Gleanings from Irish History*, pp. 63, 68, 156 (map) and 171–2
4 See D. S. Thomson, "The MacMhuirich Bardic Family", in T.G.S.I., XLIII (1966)
5 J. R. N. MacPhail (ed.), *Highland Papers*, Vol. I, 24
6 Butler *op. cit.*, 68
7 Martin Martin (ed. D. J. MacLeod), *A Description of the Western Islands of Scotland*, 177
8 p. 163

Chapter 1. The Bardic Poets

1 Edition by K. H. Jackson in *Celtica*, III, 149 ff
2 S.V.B.D., 212–14
3 S.G.S., III, 142
4 Red Book of Clanranald, Fols. 195–8
5 S.V.B.D., 6–8
6 H. Shetelig, *Viking Antiquities of Great Britain and Ireland*; see, for example, Part II, pp. 73, 159, and Part III, pp. 16, 20, etc.
7 Brøndsted, *The Vikings*, 111
8 *Ibid.*, 115
9 *Ibid.*, 131
10 For a detailed account of this poem, see the present writer's paper in *Celtic Studies: Essays in memory of Angus Matheson, 1912–1962* (ed. J. Carney and D. Greene).
11 i.e. Argyll
12 Original in S.V.B.D., 158 with literal translation. The last line of the second stanza of my translation is in the spirit rather than the letter of the original!
13 S.G.S., II, 76
14 S.V.B.D., 138
15 Adv. MS. 72.1.48, Fols. 17a–19a. Old Gaelic MS. (Nat. Lib. of Scotland.), XLVIII
16 W. J. Watson, "Classic Gaelic Poetry of Panegyric in Scotland", in T.G.S.I., xxix, 217
17 S.V.B.D., 30
18 *Ibid.*, 32

19 *Ibid.*, 56
20 S.G.S., VIII, 27
21 *Memoirs of . . . The Marquis of Clanricarde* (Dublin, 1744), cviii
22 S.G.S., III, 156
23 For original, see R.C., II, 240
24 *Ibid.*, 256
25 S.V.B.D., 152–4
26 The Irish poem was edited by Lambert McKenna in *The Irish Monthly* (1921), p. 26
27 See S.G.S., IX, 105
28 E. C. Quiggin, P.B.D., 23
29 In either 1496 or 1507 according to Mackay Mackenzie, *The Poems of William Dunbar*, 219
30 S.V.B.D., 148–50
31 *Ibid.*, 168
32 Watson, "Classic Gaelic Poetry . . .", in T.G.S.I., xxix, 22
33 R.C.II, 220
34 *Ibid.*, 238
35 *Ibid.*, 272
36 S.V.B.D., 104. The reference in the last line is to a plant, perhaps hemlock or vetch.
37 R.C.I, 133
38 J. F. Campbell, L. na F., xviii
39 R.C.II, 258
40 Carney, J. and Greene, D., *Celtic Studies*, 96
41 W. J. Watson, "Classic Gaelic Poetry", in T.G.S.I., xxix, 222
42 W. J. Watson, "Classic Gaelic Poetry", 46. The poem from which this stanza is quoted is one of two additional poems printed in a pamphlet off-printed from T.G.S.I., xxix.
43 B. Ó Cuív, *Seven Centuries of Irish Learning, 1000–1700*, 52
44 S.V.B.D., 66
45 R.C.II, 240
46 Gaelic original in R.C.II, 290
47 The reference is to husband, wife and child.
48 Gaelic original in S.V.B.D., 60
49 S.V.B.D., 200
50 R. L. Thomson, *Adtimchiol an Chreidimh*, xvii and 224
51 R.C.II, 266
52 R.C.II, 400

Chapter 2. The Song-makers and their Songs

1 *Gairm*, vol. 15, 20
2 *Journal of the Folksong Society* No. 16 (1911), 235
3 "The Solitary Reaper", from "Memorials of a Tour in Scotland, 1803".
4 Ó Cuív, *Seven Centuries of Irish Learning, 1000–1700*, 117
5 The translation is by Deòrsa Caimbeul Hay, and is published in his *Fuaran Sléibh*

6 Gaelic version in J. L. Campbell (ed.), *Gaelic Folksongs from the Isle of Barra*, 24

7 MacDiarmid MS. Collection (1770), as yet unpublished.

8 *Ibid.*

9 *MacDonald Collection*, 30

10 I remember on one occasion having a strong physical awareness of this old "culture-province". This was at Easter 1970, reading Scottish Gaelic poetry to an audience of several hundred in Cork, and listening in turn to Irish poetry being read.

11 Gaelic text from Margaret Fay Shaw, *Folksongs and Folklore of South Uist*, 254–5

12 S. Ó. Duibhginn, *Dónall Óg, Taighde ar an amhrán*

13 M. Kennedy-Fraser, *Songs of the Hebrides*, I, 68 for Gaelic text.

14 For discussion of this point see Gerard Murphy's article in *Éigse*, I, 125; for the text of Scottish Gaelic versions, see *MacDonald Collection*, 246, and *An t-Oranaiche*, 21

15 Gaelic text in *Journal of the Folksong Society*, No. 16 (1911), 227. In the last line, "linen shirt" is one possibility; the other is "close-fitting shirt".

16 A. Sinclair, *An t-Oranaiche*, 284

17 A. Carmichael, *Carmina Gadelica*, V, 136 ff

18 F. Tolmie, J.F.S. (1911), 217

19 Unpublished version heard from my mother.

20 MacDiarmid MS. Collection, 86

21 From the unpublished song *"Tha caolas eadar mi 's Iain"*

22 A. Carmichael, *Carmina Gadelica*, V, 44

23 MacDiarmid MS. Collection, 11

24 *Ibid.*, 111

25 Unpublished version heard from Mrs Johan MacLeod, *née* Campbell, Skye.

26 MacDiarmid MS. Collection, 76

27 F. Tolmie, J.F.S. (1911), 191. Lucy Broadwood thought that this nonsense-song was "closely allied to the farcical animal-songs beloved by the French peasantry".

28 See p. 27

29 See p. 30

30 W. J. Watson, *Rosg Gàidhlig*, 100, 102

31 F. Tolmie, J.F.S. (1911), 200

32 *An t-Oranaiche*, 131

33 McLagan MS. 141

34 See, for example, W. J. Watson, *Bàrdachd Ghàidhlig* (1959), 237, 239 and 242.

35 MacDiarmid MS. Collection, 75

36 *Gaelic Folksongs from the Isle of Barra*, 28

37 J. MacKenzie, *Sàr Obair nam Bàrd Gaelach*, 273, 373

38 e.g. *Dòmhnall Ruadh Chorùna*, 13, 23, 34, 58

39 J. MacKenzie, *Sàr Obair nam Bàrd Gaelach*, 373

40 *Ibid.*, 273, and *Gaelic Folksongs from the Isle of Barra*, 16. I am indebted to the latter publication for some phrases in the translation.

41 Gaelic text in W. J. Watson, *Bàrdachd Ghàidhlig* (1959), 242

42 This extract is translated from the version in K. C. Craig, *Orain Luaidh*, 87. For a shorter version with melody, see *Gairm*, Winter 1952, 45.

43 Gaelic text in A. Sinclair, *An t-Oranaiche*, 409

44 This is translated from a version heard from Fanny MacIsaac in Benbecula in 1950. Another version is printed in Gillies Collection (1786), p. 298.

45 MacDiarmid's MS. Collection, 68

46 e.g. William Shaw, *An Analysis of the Gaelic Language* (1778), 136–7, and Necker de Saussure, *Voyage en Écosse et aux Iles Hébrides* (1821), 272, 348. See discussion in J. F. Campbell and F. Collinson, *Hebridean Folksongs*, pp. 3 ff.

47 Gaelic text in *Carmina Gadelica*, V (ed. Angus Matheson), 66 ff. The translation given is that of *Carmina Gadelica*, that is to say, Alexander Carmichael's, revised by J. Carmichael Watson and Angus Matheson.

48 *Carmina Gadelica*, V, 32. Translation based on p. 33

49 Gillies Collection (1786), 205

50 *Gaelic and Scots Folktales* (1960), 34

51 Gillies Collection (1786), 204–5. There is an elaborate and different version in *Carmina Gadelica*, V, 354 ff

52 Edited, with discussion in Irish, by Seán O Tuama, *Caoineadh Airt Uí Laoghaire* (1961). See also Rachel Bromwich, "The Continuity of the Gaelic Tradition in Eighteenth-Century Ireland", in *Yorkshire Celtic Studies*, IV.

53 F. Tolmie, J.F.S. (1911), 202. A fine version is still sung in Skye.

54 Gaelic version in *An t-Oranaiche*, 124 ff

55 Gillies Collection, 69

56 *Ibid.*, 118

57 From a version of the song, recorded from the Paisley Bard, Donald Macintyre.

58 MacDiarmid MS. Collection, 172

59 The reference for this quotation eludes me.

60 Inverness Collection (1806), 125

61 Gillies Collection, 50

62 Gesto Collection (App.), 23

63 McLagan MS. 165 [A]

64 Gillies Collection, 135

65 Reading *aitinn* instead of *aiteil*

66 *An t-Oranaiche*, 425

67 Gillies Collection, 242

68 From a version sung by the late Dr Allan MacDonald of Uig, Skye.

69 See p. 82

70 Gaelic text in Gillies Collection, 246. Translation by Iain Crichton Smith.

71 Gaelic words in *Gairm*, Spring 1953, 47

72 Gaelic text in *Carmina Gadelica*, V, 12

73 Gaelic text in *Carmina Gadelica*, V, 152. The translation is basically that given there.

74 *An t-Oranaiche*, 289
75 Patrick Turner's Collection (1813), 186
76 K. C. Craig, *Orain Luaidh*, 37
77 *Carmina Gadelica*, V, 34
78 *Ibid.*, 8
79 *Ibid.*, 6
80 *Ibid.*, 2
81 Translated from a version which I recorded from Duncan Beaton, of Uig, Skye, in 1950.
82 Gaelic version in McLagan MS., 91, which is the original of Gillies 68. This song and Gillies 134 in fact share as a stereo the couplets about the silken garters and Holland shirt.

Chapter 3. Poetry in Transition

1 Murphy, *Duanaire Fin*, III, p. xli and additional note, p. 440
2 *geilt* is used of crazed persons living in woods and possessing power of levitation, but perhaps here the reference is to some kind of bird.
3 Neil Ross (ed.), *Heroic Poetry from the Book of the Dean of Lismore*, Ballad IX
4 Ross, *Heroic Poetry from the Book of the Dean of Lismore*, Ballad VII; *Duanaire Finn*, Ballad LXV.
5 F. J. Child, *English and Scottish Popular Ballads*, I, 257, V, 289
6 Fionn's wife.
7 Ross, *Heroic Poetry from the Book of the Dean of Lismore*, Ballad IV
8 W. J. Watson, *Bàrdachd Ghàidhlig* (1959), 115
9 See D. S. Thomson, "Bogus Gaelic Literature *c.* 1750–*c.* 1820" in *Trans. Gaelic Soc. of Glasgow*, vol. v
10 See e.g. D. S. Thomson, "Scottish Gaelic Folk-Poetry ante 1650", S.G.S., VIII, Part 1
11 R.C.II, 310–420
12 W. J. Watson, *Bàrdachd Ghàidhlig* (1959), 340
13 There are two versions of this poem, one attested in several sources, though deriving from a common original, the other showing signs of emendation and interpolation. I hope to discuss the matter more fully in a forthcoming article.
14 A. Maclean Sinclair, *Clàrsach na Coille*, 215, 217. The poem derives from Dr Hector MacLean's MS., compiled *c.* 1738.
15 A Gaelic text of the song is in W. J. Watson, *Bàrdachd Ghàidhlig* (1959), 244
16 For discussion and text, see article by Prof. R. A. Rankin, "Oran na Comhachaig", in *Trans. Gael. Soc. Glasgow*, vol. v, 122–71.
17 C. MacFarlane, *The Fernaig MS.*, 43
18 *Ibid.*, 45
19 *Ibid.*, 139
20 *Ibid.*, 131
21 The Gaelic original is in Fernaig, *ibid.*, 143. The editor omits an offensive word (three-letter words in Gaelic correspond to four-letter

words in English), and W. J. Watson omitted the entire stanza from his edition in *Bàrdachd Ghàidhlig*.

22 Fernaig, 119 and 123
23 *Ibid.*, 127; Watson, *Bàrdachd Ghàidhlig* (1959), 220
24 W. J. Watson, *Bàrdachd Ghàidhlig* (1959), 221
25 *Ibid.*, 217
26 *Ibid.*, 172
27 *Ibid.*, 155
28 See p. 155

Chapter 4. Clan and Politics

1 According to Alexander Webster's estimates of 1755, the five High-land counties of Perth, Argyll, Inverness, Ross and Sutherland con-tained approx. one quarter of the Scottish population of *c.* 1¼ million. In the previous century Gaelic was almost universally spoken in these counties, but also in many others, e.g. Ayrshire, Dumbartonshire, Moray and Nairn, Aberdeenshire.

2 *Orain Iain Luim* (Songs of John MacDonald Bard of Keppoch, ed. Annie M. MacKenzie) (Scottish Gaelic Texts Society, Edinburgh, 1964)

3 Dr Mackenzie is inclined to place the incident, and so the poem, in 1640. The evidence of the Baptismal Records of the Parish Kirk of Kenmore, sub. Jan. 16th, 1647, and the traditional account given in *The Dewar MSS* (ed. John Mackechnie), pp. 242–3, support the later date.

4 Original in *Orain Iain Luim*, p. 10. The translation is by Iain Crichton Smith.

5 Original in *Orain Iain Luim*, p. 20. I am indebted to Dr Mackenzie's translation for some lines and phrases.

6 For original see *ibid.*, 48 ff

7 For original, see *ibid.*, 82 ff

8 *Ibid.*, 325

9 *Ibid.*, 224

10 The question was discussed by the late Angus Matheson, in *Gairm*, II, 343, and III, 33 and 124.

11 These poems can be most conveniently consulted in the anthology made by A. Maclean Sinclair, *The Maclean Bards*, though Maclean Sinclair as an editor has to be taken on trust. The poem here referred to is *ibid.*, 35.

12 *Ibid.*, 48

13 The Gaelic text used here is that in W. J. Watson's *Bàrdachd Ghàidhlig*, p. 205.

14 The Maclean chief who fought at Harlaw was Eachann Ruadh (Red Hector), the name also for Lachlan's successor.

15 See pp. 75–81

16 Original in J. C. Watson, *Gaelic Songs of Mary Macleod*, 18–20.

17 *Ibid.*, 26

18 See p. 129

19 J. C. Watson, *Gaelic Songs of Mary Macleod* (the translation here is Watson's).

20 *Ibid.*, 52

21 *Ibid.*, 60

22 Original in *ibid.*, 90

23 Original in A. Maclean Sinclair, *Maclean Bards*, 62

24 Original in Colm Ó Baoill, *Bàrdachd Shìlis na Ceapaich*, 18

25 *Ibid.*, 154

26 *Ibid.*, 155. I take these comments on the occasion of the poem from Dr Ó Baoill's notes.

26a Original in *ibid.*, 46

27 Original in *ibid.*, 64. The significance of the third line is of course that she had reared Anna both as baby and child, and then enjoyed her mature companionship.

28 Original in *ibid.*, 70

29 *Ibid.*, 84

30 *Ibid.*, 90

31 *Ibid.*, 102 and notes, 174

32 *Ibid.*, 177

33 Original in *ibid.*, 108

34 See A. Maclean Sinclair, *The Maclean Bards*, 177–9; and Sam Maclean, "Mairearad Nighean Lachlainn" in T.G.S.I., XLII, 33–4

35 See p. 93

36 *Carmina Gadelica*, V, 16

37 I regard the "Oran do dh'Ailein", *Maclean Bards*, 215, as being in 8-line strophic stanza.

38 *Maclean Bards*, 181

39 *Ibid.*, 185

40 *Maclean Bards*, 194

41 *Ibid.*, 205. Maclean Sinclair, however, suggests that the poem may have been composed in 1750, on false news coming from Rome. Maclean died in 1751.

42 For a summary of these events see Campbell and Thomson, *Edward Lhuyd in the Scottish Highlands 1699–1700*, 18–20

43 *Maclean Bards*, 188

44 *Ibid.*, 100

45 *Ibid.*, 107–8

46 *Ibid.*, 133 ff

47 *Ibid.*, 170

48 *Ibid.*, 85

49 *Ibid.*, 84

50 J. Mackenzie, *Sàr Obair nam Bard Gaelach*, 82

51 A. and D. Stewart's Collection (1804), 488

52 Quoted in Donald Lamont, *Strath: In (the) Isle of Skye*

53 T.G.S.I., vol. 38, 529

54 J. Mackenzie, *Sàr Obair*, 68. The unwary should be warned that Mackenzie attributes poems by Iain MacAilein to Iain Dubh.

55 *Ibid.*, 72

56 Turner's Collection (1813), 138

57 *Eigg Collection*, p. 98
58 W. Matheson, *An Clàrsair Dall*, lviii
59 *Ibid.*, 4
60 *Ibid.*, 12
61 See p. 145
62 *An Clàrsair Dall*, 74
63 *Ibid.*, 46
64 *Ibid.*, 58
65 M. MacFarlane, *The Fernaig MS.*, 175
66 *Ibid.*, 195 ff
67 For discussion, see D. S. Thomson, 'The Poetry of Niall Mac-Mhuirich', T.G.S.I., xlvi, 281 ff

Chapter 5. Poetry of the Eighteenth Century

1 Further details of his connections are given in the edition of his poems ed. by A. and A. MacDonald, *The Poems of Alexander MacDonald* (Inverness, 1924). References are mainly to this edition, as it is the most accessible now.
2 *Ibid.*, 4
3 *Ibid.*, 14. I am not certain that the translation of the first line in this extract captures the poet's intention. The 1751 ed. has *spérin*, not *spéirid*, which I have translated as "vigour".
4 See *Scottish Gaelic Studies*, VIII, 53–6
5   Such themes as these the rural Maro sung
        To wide imperial Rome, in the full height
        Of elegance and taste, by Greece refined.—"Winter", ll. 52 ff
6 *The Poems of Alexander MacDonald*, 24
7 "Spring", ll. 604 ff
8 "Spring", ll. 509 ff
9 *The Poems of Alexander MacDonald*, 44
10 *Ibid.*, 24 and 26
11 *Ibid.*, 34
12 *Ibid.*, 48
13 *Ibid.*, 282
14 *Ibid.*, 70 and 74
15 See especially *ibid.*, 78, third stanza
16 *Ibid.*, 76
17 *Ibid.*, 82
18 *Ibid.*, 84. I am indebted to this source for the translation of l. 5.
19 *Ibid.*, 122
20 *Ibid.*, 324
21 *Ibid.*, 346
22 *Ibid.*, 348
23 *Ais-eiridh*, 153. Not in the 1924 edition.
24 *Ibid.*, 26. Not in the 1924 edition.
25 "Ground" is a technical term for a movement in *ceòl-mór*.
26 The *crunluath/crunlùdh* is the intricately grace-noted climax to the classical pipe composition.

27 *The Poems of Alexander MacDonald*, 218–26
28 *Ibid.*, 16
29 *Ibid.*, 18
30 *Ibid.*, 162
31 *Ibid.*, 234
32 For further detail, see J. L. Campbell's article "The Royal Irish Academy Text of 'Birlinn Chlann Raghnaill' ", in *Scottish Gaelic Studies*, IX, 39–79
33 See Angus MacLeod, *Sàr Orain*, 118
34 A. Mackenzie, *Orain Iain Luim*, 102
35 All the extracts from the "Birlinn" are translated from the edition in Angus MacLeod's *Sàr Orain*, the notes there containing many useful suggestions.
36 Angus MacLeod, *The Songs of Duncan Ban Macintyre*, 484
37 *Ibid.*, 184
38 *Ibid.*, 46
39 *Ibid.*, 68
40 *Ibid.*, 70–2
41 John Mackenzie, *Sàr Obair nam Bard Gaelach* (1877), 82
42 A. MacLeod, *The Songs of Duncan Ban Macintyre*, 116. The formal title of the poem is *"Oran d'a Chéile Nuadh-phòsda"* ("A Song to his Bride"). I am indebted to Angus MacLeod's translation.
43 *Ibid.*, 164
44 Iain C. Smith, *Ben Dorain*, 13–16. Mr Smith has a stimulating introduction to his translation.
45 J. L. Campbell, *Highland Songs of the Forty Five*
46 Eliz. E. Mackechnie, *The Poems of John Roy Stewart*, 20
47 W. Matheson, *The Songs of John MacCodrum*, 66. I am indebted to the translation there for some lines.
48 *Ibid.*, 160
49 For some detailed demonstration of this, see Donald J. MacLeod, "The Poetry of Rob Donn MacKay", in *Scottish Gaelic Studies*, XII, 3 ff
50 Hew Morrison, *Songs and Poems in the Gaelic Language by Rob Donn*, 206
51 *Ibid.*, 87
52 *Ibid.*, 84
53 *An Gaidheal*, vol. liii (1958), 59. Original in Hew Morrison, *op. cit.*, 32
54 Hew Morrison, *op. cit.*, 46
55 For original, see *ibid.*, 49
56 *Ibid.*, 106
57 *Ibid.*, 258
58 *Scottish Gaelic Studies*, X, 169
59 Lachlan MacBean, *Buchanan the Sacred Bard of the Scottish Highlands*, 132
60 *Ibid.*, 136
61 *Ibid.*, 149
62 *Ibid.*, 150–1

63 *Ibid.*, 13
64 John Macinnes, *The Evangelical Movement in the Highlands of Scotland*, 2.
65 Original in Donald Maclean (ed.), *The Spiritual Songs of Dugald Buchanan*, 34–5.
66 *Ibid.*, 18–19
67 *Ibid.*, 28
68 George Calder (ed.), *Gaelic Songs by William Ross*, 86
69 *Ibid.*, 22
70 The odd title can be attributed to the poet's first editor, John Mackenzie.
71 Iain Mac-Choinnich (ed.), *Òrain Ghàëlach le Uilleam Ròs* (1834), 122. Calder preferred not to ascribe this song to Ross.
72 George Calder, *op. cit.*, 126
73 He is said to have destroyed much of his work.
74 *Sàr Obair nam Bard Gaelach* (1877 ed.), 279
75 George Calder, *op. cit.*, 64
76 *Ibid.*, 104–6
77 *Ibid.*, 166–8
78 Original in *ibid.*, 172–4
79 The love-songs ascribed to MacDonald of Dalness are a case in point.
80 See above, p. 209
81 See John Macdonald (ed.), *Ewen MacLachlan's Gaelic Verse*
82 As yet unpublished, apart from short extracts.

Chapter 6. *Gaelic Poets in Lowlands and Highlands*

1 See Duane Meyer, *The Highland Scots of North Carolina 1732–1736*, 27
2 A. R. MacDonald (ed. D. Mackinnon), *The Truth about Flora MacDonald*, pp. 85, 88–9
3 Meyer, *op. cit.*, 86
4 D. S. Thomson, "Unpublished Letters by the Poet Ewen MacLachlan" in S.G.S., vol. XI, 203
5 Original in W. J. Watson, *Bàrdachd Ghàidhlig* (1959), 15–16
6 *Ibid.*, 9
7 For further discussion of this topic, see Charles W. Dunn, *Highland Settler*, especially chaps. 4, 5 and 6
8 George Henderson (ed.), *Dàin Iain Ghobha*, I, 84 ff
9 *Ibid.*, vol. II, 48
10 Gilleasbuig Grannda, *Dàin agus Orain*, 57
11 M. C. MacLeod, *Modern Gaelic Bards*, 83
12 Niall MacLeòid, *Clàrsach an Doire* (1924 ed.), 28
13 *Ibid.*, 69
14 Eóghan MacColla, *Clàrsach nam Beann*, *passim*
15 Iain Caimbeul, *Poems*, 31 and 36
16 Niall MacLeòid, *op. cit.*, 81
17 *Ibid.*, 156, 116 and 119
18 *Poems*, 155

19 *Clàrsach an Doire*, 44
20 M. C. MacLeod, *Modern Gaelic Bards*, 207
21 Niall MacLeòid, *Clàrsach an Doire*, 195. Original at p. 1
22 M. C. MacLeod, *Modern Gaelic Bards*, 71
23 *Clàrsach an Doire*, 131
24 *Ibid.*, 62
25 *Clàrsach nam Beann*, 46
26 *Modern Gaelic Bards*, 212
27 H. J. Hanham, *Scottish Nationalism*, 77
28 *Clàrsach an Doire*, 22
29 Iain MacPhaidein, *An t-Eileanach* (1921 ed.), 10
30 *Ibid.*, 28
31 *Ibid.*, 93
32 *Ibid.*, 49, 125 and 153
33 Dòmhnall MacEacharn, *Am Fear-ciùil*, 32
34 *Ibid.*, 68
35 *Clàrsach nam Beann*, 87
36 Poems, 74
37 *Am Fear Ciùil*, 94
38 *Modern Gaelic Bards*, 205
39 *Ibid.*, 79
40 *Clàrsach an Doire*, 9
41 *Ibid.*, 33
42 *Ibid.*, 77
43 Hector Cameron (ed.), *Na Bàird Thirisdeach*, 143
44 *Ibid.*, 180
45 Uilleam MacDhunléibhe, *Duain agus Orain*, xii
46 *Ibid.*, 1 and 61
47 *Ibid.*, 55, 45, 101
48 *Ibid.*, 129
49 *Ibid.*, 205
50 *Ibid.*, 151
51 Iain N. MacLeòid, *Bàrdachd Leódhais*, 99
52 *Ibid.*, 90
53 *Ibid.*, 89
54 *Ibid.*, 88
55 See, for example, MacDiarmid, J. M., *The Deer Forests and how they are bleeding Scotland white.*
56 *Bàrdachd Leódhais*, 124
57 *Ibid.*, 125
58 *Ibid.*, 116
59 *Ibid.*, 118
60 *Ibid.*, 76–84
61 Màiri Nic-a-Phearsain, *Dàin agus Orain Ghàidhlig*, 63
62 Recording, B.B.C. Archives, Glasgow
63 *Dàin agus Orain Ghàidhlig*
64 *Ibid.*, 110
65 *Ibid.*, 238
66 *Ibid.*, 125

67 *Ibid.*, 45
68 *Ibid.*, 15
69 *Ibid.*, 28

Chapter 7. *Renaissance*

1 I am thinking in particular of the more ornate passages in his long poem "*Cnoc an Fhradhairc*" or his novel *An t-Ogha Mór.*
2 See Alasdair I. MacAsgaill (ed.), *Luach na Saorsa* (Diary, Poems and Essays by Murdo Murray).
3 *Ibid.*, 76, 73, 74
4 Original in *ibid.*, 85–6. Earlier published in Thomson, J., *An Dìleab.*
5 See original and translation by Hugh MacDiarmid, in Maurice Lindsay (ed.), *Modern Scottish Poetry*, 44
6 Seumas MacThómais, *Fasgnadh*, 50
7 *Ibid.*, 74
8 *Ibid.*, 69
9 *Gairm*, vol. 8, 17
10 *Ibid.*, vol. 9, 69
11 *Ibid.*, vol. 7, 71
12 Somerled Macmillan (ed.), *Sporan Dhòmhnaill*, was published in 1968, four years after the poet's death.
13 *Ibid.*, 315
14 *Ibid.*, 327
15 *Ibdi.*, 262
16 *Ibid.*, 266
17 *Ibid.*, 211
18 *Ibid.*, 147–52
19 See p. 252 above
20 See *Domhnall Dòmhnallach, Dòmhnall Ruadh Chorùna*, 23, etc.
21 Norman MacLeod (ed.), *Bàrdachd á Leódhas*
22 Aonghas Caimbeul, *Moll is Cruithneachd*, 48
23 Aonghas Caimbeul, *Suathadh ri Iomadh Rubha*
24 Aonghas Caimbeul, *Moll is Cruithneachd*, 33–8
25 Original in *Gairm*, vol. 8, 153
26 Original in *Gairm*, vol. 14, 127
27 Iain Mac a' Ghobhainn, *Bìobuill is Sanasan-reice*, 21
28 Somhairle MacGhillEathain, *Dàin do Eimhir*, 31. I am indebted to the author's translation for many suggestions and phrases.
29 Ruaraidh MacThómais, *Eadar Samhradh is Foghar*, 45
30 Original in *Dàin do Eimhir*, 54
31 Original in *Seòbhrach ás a' Chlaich*, 69
32 *An Gaidheal*, vol. 38, 139. Later published in *An Dealbh Briste*, 11
33 Deòrsa Caimbeul Hay, *Fuaran Sléibh*, 31
34 Deòrsa Caímbeul Hay, *O na Ceithir Airdean*, 22
35 *Ibid.*, 20. The translation is indebted to the poet's own.
36 R. MacThómais, *Eadar Samhradh is Foghar*, 38
37 Dòmhnall MacAmhlaigh, *Seòbhrach ás a' Chlaich*, 42. The translation is the poet's own.

38 Deòrsa Caimbeul Hay, *O na Ceithir Airdean*, 11
39 *Ibid.*, 39
40 *Dàin do Eimhir*, 24
41 *Ibid.*, e.g. pp. 11, 16 and especially 37
42 *Bìobuill is Sanasan-reice*, 35
43 *An Dealbh Briste*, 27
44 *An Rathad Cian*, e.g. pp. 10, 56
45 *Seòbhrach ás a' Chlaich*, 65
46 *Bìobuill is Sanasan-reice*, 13
47 Iain C. Smith, *Poems to Eimhir*, 33. Original in *Dàin do Eimhir*, 23
48 *Gairm*, vol. 19, 162
49 *Seòbhrach ás a' Chlaich*, 15
50 *Lines Review* No. 39, 19. Original in *An Rathad Cian*, 17
51 See above p. 267
52 Original in *Bìobuill is Sanasan-reice*, 23. I am indebted to the author's translation at many points.
53 Original in *Seòbhrach ás a' Chlaich*, 35. The translation is the poet's own.
54 *Poems to Eimhir*, 51. Original in *Dàin do Eimhir*, 37
55 Original in *An Dealbh Briste*, 46
56 *Cúirt Fhilíochta, Eire—Alba 1972*, 12, a booklet issued by Comhdháil Náisiúnta na Gaeilge, Dublin
57 *Dàin do Eimhir*, 39
58 Original in *Gairm*, vol. 17, 343
59 *O na Ceithir Airdean*, 47–50
60 Original in *Fuaran Sléibh*, 44. I am indebted to the translation given there.
61 *O na Ceithir Airdean*, 39
62 *Ibid.*, 26
63 Original in *Dàin do Eimhir*, 53
64 *An Dealbh Briste*, 34
65 See above p. 270
66 *Eadar Samhradh is Foghar*, 67
67 Original in *Seòbhrach ás a' Chlaich*, 61

INDEXES

Index of Gaelic Poets

General Index